JAMES AND JUDE

James and Jude is the first commentary to focus exclusively on the two letters written by the "brothers of the Lord." The letter of James is held to be one of the oldest Christian writings and an early witness to the teachings of Jesus. While each letter is read on its own merit, particular attention is paid to the social worlds of James and Jude and to interpreting the significance of their messages for our day. Of special interest are the focus on the ideological texture of James and the exploration of the ethical implications of James's teaching on poverty and wealth.

William F. Brosend II is Associate Director of the Louisville Institute, a program of Lilly Endowment, Inc., based at Louisville Presbyterian Seminary, where he also serves as Adjunct Professor of New Testament and Preaching.

NEW CAMBRIDGE BIBLE COMMENTARY

GENERAL EDITOR: Ben Witherington III

HEBREW BIBLE/OLD TESTAMENT EDITOR: Bill T. Arnold

EDITORIAL BOARD
Bill T. Arnold, *Asbury Theological Seminary*
James D. G. Dunn, *University of Durham*
Michael V. Fox, *University of Wisconsin–Madison*
Robert P. Gordon, *University of Cambridge*
Judith Gundry-Volf, *Yale University*
Ben Witherington III, *Asbury Theological Seminary*

The New Cambridge Bible Commentary (NCBC) aims to elucidate the Hebrew and Christian Scriptures for a wide range of intellectually curious individuals. While building on the work and reputation of the Cambridge Bible Commentary popular in the 1960s and 1970s, the NCBC takes advantage of many of the rewards provided by scholarly research over the last four decades. Volumes utilize recent gains in rhetorical criticism, social scientific study of the Scriptures, narrative criticism, and other developing disciplines to exploit the growing edges in biblical studies. Accessible, jargon-free commentary, an annotated "Suggested Reading" list, and the entire New Revised Standard Version (NRSV) text under discussion are the hallmarks of all volumes in the series.

PUBLISHED VOLUMES IN THE SERIES
Revelation, Ben Witherington III
Judges and Ruth, Victor H. Matthews
James and Jude, William F. Brosend II

FORTHCOMING VOLUMES
Genesis, Bill T. Arnold
Exodus, Carol Meyers
Deuteronomy, Brent Strawn
Joshua, Douglas A. Knight
1–2 Chronicles, William M. Schniedewind
Psalms 1–72, Walter Brueggemann and Patrick D. Miller
Psalms 73–150, Walter Brueggemann and Patrick D. Miller
Isaiah 1–39, David Baer
Jeremiah, Baruch Halpern
Hosea, Joel, and Amos, J. J. M. Roberts
The Gospel of Matthew, Craig A. Evans
The Gospel of Luke, Amy-Jill Levine and Ben Witherington III
The Gospel of John, Jerome H. Neyrey
Paul's Letters to the Corinthians, Craig S. Keener
The Letters of John, Duane F. Watson

James and Jude

William F. Brosend II
The Louisville Institute

PUBLISHED BY THE PRESS SYNDICATE OF THE UNIVERSITY OF CAMBRIDGE
The Pitt Building, Trumpington Street, Cambridge, United Kingdom

CAMBRIDGE UNIVERSITY PRESS
The Edinburgh Building, Cambridge CB2 2RU, UK
40 West 20th Street, New York, NY 10011-4211, USA
477 Williamstown Road, Port Melbourne, VIC 3207, Australia
Ruiz de Alarcón 13, 28014 Madrid, Spain
Dock House, The Waterfront, Cape Town 8001, South Africa

http://www.cambridge.org

© Cambridge University Press 2004

This book is in copyright. Subject to statutory exception
and to the provisions of relevant collective licensing agreements,
no reproduction of any part may take place without
the written permission of Cambridge University Press.

First published 2004

Printed in the United States of America

Typeface Minion 10/12 pt.   *System* LaTeX 2_ε [TB]

A catalog record for this book is available from the British Library.

Library of Congress Cataloging in Publication Data
Brosend, William F. (William Frank), 1954–
James and Jude / William F. Brosend II.
    p.   cm. – (New Cambridge Bible commentary)
Includes bibliographical references and index.
ISBN 0-521-81482-0 – ISBN 0-521-89201-5 (pbk.)
1. Bible. N.T. James – Commentaries.   2. Bible. N.T. Jude – Commentaries.   I. Title.   II. Series.
BS2785.53.B76   2004
227′.91077 – dc22   2003060535

ISBN 0 521 81482 0 hardback
ISBN 0 521 89201 5 paperback

Contents

Preface	page xi
A Word about Citations	xiii
Abbreviations and Acronyms	xv

I. INTRODUCTION — 1

Authors	2
Dates	5
Occasions	7
Literary Relationships	9
Reception and Interpretation	12
The Texture of Texts	15

II. SUGGESTED READING — 21

Inner Texture and Intertexture	21
Sociocultural Texture	22
Ideological Texture	22
Sacred and Homiletical Textures	23
Commentaries on the Letter of James	23
Studies on James	24
Articles on the Letter of James	25
Commentaries and Books on Jude	26
Studies and Articles on Jude	26
Special Studies	27

III. COMMENTARY — 29

James 1:1–27 – That You May Be Mature and Complete	29
James 1:1	29
James 1:2–8	33
A Closer Look – Climbing James's Ladder	34

James 1:9–11	39
James 1:12–18	44
James 1:19–27	48
A Closer Look – God and Righteousness	50
A Closer Look – Through a Glass Darkly?	51
Bridging the Horizons – Out of Silence	54
James 2:1-26 – I By My Works Will Show You My Faith	55
James 2:1–13	56
A Closer Look – Synagogue, Story, and Setting	61
A Closer Look – James's Use of Law	66
James 2:14–26	70
A Closer Look – A Confusing Verse	74
A Closer Look – Paul and James	78
Bridging the Horizons – Faith Is All about the Practice	82
James 3:1–18 – Teachers, Tongues, and Righteousness	86
James 3:1–12	86
Bridging the Horizons – Sacred and Homiletical Textures	97
James 3:13–18	98
Bridging the Horizons – The Preacher as Practitioner	104
James 4:1–17 – Conflict, Friendship, and What Tomorrow May Bring	105
James 4:1–10	106
A Closer Look – The Language of Desire	107
Bridging the Horizons – Friendship with God in the World	115
James 4:11–12	116
James 4:13–17	122
A Closer Look – Text-Critical Issues	124
Bridging the Horizons – When the Text Is Tough	128
James 5:1–20 – Cries, Patience, and Prayer: The Lord Is Near	130
James 5:1–6	131
A Closer Look – James's Use of the Greek Tense	132
James 5:7–11	141
A Closer Look – James's Thoroughgoing Eschatology	146
James 5:12–20	148
A Closer Look – James and Jesus on Swearing an Oath	150
Bridging the Horizons – Preaching James	164
The Letter of Jude – Have Mercy on Some Who Are Wavering	166
Jude 1–2	167
A Closer Look – "Jude" in the NT	167
Jude 3–4	169
Jude 5–10	172
Jude 11–16	176
Jude 17–23	180

A Closer Look – The Text of Jude 22–3	181
Jude 24–5	182
A Closer Look – A Challenge to Jesus' Honor	184
Bridging the Horizons – Preaching Jude	191
Author Index	195
Scripture and Extra-Biblical Texts Index	197
Subject Index	205

Preface

The invitation to write the present commentary preceded by a few months the trip that proved decisive in determining its shape. In 2001 I was able to fulfill a long postponed commitment to teach and preach in Nicaragua. As the guest of the Rev. Gustavo Parajón, MD, pastor of the First Baptist Church of Managua and founder of CEPAD, the evangelical council of churches, and Providenic, a group of public health clinics, I was privileged to study the letter of James with pastors around the country. The debt I owe to Dr. Parajón and the pastors I met in Nicaragua is evident on every page. A second and more obvious debt is to the work of Vernon Robbins. The exegetical taxonomy found in *Exploring the Texture of Texts* and his encouragement to include the homiletical texture provide the architecture of this commentary.

Ben Witherington III, the editor of this series, and Andrew Beck, humanities editor for Cambridge University Press, have been invaluable and unceasing supporters, as has Dr. Jim Lewis, executive director of the Louisville Institute, and the staff and board of the institute. ¡Muchas gracias!

The commentary is offered to the Church in memory of my parents, the late Rev. Frank Brosend and Lucille Brosend, with loving thanks to "my girls," Christine and Emily.

Soli deo gloria
Thanksgiving 2003

A Word about Citations

All volumes in the New Cambridge Bible Commentary include footnotes, with full bibliographical citations included in the note when a source text is first mentioned in a chapter. Subsequent, nonconsecutive citations in the same chapter include the author's initial or initials, full last name, abbreviated title for the work, and date of publication. Most readers prefer this citation system to endnotes, which require searching through pages at the back of the book.

The Suggested Reading lists, also included in all NCBC volumes after the introductions, are not a part of this citation apparatus. Annotated and organized by publication type, the self-contained Suggest Reading lists are intended to introduce and briefly review some of the most well-known and helpful literature on the biblical text under discussion.

Abbreviations and Acronyms

ABD	*Anchor Bible Dictionary* (6 vols., D. N. Freedman, ed.; New York: Doubleday, 1992)
CTJ	*Calvin Theological Journal*
CBQ	*Catholic Biblical Quarterly*
HE	*Historia Ecclesiastica* (Eusebius)
ICC	International Critical Commentary on the Holy Scriptures of the Old and New Testaments
JBL	*Journal of Biblical Literature*
JSNT	*Journal for the Study of the New Testament*
KJV	King James Version (or Authorized Version)
LCL	Loeb Classical Library
LXX	Septuagint
NEB	New English Bible
NIBC	New International Bible Commentary
NIGTC	New International Greek Text Commentary
NIV	New International Version
NovT	*Novum Testamentum*
NovT Sup	*Novum Testamentum Supplement*
NRSV	New Revised Standard Version
NT	New Testament
NTS	*New Testament Studies*
OT	Old Testament
RSV	Revised Standard Version
TDNT	Theological Dictionary of the New Testament
TEV	Today's English Version
ZNW	*Zeitschrift für die Neutestamentliche Wissenschaft*

I. Introduction

I intended to write that the present commentary was an attempt to address the status of the letters of James and Jude as "overlooked, ignored, and forgotten." As the Suggested Reading list shows, this is really no longer the case. And now, following the announcement in November 2002 that an Israeli antiquities dealer was in possession of an ossuary, or bone box, with an inscription reading "James, son of Joseph, brother of Jesus," James is enjoying unprecedented publicity.[1]

James then, and to a lesser extent Jude, may now be said to be well studied and fairly treated. To be sure, both letters still suffer from a traditional tendency to read them along with the wrong conversation partners – James and Paul, Jude and 2 Peter – as if the only questions of importance were the relationship of the apostles Paul and Peter and the letters James and Jude, respectively. But the work of Richard Bauckham, Luke T. Johnson, and Jerome Neyrey, among others, has done much to correct biases even as longstanding as these.

Why and for whom is this volume written? It is written for the Church by one who has spent most of the last quarter century as a parish pastor and as a seminary professor, not always balancing the two roles as well as might be wished but always trying to allow each role to inform, question, and shape the other. This reading of the letters of James and Jude is very much indebted to the readings, formal and informal, emerging from the Church in years past and is submitted not as a corrective but in the hope of furthering the conversation

---

[1] See Hershel Shanks and Ben Witherington III, *The Brother of Jesus: The Dramatic Story and Significance of the First Archaeological Link to Jesus and His Family* (New York: Harper SanFrancisco, 2003). Having viewed the ossuary myself I have no doubt about its antiquity but recognize there are disagreements over its authenticity and over the claims of some for its significance. A few years earlier a smaller splash was made by Robert Eisenman with the publication of *James the Brother of Jesus: The Key to Unlocking the Secrets of Early Christianity and the Dead Sea Scrolls* (New York: Viking Press, 1997). Eisenman argued, to almost universal rejection and no small amount of ridicule, that James was the "teacher of righteousness" in the documents of Qumran.

and encouraging others to attend more seriously to what James and Jude say to us today. It is also an attempt to read the letters in light of the insights of sociorhetorical interpretation, particularly as found in the work of Vernon Robbins, a method that will be presented more fully at the end of the Introduction, following consideration of authorship, dating, occasion, and other customary issues. The commentary likewise brings to bear the significant insights of a generation of biblical criticism informed by the social sciences, particularly cultural anthropology, something that Neyrey has done for Jude but that has largely not been applied to James.

Bauckham notes, "Most introductory issues can really only be settled as a result of detailed exegesis."[2] One must start somewhere, however, and because my conclusions about the authorship of the letters of James and Jude both keep with the tradition and step outside of much current scholarship, it is a good place to begin. That said, conclusions about authorship, dates, and occasions of composition are interrelated, and the reader is invited to consider all three before making an evaluation of any one.

AUTHORS

Trends in scholarly opinion ebb and flow. As we will see in the section on reception and interpretation, Martin Luther was not the first to have questions about the letter of James, and the letter of Jude seems to have received a mixed reception almost from its composition. There were also early doubts about the identity of the letters' authors. Nevertheless, conventional opinion identified both letters with one or another of the New Testament (NT) personages bearing the name James (Gk. *Iakōbos*) or Jude (Gk. *Ioudas*), traditionally the two brothers of the Lord.

Fairly early in the history of modern, critical, biblical scholarship, and certainly by the time of F. C. Baur and the flourishing of the Tübingen School (mid-nineteenth century), conventional opinion changed, largely as a result of the late dating of both letters, the topic of the next section. The reasoning was, and remains, clear-cut: because the letters of James and Jude were understood to show evidence of concern for issues thought to be "early Catholic" (dulled eschatological expectations and organizational, *episcopal* concerns, etc.), they must be dated in the nineties CE or after, making it impossible for James, who was executed in 62, and unlikely for Jude to be the authors. Additionally, because James was generally read as if written in conversation and/or dispute with Paul, the letter has been held to be in response to Paul, and so again dated to a time after the death of James. And because Jude is read largely with regard to its

---

[2] Richard Bauckham, *Jude and 2 Peter*, Word Biblical Commentary, vol. 50 (Waco, TX: Word Books, 1983), p. 3.

Introduction 3

relationship to 2 Peter, it is often dated alongside (or after, depending on the decision about priority of Jude/2 Peter) the usual late dating of that letter.

Questions of authorship seem often answered in tandem with questions of dating, and because there is generally held to be more "evidence" within the letters suggestive of date, authorship is circumscribed by date. But what happens if one separates the two? Moreover, what happens when one reads the letters of James and Jude on their own merits and not in light of any real or imagined relationship to the letters of Paul and Peter? Then the question changes, and the presumption returns to more traditional identifications. One is compelled to ask, what are the reasons to deny authorship to James and Jude, the brothers of the Lord?[3] First, one must identify the "James" and "Jude" in question.

Jude is the conventional rendering of Judas in the first verse of the epistle, but the Greek is *Ioudas*, so the task is to distinguish, or identify, the Judas of the letter from the other Judases in the NT, for the name occurs thirty-six times.

- twenty-two times the reference is to Judas ("Iscariot"), the betrayer.
- two times (Lk 6:16, Acts 1:13) the reference is to "Judas of James" (*Ioudas Iakōbou*) in Luke's list of the twelve.
- three times in Acts 15 the reference is to "Judas Barsabbas."
- Acts (9:11) mentions a Judas who hosts Saul before his sight is restored and a "Judas the Galilean" (5:37) whose revolt against the census in 6 CE is discussed by Josephus.
- Jn (14:22) includes a question from Judas identified in the Greek text as *ouch ho Iskariōtēs* ("not the Iscariot"), a phrase omitted in New Standard Revised Version (NRSV).
- Mt 13:55 and Mk 6:3 relate the Nazarean synagogue member's identification of Jesus as the "brother of James and Joses and Judas and Simon."

While from time to time one or another writer has argued otherwise, the vast majority of scholars agree that the letter of Jude intends its author to be understood as one of the brothers of Jesus.

Is this identification authentic? I conclude that it is, insofar as one can identify any biblical author with a historical person. First, removing the late dating limits the reasons not to accept this identification to one or another version of the "early Catholic" canard and to the objection that a Galilean farmer or craftsman could

---

[3] While I understand the Marian issues that bear upon discussions of the fraternal relationship of Jesus, James, and Jude, there is not room to discuss them, nor does it impact the commentary to follow. The interested reader may turn to Richard Bauckham, *Jude and the Relatives of Jesus* (Edinburgh: T & T Clark, 1990), pp. 19–32.

not write sophisticated Greek. As we will see in the commentary, there is nothing "early Catholic" about Jude.[4] The letter pulses throughout with anticipation of the Lord's return, cares nothing for office or position, and deals with a dispute easily understood as possible in earliest Jewish Christianity. As for writing Greek, Sevenster[5] and others have seriously called into question the depiction of the apostles as "illiterate Galilean fishermen," and if that does not convince, one always has recourse to the use of scribes, something we know happened in at least some NT writings (2 Th 3:17). In other words, there is no good reason *not* to accept the letter of Jude as coming from the brother of James. But did *this* brother write the letter attributed to him? And why did neither come right out and self-identify as a "brother of the Lord"?

"James" (*Iakōbos*) occurs forty-two times in the NT.

- twenty-one references are to the "son of Zebedee, brother of John," whose execution in 44 CE is recorded in Acts 12:2, the last mention of this member of the inner circle of the twelve.
- four references are to the "son of Alphaeus," one of the twelve.
- four references are to the "son of Mary" and "brother of Joses/Joseph" at the burial of Jesus.
- two references are to the father of Judas.
- two references are to the brother of Jesus by the Nazarean synagogue members.
- eight references are without designation.
- one reference, Gal 1:19, is to James, "the Lord's brother."

The last three sets are all accepted as one and the same person, for in early Christian history there is only one "James" who needed no further introduction: James, the brother of the Lord, who according to Josephus (*Antiquities* 20.200) was executed in 62 CE.

Did this James compose the letter of the same name? Certainly, as in the case of Jude, the letter was understood by its author to have been written by someone who needed no further introduction. On this everyone agrees. The letter of James purports to have been written by the brother of the Lord. But was it in fact? Here the burden, it seems to me, shifts to those who think that it was not, and they of course are many. But their reasons are few and generally cluster around a late dating, which will be discussed, a "tension" between the concerns of James found in the letter and the depiction of James's concerns in Acts and Galatians, and the sophisticated level of composition, which is denied, almost in

---

[4] This is not to assume that the designation "early Catholic" is still useful. Recent research into the trajectories of early Christianity have largely put aside this nineteenth-century interpretation.

[5] "Do You Know Greek? How Much Greek Could the First Jewish Christians Have Known?" *Novum Testamentum Supplement* 19 (1968).

Introduction

the spirit of Nathaniel's "Can anything good come out of Nazareth?" (Jn 1:46), to James. As seen with regard to Jude, the argument about composition is not telling. Nor, I think, is the very small glimpse of James found in Acts 15 and 21 and Gal 1–2 decisive. That Paul's rhetoric in Galatians and likely his attitude were tendentious, is indisputable. The danger of allowing Paul to have the deciding vote about the character and priorities of James is well evidenced by Luther. To say that the concerns evidenced in Acts do not match those of the letter is to forget that Paul is the center of the second half of Acts, so that James is likely to have been somewhat caricatured. There is also a tendency to overstate the significance of the two-part requirement of Acts 15:29 and 21:25 (abstain from certain meats and from fornication), and in turn to read the ethical concerns in the letter of James as if James had no interest in purity issues, thereby creating a tension between the depiction of "James" in Acts and the "James" apparent in the letter. That this tension is an artificial creation is evidenced, for example, by the very real purity concerns in James 3:17 and 4:8.

Among authors who have influenced this commentary, Martin Dibelius, Hubert Frankemölle, Sophie Laws, Pheme Perkins, and Bo Reicke deny authorship to James, and Ralph Martin and Robert Wall make recourse to later editing of Jacobean tradition, while James Adamson, Richard Bauckham, Patrick Hartin, Luke Johnson, and Douglas Moo affirm the traditional designation. Because I am unconvinced by arguments for a late dating and, as will be indicated in the commentary, hold that the work itself shows every evidence of being very early indeed, and because I am not persuaded that we know enough to deny authorship based on theories of what early Christians could or could not write, with or without use of a scribe, I accept the traditional designation as the basis for my reading. *James and Jude, the authors of the letters bearing their names, were the brothers of Jesus.* The really interesting question is what happens when one reads the letters based on this position.

DATES

Having claimed that our authors are "the brothers of the Lord" I have implicitly accepted a *terminus ad quem* of 62 CE for James and presumably not much later for Jude. I believe the internal evidence of both letters supports this conclusion. Johnson outlines six points in favor of an early date for James. The first four are most telling.

1. "James lacks any of the classic signs of late, pseudonymous authorship" (elaboration of author's identity, rationalization for delay of "parousia," tradition viewed as "deposit" rather than process, etc.).
2. "James reflects the social realities and outlooks appropriate to a sect in the early stages of life."

3. The shape of Jesus' sayings in James is similar to that of Q, so the arguments for placing Q within early Palestinian Christianity should also apply to James.
4. "The best way to account for the similarity and difference" between the language of James and Paul "is to view them both as first generation Jewish Christians deeply affected by Greco-Roman moral traditions yet fundamentally defined by an allegiance to the symbols and story of Torah."[6]

In the present commentary particular attention will be given to the sociocultural realities (2) and to the way James uses material we now identify as sayings of Jesus (3). The ecclesial and cultural realities seem best dated before the fall of Jerusalem and placed within Palestine, while the rather nonchalant handling of Jesus material is evidence of a time very early in the tradition. For these reasons I join with Adamson, Bauckham, Hartin, and Johnson in *dating the composition of the letter of James to the fifties CE, making it one of the earliest writings in the NT*.[7]

Jude is likely not dated quite so early and has one internal piece of evidence that must be explained.[8] Jude 17 says, "But you, beloved, must remember the predictions of the apostles of our Lord Jesus Christ." The verse will be considered in detail in the commentary, but the idea that predictions said by apostles must be remembered suggests to many an *apostolic age* that is past, even long past, by the time the letter of Jude is written. Yet there is nothing in the construction itself that suggests a distant past, just a prior action, in this case action by apostles, perhaps but likely not including the author. Moreover, Paul calls to mind prior teachings (1 Th 4:1–2; Gal 1:9; 1 Cor 15:1) and refers to a central portion of his own teaching as "received from the Lord" (1 Cor 11:23); yet this is not thought to suggest a late date for his letters. When the objections to v. 17 are removed, and one appreciates that the words and actions of the opponents are hardly inconsistent with that of Paul's descriptions of the Corinthians, for example, what stands out is the sense of being in "the last times" (v. 18) when readers should "look forward to the mercy of our Lord Jesus Christ that leads to eternal life" (v. 21) – in other words, an expectation usually identified with earliest Christianity. While it is not possible to offer a precise date, nor is there a *terminus* provided by the date of Jude's death, which is not mentioned in any source, *it seems best to interpret the letter as*

---

[6] Luke T. Johnson, *The Letter of James*, Anchor Bible 37A (New York: Doubleday, 1995), pp. 118–21.

[7] John A. T. Robinson, *Redating the New Testament* (Philadelphia: Westminster Press, 1976), pp. 118–39, attempted to place James on "the frontier between Judaism and Christianity" and dated it to before the Jerusalem council, i.e., 47–8.

[8] Scholarship's more sophisticated understanding of gnosticism has resulted in setting aside the idea that Jude's opponents were either gnostic or proto-gnostic. See R. Bauckham, *Jude and 2 Peter* (1983), pp. 11–13.

Introduction 7

having been written prior to the fall of Jerusalem and thus sometime before 70 CE.[9]

OCCASIONS

Jude makes it easy. Whatever one concludes about who he was, when he wrote, and to whom he was writing, he tells us why he wrote. He even tells us why he was going to write a letter he apparently never got around to writing. "Beloved, while eagerly preparing to write to you about the salvation we share, I find it necessary to write and appeal to you to contend for the faith that was once for all entrusted to the saints" (v. 3). In form (sender, v. 1a; addressee, v. 1b; blessing, v. 2; thesis, vv. 3–4; body, vv. 5–23; doxology, vv. 24–5) Jude is clearly a letter, and by the letter's own admission it was written as warning, condemnation, and encouragement to a community confronted with suspect teachers and/or leaders.

The genre of the letter of Jude is clear, but what of its character? A fuller discussion must wait for the commentary. To anticipate the conclusions, Jude can be fairly characterized in rhetorical terms as exhibiting a mixed species of deliberative (giving advice and encouraging or discouraging a specific course of action) and epideictic (praise and blame, seeking assent to some value) rhetoric (Duane Watson). In sociocultural terms it may be characterized as a response, or riposte, to a challenge to the author's honor (Neyrey) and in ideological terms as an expression of early Christian apocalyptic, particularly as opposed to prior declarations that the letter's ideology was "early Catholic" (Bauckham).

While there are few if any clues as to provenance, recent interpreters have returned to Jerusalem as a likely location, given the identification of the family of Jesus with the Jerusalem church. As we will see in the commentary, however, little of this matters to the interpretation and appreciation of the letter.

The letter of James is another matter altogether. Although the most recent and best interpreters have begun to lay such questions to rest, it is still necessary to consider to whom (Jews, Christians, Jewish Christians?) and why (correction, reproof, encouragement?) James was writing, where author and audience were located, and whether the letter of James is even a letter.

Is the letter of James a letter, and if not, what is the genre of James?[10] The text itself purports to be a letter. In classic form it begins with the sender, then the addressee, followed by the traditional greeting, *chairein* (greetings). Is that enough to qualify James as a letter? Yes. First, despite the pervasive influence of Paul, there is not a single model in the NT of what a letter looks like. NT letters

---

[9] J. A. T. Robinson, *Redating the New Testament* (1976), pp. 169–99, dates Jude (and 2 Pet) to "61–2" (p. 198).
[10] Throughout this commentary I use the designation "letter" to avoid any echo of the once popular debate distinguishing "letter" and "epistle" fostered by Gustav Deissmann, *Light from the Ancient East* (London: Hodder and Stoughton, 1911).

vary in length, audience, outline, and topics, from the "letters" in Acts to the "letter to the Romans." To argue that James cannot be a letter because it lacks final greetings is like arguing that Mark is not a gospel because it originally had no resurrection appearance, nor John because it has no birth narrative.[11] Second, to disqualify James as a letter because the majority of its verses are devoted to *paranesis* (traditional moral instruction) and *diatribe* (moral exhortation) is to confuse form and content. By this standard one would also disqualify Romans. Johnson's solution is simple and persuasive, even if one may disagree with his final designation that James "can be appropriately considered protreptic discourse in the form of a letter."[12] More generally, and particularly in light of the discussion of homiletical texture in the final section of the Introduction, James may be thought of as a homiletical letter intended to be circulated and read aloud (as were all letters) by early Christian communities influenced by the Jerusalem church. Whether one thinks of it as a letter in the form of a sermon or as a sermon in the form of a letter, it was a vehicle for sharing the teaching of James with the extended early Jewish Christian community – the "twelve tribes of the Dispersion" (Gk *diaspora*).

This latter designation is explicitly metaphorical[13] and bridges a divide (Jew–Christian) experienced more in our day than in James's. Certainly it is a divide experienced more sharply. That James uses a traditional designation for the children of Israel, "the twelve tribes," and extends it to the early Christian community in a way that also speaks to the realities of the Jewish diaspora (a population that even in James's day far outnumbered that of Judah and Galilee) speaks to the absence of a boundary we have come to take for granted but cannot clearly place: the boundary between prerabbinic Judaism and earliest Christianity. Further evidence is found in debates over whether James is a "Christian" or "Jewish" writing, for Jesus is only mentioned by name at 1:1 and 2:1, and these verses have from time to time been held as insertions to an originally Jewish document. Such proof texting proves little, except the inadequacy of the categories to describe a newly emerging reality. What seems clear in the twenty-first century was hardly so in the middle of the first. Was James a Jew? Yes. Was James a Christian? Yes. Little wonder his letter reads as if written by a Jewish Christian. It was.

---

[11] William G. Doty, *Letters in Primitive Christianity* (Philadelphia: Fortress Press, 1973) follows Deissmann in denying that James and Jude are "real letters" (p. 68). That he devotes his longest chapter entirely to Paul and discusses James and Jude in less than a paragraph is comment enough. The much more thorough treatment by Stowers classifies James among "letters of exhortation and advice" (pp. 96–7) but does not treat Jude. Stanley K. Stowers, *Letter Writing in Greco-Roman Antiquity*, Library of Early Christianity (Philadelphia: Westminster Press, 1986).
[12] L. T. Johnson, *Letter of James* (1995), p. 24.
[13] See Robert W. Wall, *Community of the Wise* (Valley Forge, PA: Trinity Press International, 1997), pp. 11–18.

Introduction 9

The geographical location of James and his audience is also hard to fix. To the extent that James intended his designation of addressee to mean at some level those outside Judah and Galilee, his own traditional location in Jerusalem is confirmed. But if "twelve tribes of the Dispersion" is wholly metaphorical, referring as Wall and others suggest to their social location and not to their geographical location within Jewish Christianity, no support for the traditional identification of Jerusalem as James's place of writing can be adduced. Discussion of the character of the letter of James is deferred to the section on literary relationships.

To summarize: Jude and James are both real letters written to real audiences with real issues in mind, another reason the designation "general" or "catholic" is not apt. Jude wrote to warn a beloved community to be careful of certain teachers/leaders and to hold firm to the teaching they had already received. James wrote to encourage a community or communities, reminding them of key features of his teaching, using the letter as a sermon in absentia.

There are two names notably missing from this brief discussion of the occasion for the writing of the letters of James and Jude: Paul and Peter. As we will see in the next section, I do not believe that James was written with Paul in mind, nor Jude with Peter, and I endeavor to read each letter accordingly.

LITERARY RELATIONSHIPS

In discussion of intertexture in the last section of the Introduction and in our examination of intertexture in the Commentary, literary relationships are understood to run in two directions. The focus in this section is on the textual traditions that have impacted the works under consideration.

The most obvious influence is the Hebrew Bible, for James in translation (LXX [Septuagint]) and for Jude perhaps not.[14] Whether in Hebrew or Greek, in the text both authors are deeply indebted to the tradition. Jude's references are fewer in number and so are easier to identify. As with James, they are discussed in detail in the Commentary, with citations and references, and need only be listed here to give the reader some sense of just how thoroughly imbued both books are with OT (Old Testament) tradition. Jude's biblical references tend to come from the Torah, and James draws on Torah, prophets, and, to an even greater extent, the full range of the Wisdom tradition.

Citations and References in Jude	*Citations and References in James*
Gen 4:3–8; 19:4–25	Gen 1:26–7; 4:10; 22:9, 12
Ex 12:51; 34:8	Ex 20:5, 13, 14; 34:6
Num 14:29–30, 35; 22:7; 31:16	Lev 19:13–18
Isa 57:20	Deut 5:17–18; 11:14; 24:14–15

[14] See R. Bauckham, *Jude and 2 Peter* (1983), p. 7.

Eze 34:8	Josh 2:4, 15; 6:17
Amos 4:11	1 Kgs 17:1; 18:42–5
Zech 3:2; 14:5	Job 5:11; 34:19
	Psa 18:6; 21:9; 34:13; 39:1; 102:4, 11; 103:8; 111:4; 140:3; 141:3
	Prov 3:34; 10:12; 27:1
	Eccl 7:9
	Isa 5:9; 40:6–7
	Jer 5:24
	Dan 12:12
	Zech 1:3
	Mal 3:5, 7
	Sir 5:11; 15:11–13

Biblical citations hardly exhaust the literary relationships of Jude and James. Jude famously cites from two apocryphal, pseudepigraphical works – *1 Enoch* and *Testament of Moses* – along with an otherwise unrecorded saying of "the apostles." Johnson details a wealth of influences and possible parallels, if not precisely literary relationships, that form an important backdrop to James.[15] Two are key: the traditions of OT and Jewish Wisdom literature and the teachings/sayings of Jesus.

OT and Jewish Wisdom traditions are, of course, important to the entire NT but perhaps not to the extent of the letter of James. Bauckham has shown in *James: Wisdom of James, Disciple of Jesus the Sage* the full extent of this influence, for as is the case with all the influences on James it is not simply a matter of citation. James obviously felt it unnecessary to give chapter and verse. Nor is it limited to possible parallels, such as those included in the lists just provided. Instead it is the way in which the spirit of OT and Jewish Wisdom traditions imbue the entire letter, so that it would be fair to characterize the ideology of this homiletical letter as very much a part of the sapiential tradition, yet with strong "alternative wisdom" leanings.[16]

No doubt the most intriguing question in any discussion of the literary relationships of James is the relationship of James to the sayings of Jesus. The most thorough examination of Jesus' sayings in the letter of James is found in

---

[15] L. T. Johnson, *Letter of James* (1995), pp. 26–46.
[16] On OT and Jewish Wisdom, see the introductions by Anthony R. Ceresko, OSFS, *Introduction to Old Testament Wisdom: A Spirituality for Liberation* (Maryknoll, NY: Orbis Books, 1999) and James L. Crenshaw, *Old Testament Wisdom: An Introduction*, rev. ed. (Louisville, KY: Westminster/John Knox Press, 1998). Crenshaw is the standard introduction, while Ceresko's approach emphasizes the ideological stream of wisdom that the letter of James itself reflects. On wisdom and James, see Ben Witherington III, *Jesus the Sage* (Minneapolis, MN: Fortress Press, 1994), pp. 236–47. In the Commentary I will argue against Witherington in finding that James's ideology more closely fits the model of alternative wisdom than is recognized in *Jesus the Sage*.

Introduction

the 1989 Amsterdam dissertation of Dean B. Deppe.[17] Deppe concludes that scholars often overstate the number of allusions to Jesus material in the letter and attributes this to a lack of precision in determining what constitutes an allusion. His own standards are high, and by defining an allusion as the presence of "substantial verbal similarities as well as a common context and emphasis of content," he finds only eight allusions:

James 1:5 = Mt 7:7; Lk 11:9	ask and you will receive
James 4:2c–3 = Mt 7:7; Lk 11:9	ask and you will receive
James 2:5 = Lk 6:20b; Mt 5:3	kingdom belongs to poor
James 5:2–3a = Mt 6:19–20; Lk 12:33b	do not treasure up wealth
James 4:9 = Lk 6:21, 25b	those who laugh will mourn
James 5:1 = Lk 6:24	woe to the rich
James 5:12 = Mt 5:33–7	oaths
James 4:10 = Mt 23:12; Lk 14:11; 18:14b	humble are exalted

That Deppe's standards may be too high is suggested to the student of the NT by the absence from this list of very familiar sayings; for example, about being doers of the word (James 1:22–5; 2:14-17 cf. Mt 7:24–7; Lk 6:46–9), against judging others (James 4:11–12 cf. Mt 7:1–2; Lk 6:37), against anger (James 1:19–20 cf. Mt 5:22), fruit from the tree (James 3:12 cf. Mt 7:16; Lk 6:44), blessing on those who endure (James 1:12; 5:10–11 cf. Mt 5:11–12; Lk 6:22–3), being peacemakers (James 3:18 cf. Mt 5:9), the results of mercy (James 2:13 cf. Mt 5:7), and more. Indeed, when one tallies not only allusions but parallels of content and/or terminology and common references, Deppe's list grows from eight to thirty-six, and this does not include nine themes common to the preaching of Jesus and the letter of James.[18]

What stands out most, however, is not the large number of allusions, references, and parallels, but the complete absence of citations. For all the common themes, sayings, and ideas, never once does James "quote" Jesus, which suggests not a lack of awareness or familiarity with Jesus traditions but a casual approach to those sayings. Far from being "gospel," at the time James was writing the sayings of Jesus were not yet fixed within the tradition. Instead they were part of a growing and gathering body of material, from which James freely and easily borrowed and to which his letter contributed.[19] This is, perhaps more than anything, the clearest evidence for an early dating of James.

---

[17] Dean B. Deppe, *The Sayings of Jesus in the Epistle of James* (Chelsea, MI: Bookcrafters, 1989).

[18] Ibid., pp. 219ff.

[19] I am not convinced, as is Patrick Hartin, *James and Q Sayings of Jesus* JSNT Supplement Series 47 (Sheffield, England: JSOT Press, 1991), that the letter of James knows the Jesus material via Q. Instead I think James and Q reflect a common, but unshared, early stage of development.

Jude, too, was in his own way fairly nonchalant in his use of traditional materials, quoting from and referring to the Hebrew Bible, the apocryphal work *1 Enoch*, the pseudepigraphic *Testament of Moses*, and an otherwise unknown saying of the apostles in more or less the same fashion, as if all were a piece. Also, it seems to be evidence for an early date.

Before turning briefly to the reception and history of interpretation of James and Jude, the relationship of Jude and 2 Peter, and of James and Paul, must be considered. The first is rather easy – and this may be the last time that anything can be said to be easy in our consideration of Jude. I will make every effort to read Jude without regard to 2 Peter, understanding, along with the majority of recent interpreters, that 2 Peter 2 is itself the first reading and appropriation of Jude.[20]

For the purpose of this commentary, the relationship of James and Paul, in its own way, is also simple. Along with Bauckham, Johnson, and many others, I am convinced that appreciation, interpretation, and appropriation of James has been consistently undermined by the long habit of reading James "in light of" (as the saying goes, but actually "in the shadow of") Paul. This commentary will, by way of corrective, endeavor to read the letter of James with as little reference to the letters of Paul as may be responsibly attempted. Convinced as I am that the differences between Paul and James have been consistently exaggerated and that the pivotal terms of law, faith, work, and righteousness mean slightly but significantly different things to each author, I want to explore what happens when we read James on his own terms and read James without reference to Paul as much as possible.

RECEPTION AND INTERPRETATION

That the letters of Jude and James have experienced a mixed reception in the Church, east and west, is both a commonplace and an understatement. In their own ways, each struggled to be received into the canon, and as late as Eusebius's *Ecclesiastical History* (324–5 CE) both were listed as "disputed" writings (*antilegomenoi*; *HE* 3.25.3). Even after their inclusion in the list of twenty-seven writings found in Athanasius's "festal letter" (c. 367 CE), a point often used to demark the closing of the NT canon, James's and Jude's authenticity and canonicity continued to be questioned and perhaps more significantly, often ignored. The reasons were shared and unique.

---

[20] The work of Duane Watson is particularly important here. Recognizing the difficulty of using redactional criticism to establish the priority of Jude over 2 Peter, or vice versa, Watson carefully applied rhetorical criticism. He concluded, "Often the priority of neither can be asserted, the verbal correspondences being equally suited to the rhetoric of either work. Occasionally the priority of 2 Peter is indicated. However, by a considerable margin, *the priority of Jude is strongly affirmed*" (my emphasis). Duane Watson, *Invention, Arrangement, and Style* (Atlanta: Scholars Press, 1988), esp. pp. 163–88. Also, see R. Bauckham, *Jude and the Relatives of Jesus* (1990), pp. 134–77.

The most likely trajectory is as follows. Both letters were initially (c. 65–125 CE) well and widely received, a reflection of the recognition of the authors as "brothers of the Lord" and of the honored place of the Jerusalem church, with which they were closely identified. The ascendance of the legacies and reputation of Peter and Paul in the growing church and the geographical and theological shift away from Jerusalem as the center of emergent Christianity resulted in a decline in reputation for James and Jude. The spread of the canonical gospels, in which Jude and James play no real part, further eclipsed the letters bearing their names. By the third century, that James and Jude lacked clear apostolic credentials pushed the letters to the margins of the Church's favored reading. The tendency to read James with Paul and Jude with 2 Peter was almost their undoing. To the extent that James was understood to be challenging Paul, the letter was set aside as inferior. To the extent that Jude was read as an excerpt of 2 Peter, the letter was set aside as a pale imitation of the work of the rock upon which the Church was being built. More telling for Jude, as the biblical canon took on clearer shape, was that the letter cites *1 Enoch* and *Testament of Moses*. Would a work worthy of inclusion in the canon quote works that were not?

At one level, then, it is a wonder the letters of Jude and James survived at all. Certainly their earlier acceptance was crucial. At a practical level, this acceptance yielded sufficient copies to keep the letters available and read. Nor were the letters without champions. Foremost for Jude were Clement and Origen in Alexandria, but there was also Tertullian. The letter is included in the Muratorian Canon and finally, if grudgingly, accepted by Eusebius and Jerome. And assuming the order of composition most widely held today (see note 9), the strongest testament to the acceptance of Jude is 2 Peter. Given this history it is not surprising that other than the relationship to 2 Peter two issues have dominated the treatment of Jude in biblical scholarship: the identity of Jude's opponents and the sources of Jude's citations, questions that will be considered in the commentary on Jude.

The reception and interpretation of the letter of James has been, if possible, more troubled and controversial than that of Jude. Johnson devotes almost forty pages to this topic in his *Letter of James* (pp. 124–61), an excellent analysis to which the interested reader is encouraged to turn, for it cannot be duplicated in this commentary, where we must settle for a brief summary.

The opinion of Martin Luther (in)famously casts a shadow over any discussion of the reception of James, but Luther was hardly the first voice to raise questions about the letter of James and its place in the canon. While *1 Clement* (c. 95 CE) and *The Shepherd of Hermas* (c. 140 CE) seem to know the letter of James (especially the latter, which shares James's use of the unusual term *dipsuchos* [double-minded] and a number of important themes), if not borrow from it, James is not mentioned in the Muratorian fragment (c. 190 CE), although all three later documents are usually identified with Rome. This may well be evidence of the declining reputation of the letter of James in the West after the middle of the second century. James fared better in Alexandria, where Clement and Origen cited James frequently (thirty-six times according to Johnson's count) and where Didymus the Blind (313–98 CE) wrote a commentary on James, and in the East generally, where Athanasius, Cyril of Alexandria, Cyril of Jerusalem, and others include James in their lists of accepted documents and cite the letter in their own writing.

Eusebius (c. 325 CE) wrote that to James "is attributed the first of the 'general' epistles. Admittedly its authenticity is doubted, since few early writers refer to it, any more than to 'Jude's', which is also one of the seven called general. But the fact remains that these two, like the others, have been regularly used in very many churches."[21] Later in the fourth century James found new champions in Jerome and Augustine, the latter writing a commentary on the letter. The letter is well attested in the fourth–sixth centuries and received a marvelous commentary from the Venerable Bede, still extant, in the late seventh century.

Prior to Luther, Erasmus and Cajetan both expressed doubts about the worthiness of the letter of James. The late Raymond Brown, SS, offered a succinct and unbiased summary of Luther's views in his *Introduction to the New Testament*.

In the (September) 1522 edition of his translation into German, Luther attempted to put Jas with Heb, Jude, and Rev at the end of the NT as of lesser quality than "the true and certain, main books of the New Testament." Major factors in the Reformation opposition to Jas, besides disputes in antiquity, were the support it gave to extreme unction as a sacrament and its affirmation, "Faith apart from works is useless" (2:20), which conflicted with Luther's exaltation of faith. Even though Luther found many good sayings in it, Jas was a strawlike epistle when compared to the true gold of the gospel. As late as the 1540s in his "Table Talk" he was wishing that Jas be thrown out of discussion at the University of Wittenberg, for it did not amount to much.[22]

Brown goes on to note that Luther's attempt to rearrange the canon was later abandoned.

Since Luther the fate and fortune of James largely followed a path that would have been to the Reformer's liking. Consistently read alongside Paul, and found wanting, James the author began to disappear from the scene as nineteenth-century commentators, following the lead of F. H. Kern, began to read (or not read) the letter along the lines of larger currents and disputes in biblical

---

[21] *The History of the Church*, HE 2.24, trans. G. A. Williamson (Minneapolis, MN: Augsburg, 1975) p. 103.

[22] Raymond Brown, *An Introduction to the New Testament* (New York: Doubleday, 1997), p. 744. Luther himself never retracted the opinion given in the 1522 "Preface to James": "I therefore refuse him a place among the writers of the true canon in my Bible; but I would not prevent anyone placing him or raising him where he likes, for the epistle contains many excellent passages." *Martin Luther: Selections from His Writings*, ed. John Dillenberger (New York: Anchor Books, 1961), p. 36.

scholarship. Adolf Jülicher betrayed his Lutheran sensibilities when he wrote in his NT introduction (1894) that James was the "least Christian book" of the New Testament. It was not long after that L. Massibieau put forward the thesis that James was a Jewish composition to which 1:1 and 2:1 had been added, a position supported by the work of F. Spitta. The letter has been on the defensive ever since. As Johnson writes, "What the thesis of Massibieau and Spitta most vividly illustrates is the way in which the logic of the scholarly discussion in some circles had led to the removal of James from serious consideration as properly 'Christian' literature at all, whether early or late!"[23] Because the present commentary joins the discussion at about this juncture, I need only mention that twenty years or so after Spitta convinced many that the letter of James was not Christian, Dibelius argued that the letter was not really a letter! Fortunately, the fortunes of the letter of James, both in the level of attention paid to it and in the competency of the scholarship applied to it, would increase throughout the twentieth century, culminating in Johnson's marvelous Anchor Bible commentary, *Letter of James*, in 1995.

THE TEXTURE OF TEXTS

This commentary is an attempt to apply the methods of sociorhetorical criticism to the interpretation of the letters of James and Jude. "Socio-rhetorical criticism challenges interpreters to explore human reality and religious belief and practice through multiple approaches to written discourse in texts. As an interpretive program that moves toward a broad-based interpretive analytics, it invites investigations that enact integrated interdisciplinary analysis and interpretation."[24] As practiced by Robbins, his students, and colleagues, sociorhetorical criticism is not a new method, but a disciplined attempt to bring what is better seen as a *series* of methods to the reading of biblical texts. In his "guide to socio-rhetorical interpretation," *Exploring the Texture of Texts* (1996), and the companion study, *The Tapestry of Early Christian Discourse* (1996), Robbins details the five textures found in any and every biblical text. Because the exegesis of the letters of James and Jude is informed and organized by these textures, plus a sixth that extends the method to include preaching, it is important to summarize them now.

Inner Texture

Robbins refers to inner texture as "getting inside a text." To study inner texture is to explore "features in the language of the text itself,"[25] that is, the rhetorical

---

[23] L. T. Johnson, *Letter of James* (1995), p. 151.
[24] Vernon K. Robbins, *The Tapestry of Early Christian Discourse* (London: Routledge, 1996), p. 13.
[25] Vernon K. Robbins, *Exploring the Texture of Texts* (Valley Forge, PA: Trinity Press International, 1996) p. 7.

patterns and strategies used by the author to communicate with the reader. One explores inner texture with nothing but the text, perhaps in more than one translation, and a dictionary or lexicon. To study inner texture is to experience and appreciate the power of the text to create a world, to create meaning, to persuade, dissuade, and cajole, without reference to other texts, textual history, sociohistorical and cultural-anthropological insights, etc. Just the author and the reader, with the text as mode of communication. Consider, for example, James 1:2–5, a passage with a typically rich inner texture.

2 My brothers and sisters, whenever you face trials of any kind, consider it nothing but joy, 3 because you know that the testing of your faith produces endurance; 4 and let endurance have its full effect, so that you may be mature and complete, lacking in nothing. 5 If any of you is lacking in wisdom, ask God, who gives to all generously and ungrudgingly, and it will be given you.

When the passage is read aloud, and read closely, its inner-textual richness is clear, even more so if one is able to read in Greek, so that the alliteration and poetic resonance may be appreciated. In any language, however, the gentle opening ("My brothers and sisters"), the immediate (this is v. 2, after all) introduction of "trials of any kind," and the unexpected juxtaposition of "trials" and "joy" stand out. Perhaps most notable is the careful, stair-step construction known to rhetoricians as *gradatio* (climax): the reader climbs from trials to testing to endurance, from endurance to "full effect" (Gk. *teleion*), from "mature and complete" (Gk. *teleioi*) to "lacking in nothing" to "lacking in wisdom" to the God who "gives to all" and "it will be given you." The study of inner texture brings the interpreter as deeply as possible into the words and ways of the text, to the appreciation of its structure and shape, without recourse to anything outside the text itself.

Intertexture

"Intertexture is a text's representation of, reference to, and use of phenomena in the 'world' outside the text being interpreted. In other words, the intertexture of a text is the interaction of the language in the text with 'outside' material and physical 'objects,' historical events, texts, customs, values, roles, institutions, and systems."[26] When we explore intertexture the relation of the text under study is first and foremost to others texts and secondarily to the "world" behind the other texts. Robbins identifies intertexture as being either oral-scribal, cultural, social, or historical. An example from James 5:12 will help.

Above all, my beloved, do not swear, either by heaven or by earth or by any other oath, but let your "Yes" be yes and your "No" be no, so that you may not fall under condemnation.

Study of the inner texture would note the repetition of "beloved" (Gk. *adelphoi*) followed by a stern imperative prohibition, and so on. Study of

---

[26] Ibid., p. 40.

intertexture says, "Doesn't that sound like something Jesus and Paul said?" (yes, Mt 5:33–7 and 2 Cor 1:17ff.) and asks, "Isn't there something about swearing in the Hebrew Bible?" (yes, Lev 19:12). Study of intertexture would go on to ask about the attitude toward swearing an oath in Jewish and other ancient sources (cultural intertexture), how oaths figured in the social roles and codes of the ancient world (social intertexture), and whether we have inscriptions, coins, or other things that might provide evidence of these attitudes and values (historical intertexture). When the interpreter considers intertexture she or he moves beyond the text to examine other texts that have greater (in our example, the text from Mt 5) or lesser (Lev 19) degrees of relationship to the text under study and to the world behind those texts.

Sociocultural Texture

Examination of the sociocultural texture of a text immerses the interpreter in the world of the text and the world presupposed and evidenced by the text. We attempt to understand the world that produced the text, what it would mean to live in that world, and how our understanding of what it would mean to live in such a world impacts how we understand what it means to "live" the text in our own world. Much more than a consideration of "everyday life in Bible times," fully exploring a text's sociocultural texture means studying the insights of social-scientific criticism, cultural anthropology, and more. Robbins sketches it this way:

The social and cultural texture of text emerges in specific social topics, common social and cultural topics, and final cultural categories. . . . The social and cultural systems presupposed in the text may be significantly distinct from the social and cultural systems in which the interpreter himself or herself lives. Analysis and interpretation of the common social and cultural topics in a text may take an interpreter beyond his or her own presuppositions into the foreign social and cultural world of the text. When this happens, a deeper level of the social and cultural texture of the text begins to emerge as well as a clearer understanding of the implications in the text about living a committed religious life in the world.[27]

Sociocultural texture is multilayered, helping us to understand a world where communal values outweigh individual preferences, where family and village ties truly bind, patriarchy reigns unquestioned, patronage controls the economy, and where honor and shame are dominant cultural values. Let us here take an example from Jude 4.

For certain intruders have stolen in among you, people who long ago were designated for this condemnation as ungodly, who pervert the grace of our God into licentiousness and deny our only Master and Lord, Jesus Christ.

---

[27] Ibid., p. 71. Although Robbins refers to "social texture" and "cultural texture" I will collapse the two into "sociocultural texture" to facilitate consideration of sociocultural and ideological textures in the same section.

Almost instinctively the reader wants to know the identity of the "certain intruders" and what it is that Jude has against them. As we will see in the Commentary, the level of invective is high and tends to overwhelm other dynamics in the text. But behind the invective we find social and cultural values, values important to Jude but apparently not to his opponents, or perhaps more accurately, values important enough to Jude and his community that to accuse his opponents of not sharing them is damning indeed. That the opponents are referred to as "intruders" who have "stolen in" is more than name-calling. It is evidence of a premium placed on honesty, openness, and a propriety of place. To be out of place is to be impure, polluted (see Jude 6, where some "angels" do not "keep their own position but left their proper dwelling"). The value of the ancient over the new and the importance of prophetic anticipation are clear, as are the place and value of grace, and the cultural rejection of "licentiousness." Perhaps more telling of one who begins the letter by referring to himself as a "slave" (NRSV "servant" but Gk. *doulos*) is the denial of "our only Master," which in sociocultural terms is a repudiation of appropriate social roles within the community of believers. All of this, and much more, is part of the sociocultural texture of this text. In the Commentary we will explore this texture much more fully, along the way developing our understanding of the important values and roles apparent in the cultures of James, Jude, and their readers.

Ideological Texture

In exploring ideological texture interpreters put their cards on the table, for the ideological texture is at least as much about the interpreter as it is about the text. Robbins writes, "The issue is the social, cultural, and individual location and perspective of writers and readers. Ideological analysis of a text, then, is simply an agreement by various people that they will dialogue and disagree with one another with a text as a guest in the conversation."[28] Sounds like fun. This is not to say that texts under study have no ideological biases. Clearly this is not the case with the letters of James and Jude. But it is the interpreter's bias, along with the ideology implicit in any methodology, that is most under scrutiny in this texture.

The letter of James provides a particularly dense ideological texture in its treatment of wealth and poverty. Consider James 1:9–11.

9 Let the believer who is lowly boast in being raised up, 10 and the rich in being brought low, because the rich will disappear like a flower in the field. 11 For the sun rises with its scorching heat and withers the field; its flower falls, and its beauty perishes. It is the same way with the rich; in the midst of a busy life, they will wither away.

---

[28] Ibid., p. 95.

Introduction

Setting aside the poetic inner texture, the multiple intertextures, and the values apparent in the sociocultural texture, what does James (and perhaps his community) appear to believe about rich and poor? What does the reader believe? How will what the reader believes impact how she or he will understand what James seems to believe and what the text says? How is this text read differently at the church where I worship in suburban Louisville, Kentucky, from the way I read it with a group of pastors in the town of San Marcos, Nicaragua? Our answers to questions like these explore and reveal both our ideology and what we learn of the ideology apparent in the letter of James.

Sacred Texture

From time to time in my own seminary studies, when confused in our grasp of Husserlian phenomenology or lost in some corner of structuralist hermeneutics, we would ask, "What does this have to do with Jesus?" That is to explore the sacred texture. "People who read the New Testament regularly are interested in finding insights into the nature of the relation between human life and the divine. In other words, these readers are interested in locating the way the text speaks about God or gods, or talks about realms of religious life."[29]

For many people this is the reason for biblical study in the first place. What does this text tell me about God, about Jesus, about salvation, about the nature of the Christian life? How does my understanding of the other textures of this text inform my faith and practice as a believer, or my search for faith? What will I do differently today because I have grappled with this text? Jude (vv. 22–3) provides another example.

> 22 And have mercy on some who are wavering; 23 save others by snatching them out of the fire; and have mercy on still others with fear, hating even the tunic defiled by their bodies.

Jude, as we have already seen, has an ax or two to grind. He knows who his opponents are, and he knows what he wants to see happen to them. But he also seems to know, along with James (5:20, a bit of intertexture), "that whoever brings back a sinner from wandering will save the sinner's soul from death and will cover a multitude of sins." There is ideology here as well, and the many interpretive textures will be dealt with in the Commentary. For now we note the important role given to "mercy," which as James says, "triumphs over judgment (2:13, more intertexture), and the call to "save others" and "save the sinner's soul." When all is said and done, in these verses both Jude and James are offering paranesis, and our response to this instruction is not just to parse and deconstruct it, to appreciate its many textures and its multiple implications, as

---

[29] Ibid., p. 120.

important as these are. Our response is our choice to reach out to others, or to not, a choice presented in the sacred texture of the texts.

Homiletical Texture

At the 1998 Annual Meeting of the Society of Biblical Literature, the Rhetoric and the New Testament section devoted a session to the work of Vernon Robbins. I was privileged to present a paper calling for consideration of an additional texture, a homiletical texture. Professor Robbins graciously agreed that there was indeed a place for consideration of the implications within the text for how the text may itself be proclaimed. In exploring the homiletical texture of a text the interpreter looks first for clues to its proclamation within the text itself, both the verses in question and the dynamics of the work as a whole. Rhetorical structure, argumentation, topics, and so forth, that is the inner texture, are again examined with care, but this time for guidance in preaching. Second, the intertexture and sociocultural texture are reconsidered from a homiletical perspective, as are the ideological and sacred textures. The guiding question is this: what does this text, the texts to which it interrelates, and the sociocultural world from which and to which it was written reveal about how it might best be preached? A final example from James clarifies, in this case the conclusion to 1:2–8.

6 But ask in faith, never doubting, for the one who doubts is like a wave of the sea, driven and tossed by the wind; 7, 8 for the doubter, being double-minded and unstable in every way, must not expect to receive anything from the Lord.

James begins the letter, as noted earlier, with a wonderful *climax* inviting the readers to ask for wisdom if they lack it, promising that God will grant it – good advice from any author to readers at the beginning of the time they will spend together. But what James offers with his left hand he seems to take back with his right, at least in part. It is only when we "ask in faith, never doubting." Already the text is suggesting a form, *gradatio*, and a focus: what sort of "asker" does James have in mind and what if we do not seem to fit that mold? What does it look like to be a "doubter" or "double-minded"? One could easily imagine a message that builds to its own climax in addressing the doubts of the audience as to their own readiness to ask and receive from God, even if God "gives to all generously and ungrudgingly."

In the Commentary the letters of James and Jude will be examined in detail, considering each passage in a three-fold form: (1) inner textures and intertextures; (2) sociocultural and ideological textures; and (3) sacred and homiletical textures.

II. Suggested Reading

The following bibliography is neither exhaustive nor exhaustively annotated. It is offered as a guide to further reading and research. The few abbreviations used follow the standard forms stipulated by the *Journal of Biblical Literature*.

INNER TEXTURE AND INTERTEXTURE

Aristotle, *The "Art" of Rhetoric*, trans. J. H. Freese. Loeb Classical Library (Cambridge, MA: Harvard University Press, 1926–82). *The beginning point for students and preachers serious about the study of rhetoric. Available in multiple editions, but the Loeb has both Greek and English.*

George A. Kennedy, *New Testament Interpretation through Rhetorical Criticism* (Chapel Hill: University of North Carolina Press, 1984), 171 pp. *Basic to intermediate introduction and exposition of the application of classical rhetorical categories to NT texts. The more advanced student may also want to read his* Classical Rhetoric and Its Christian and Secular Traditions from Ancient to Modern Times *(Chapel Hill: University of North Carolina Press, 1980), 291 pp.*

Burton L. Mack, *Rhetoric and the New Testament* (Minneapolis, MN: Fortress Press, 1990), 110 pp. *A guide to rhetorical criticism of the NT by a scholar better known for his controversial theories on NT origins. Very useful for the beginning student.*

Burton L. Mack and Vernon K. Robbins, *Patterns of Persuasion in the Gospels* (Sonoma, CA: Polebridge Press, 1989), 234 pp. *A very helpful introduction to how rhetoric works in the gospels with more advanced applications than Mack's* Rhetoric and the New Testament.

Vernon K. Robbins, *Exploring the Texture of Texts* (Valley Forge, PA: Trinity Press International, 1996), 148 pp., and *The Tapestry of Early Christian Discourse* (London: Routledge, 1996), 278 pp. *These two volumes will thoroughly introduce the interested student to Robbins's sociorhetorical method. The first is something of a textbook, the second a more theoretical development.*

Wesley H. Wachob, *The Voice of Jesus in the Social Rhetoric of James* (Cambridge: Cambridge University Press, 2000), 251 pp. *In an earlier form this volume was the author's 1993 Emory University doctoral thesis, directed by Vernon Robbins. It is especially good on the inner texture and intertexture of James 2:1–13, devoting ninety-four pages to the task.*

SOCIOCULTURAL TEXTURE

K. C. Hanson and Douglas E. Oakman, *Palestine in the Time of Jesus: Social Structures and Social Conflicts* (Minneapolis, MN: Fortress Press, 1998), 235 pp. *An excellent introductory textbook on social-scientific criticism by two able practitioners. Very readable, light on jargon. Emphasizes economic and family issues.*

Gerhard Lenski and Jean Lenski, *Human Societies: A Macrosociological Approach*, 7th ed. (New York: McGraw-Hill, 1994), 511 pp. *The anthropological/sociological foundation for many social-scientific biblical critics. A textbook not for the faint-hearted but required reading for those serious about this approach to understanding biblical cultures.*

Bruce J. Malina, *The New Testament World: Insights from Cultural Anthropology*, rev. ed. (Louisville, KY: Westminster/John Knox Press, 1993), 200 pp. *Another outstanding introduction, this volume does an excellent job of introducing the theoretical underpinnings of social-scientific criticism. Emphasizes honor/shame and purity issues more than Hanson and Oakman.*

Jerome H. Neyrey, ed., *The Social World of Luke-Acts: Models for Interpretation* (Peabody, MA: Hendrickson, 1991), 436 pp. *With chapters by Robbins, Malina, and other scholars, this volume introduces the practice of social-scientific criticism by applying key social-cultural values to selected themes and texts from Luke–Acts. A classic.*

John J. Pilch and Bruce J. Malina, eds., *Biblical Social Values and Their Meaning: A Handbook* (Peabody, MA: Hendrickson, 1993), 199 pp. *This is an "A–Z" guidebook (literally! from "activeness/passiveness" to "zeal") briefly explaining key terms and values by a group of leading scholars.*

IDEOLOGICAL TEXTURE

Craig L. Blomberg, *Neither Poverty nor Riches: A Biblical Theology of Material Possessions* (Grand Rapids, MI: Eerdmans, 1999), 300 pp. *A fine study of critical passages for understanding biblical views on money and possessions. That the author has some ideological commitments on the topic is indicated by a note on the frontispiece, indicating that all royalties from the book will go to charities "currently implementing significant aspects of the biblical themes surveyed here."*

Justo L. González, *Faith and Wealth: A History of Early Christian Ideas on the Origin, Significance, and Use of Money* (San Francisco: Harper and Row, 1990). *An exploration of a topic central to the letter of James by a leading Hispanic scholar. See especially chapter 3 on the "Roman Economy."*

Elsa Tamez, *The Scandalous Message of James: Faith without Works Is Dead*, trans. John Eagleson (New York: Crossroad, 1990), 102 pp. *This slim volume by a leading Latina biblical theologian examines the letter of James from a Central American perspective. A fine example of ideologically committed biblical scholarship.*

Sondra E. Wheeler, *Wealth as Peril and Obligation: The New Testament on Possessions* (Grant Rapids, MI: Eerdmans, 1995), 158 pp. *While the author might object to being*

Suggested Reading

classified under this heading, the force of her work, including the chapter on James 5:1–6 (pp. 91–106), is to highlight the issues of wealth and possessions in a way that is almost inevitably seen as ideological. A valuable resource.

SACRED AND HOMILETICAL TEXTURES

Robert Alter, *The Art of Biblical Narrative* (New York: Basic Books, 1981), 195 pp. *Although about the Hebrew Bible, and more than twenty years old, this classic of interpretation helps all readers of Scripture appreciate more fully the sacred texture of the biblical text.*

Dorothy Bass and Craig Dykstra, eds., *Practicing Our Faith* (San Francisco: Josey Bass, 1997). *This volume and ones by Bass and Stephanie Paulsell already published and others to follow introduce the understanding of Christian practice discussed in the commentary.*

Jerry Camery-Hoggatt, *Speaking of God: Reading and Preaching the Word of God* (Peabody, MA: Hendrickson, 1995), 277 pp. *Combines the insights of reader-oriented biblical criticism (see Reese's volume on Jude under "Studies and Articles on Jude") with concern for preaching. An interesting approach to the homiletical texture.*

Patrick J. Hartin, *A Spirituality of Perfection: Faith in Action in the Letter of James* (Collegeville, MN: Liturgical Press, 1999), 192 pp. *Fr. Hartin explores the theme of perfection (telos) as developed in the letter of James. A good example of focusing on the sacred texture of a text, building on his dissertation (see under "Studies on James").*

Thomas G. Long, *Preaching and the Literary Forms of the Bible* (Philadelphia: Fortress Press, 1989), 144 pp. *A good introduction to the implications of the homiletical texture of a variety of biblical texts from the homiletical side of the exegesis/preaching equation.*

Henri Nouwen, *The Way of the Heart* (New York: Ballantine, 1981), 81 pp. *A powerful reflection on solitude, silence, and prayer informed by the letter of James.*

Amos N. Wilder, *Early Christian Rhetoric: The Language of the Gospel* (New York: Harper and Row, 1964), 143 pp. *A classic, inviting deep reflection on both the sacred and homiletical textures of the biblical text.*

COMMENTARIES ON THE LETTER OF JAMES

James Adamson, *The Epistle of James* (Grand Rapids, MI: Eerdmans, 1976), 227 pp. *Although somewhat dated, it remains a helpful reading by a scholar/pastor.*

Peter H. Davids, *The Epistle of James: A Commentary on the Greek Text* (Grand Rapids, MI: Eerdmans, 1982), 226 + xxxviii pp. *This volume in the NIGTC series is essentially limited to the inner texture and intertexture of James. He later published a revised, shorter commentary,* James. *NIBC (Peabody, MA: Hendrickson, 1983–5).*

Martin Dibelius, *The Letter of James*, revised by Heinrich Greeven, trans. M. A. Williams. Hermeneia (Philadelphia: Fortress Press, 1975), 285 pp. *Written in the 1920s and revised in 1964, this volume remains the starting point for the study of James. Dibelius, the founder of form criticism, brought all his skills to bear in this reading. He cannot hide his preferences for Paul, and his approach to the letter, some eighty years later, is finally beginning to show its age. The footnotes alone, however, remain invaluable.*

Hubert Frankemölle, *Der Brief des Jakobus* (Gütersloh: Gütersloher Verlagshaus; Würzburg, Germany: Echter Verlag, 1994), 2 vols. *A dense, exhaustive (and exhausting!) work of interest primarily to the specialist.*

Luke Timothy Johnson, *The Letter of James*. Anchor Bible 37a (New York: Doubleday, 1995), 412 pp. *This is the best, most comprehensive commentary on the letter of James available. While the Anchor Bible format is at times frustrating, the command of the literature, comprehensive introduction, and voluminous notes and bibliographies make this volume well worth the price. Mention should also be made of his much shorter treatment of James in the* New Interpreter's Bible, vol. 12 (Nashville, TN: Abingdon Press, 1998), pp. 177–225.

Sophie Laws, *The Epistle of James* (Peabody, MA: Hendrickson, 1980), 273 pp. *This volume, first published in London (A & C Black, Ltd.) remains a solid, if somewhat dated, reading of James. The exegesis is sound, and the incorporation of notes and references in the body of the text aids the reader.*

Ralph Martin, *James*. Word Biblical Commentary, vol 48 (Waco, TX: Word Books, 1988), 240 pp. *One of the best commentaries in this series, it is of the high quality one has come to expect from Professor Martin, who also served as NT editor for the series. From time to time he may overhistoricize the community to which James wrote.*

Douglas J. Moo, *The Letter of James* (Grand Rapids, MI: Eerdmans, 2000), 271 pp. *Good and balanced reading of the letter based on the* New International Version *(NIV) translation. Small bibliography.*

James Hardy Ropes, *A Critical and Exegetical Commentary on the Epistle of St. James*. ICC (New York: Charles Scribner's Sons, 1916), 319 pp. *Despite its advanced years, this volume continues to contribute in important ways to the conversation about the letter of James.*

Robert W. Wall, *The Community of the Wise* (Valley Forge, PA: Trinity Press International, 1997), 354 pp. *This fine study of the letter of James offers a "canonical reading" of James. The author views the letter as "midrashic literature" organized according to the "thesis statement" Wall identifies at 1:19, "let everyone be quick to hear, slow to speak, slow to anger." Notes and bibliography are limited.*

STUDIES ON JAMES

James B. Adamson, *James: The Man and His Message* (Grand Rapids, MI: Eerdmans, 1989), 553 pp. *An impressively long, thematic study of the letter of James by a Presbyterian scholar/pastor.*

Richard Bauckham, *James: Wisdom of James, Disciple of Jesus the Sage* (London: Routledge, 1999), 246 pp. *A marvelously insightful study of James and Jesus that goes beyond aligning similar sayings to exploring their shared worlds and theologies. Includes a fascinating chapter on Kierkegaard's love of James, a topic that unfortunately could not be fit into this commentary.*

Bruce Chilton and Jacob Neusner, eds., *The Brother of Jesus* (Louisville, KY: Westminster/John Knox Press, 2001), 210 pp. *This volume, which includes excellent chapters by Craig Evans, Richard Bauckham, Wiard Popkes, the editors, and others, emerged from the work of the Consultation on James of the Society of Biblical Literature.*

Dean B. Deppe, *The Sayings of Jesus in the Epistle of James* (Chelsea, MI: Bookcrafters, 1989), 299 pp. *This fine Amsterdam dissertation addresses an important question in the study of the letter of James. Unfortunately it is only available through the author, who teaches at Calvin Seminary.*

Patrick J. Hartin, *James and the Q Sayings of Jesus.* JSNT Supplement Series 47 (Sheffield, England: JSOT Press, 1991). *Originally the author's doctoral thesis, exploring the relationship of "Jesus material" in James and the sayings source Q.*

John Painter, *Just James: The Brother of Jesus in History and Tradition* (Minneapolis, MN Fortress Press, 1999), 326 pp. *This volume is something of a sourcebook for the study of the letter of James, with chapters on the family of Jesus, Paul, and James. The majority of the book is devoted to early Christian literature about James.*

Pedrito U. Maynard-Reid, *Poverty and Wealth in James* (Maryknoll, NY: Orbis Books, 1987), 136 pp. *This short study could easily have been classified under "Sociocultural Texture" or "Ideological Texture" but is placed here because it is organized according to its exegesis of select passages, passages that just happen to have the sharpest ideological edge and greatest sociocultural implications.*

ARTICLES ON THE LETTER OF JAMES

There are scores of articles worthy of inclusion in this section and the one on Jude. Listed are works representative of biblical scholarship since 1980, plus a couple of older articles of importance. Fuller lists are available on James in the commentary by Luke T. Johnson.

Peter H. Davids, "Controlling the Tongue and the Wallet: Discipleship in James" in *Patterns of Discipleship in the New Testament,* ed. Richard N. Longnecker (Grand Rapids, MI: Eerdmans, 1996), pp. 225–47.

Lewis R. Donelson, "James" in *From Hebrews to Revelation: A Theological Introduction* (Louisville, KY: Westminster/John Know Press, 2001), pp. 35–60. *Outlines the important issues in the study of James.*

John H. Elliott, "The Epistle of James in Rhetorical and Social Scientific Perspective: Holiness-Wholeness and Patterns of Replication" *Biblical Theology Bulletin* 23 (1993): 71–81.

Fred O. Francis, "The Form and Function of the Opening and Closing Paragraphs of James and I John" *Zeitschrift für die neutestamentliche Wissenschaft* 70 (1970): 110–26.

Donald E. Gowan, "Wisdom and Endurance in James" *Horizons in Biblical Theology* 15 (1993): 145–53.

Luke T. Johnson, "The Use of Leviticus 19 in the Letter of James" *Journal of Biblical Literature* 101 (1982): 391–401.

"James 3:13–4:10 and the *Topos* ΠΕΡΙ ΦΘΟΝΟΥ" *Novum Testamentum* 25 (1983): 327–47.

"Friendship with the World/Friendship with God: A Study of Discipleship in James" in *Discipleship in the New Testament,* ed. Fernando F. Segovia (Philadelphia: Fortress Press, 1985), pp. 166–83.

"The Mirror of Remembrance (James 1:22–25)" *Catholic Biblical Quarterly* 50 (1988): 632–45.

Stanley E. Porter, "Is *dipsuchos* (James 1,8; 4,8) a 'Christian' Word?" *Biblica* 71 (1990): 469–98.

Luis Alonso Schöckel, "James 5,2 and 4,6" *Biblica* 54 (1973): 73–6.

John J. Schmitt, "You Adultresses! The Image in James 4:4" *Novum Testamentum* 28 (1986): 327–37.

Robert W. Wall, "James as Apocalyptic Paraenesis" *Restoration Quarterly* 32 (1990): 11–22.

Duane F. Watson, "James 2 in Light of Greco-Roman Schemes of Argumentation" *New Testament Studies* 39 (1993): 94–121.

"The Rhetoric of James 3:1–12 and a Classical Pattern of Argumentation" *Novum Testamentum* 35 (1993): 48–64.

COMMENTARIES AND BOOKS ON JUDE

Richard Bauckham, *Jude, 2 Peter*, Word Biblical Commentary, vol. 50 (Waco, TX: Word Books, 1983), 357 pp. (Jude, pp. 1–127). *Despite its age, this remains the best general commentary on the letter of Jude. Bauckham's mastery of the intertextures of Jude is impressive.*

J. N. D. Kelly, *A Commentary on the Epistles of Peter and Jude* (New York: Harper and Row, 1969), 387 pp. (Jude, pp. 223–94). *A classic, middle-of-the-road reading of the letter, now fairly well dated.*

Jerome H. Neyrey, *2 Peter, Jude*. Anchor Bible 37c (New York: Doubleday, 1993), 287 pp. (Jude, pp. 21–105). *Neyrey, one of the leading practitioners of social-scientific criticism of the NT, brings his strengths to bear on the letter of Jude in a compelling way. The categories and methods he uses, while perhaps inevitably giving less attention than one might wish to textual and theological questions, certainly make an important contribution to both the study of Jude and the extension of social-scientific methodology.*

Duane F. Watson, *Invention, Arrangement, and Style: Rhetorical Criticism of Jude and 2 Peter* (Atlanta: Scholars Press, 1988), 214 pp. *This typically well-crafted work, originally the author's dissertation, is by one of the leading scholars of classical rhetoric and the NT. Mention should also be made of his chapter on Jude in the* New Interpreter's Bible, vol. 12 (Nashville, TN: Abingdon Press, 1998), pp. 471–500.

Among the short commentaries that deal with a number of letters, including Jude, mention should be made of Fred C. Craddock, *First and Second Peter and Jude* (Louisville, KY: Westminster/John Knox Press, 1995); Pheme Perkins, *First and Second Peter, James and Jude* (Louisville, KY: John Knox Press, 1995); Earl J. Richard, *Reading 1 Peter, Jude, and 2 Peter* (Macon, GA: Smyth & Helwys, 2000); and Simon Kistemaker, *James, Epistles of John, Peter, and Jude* (Grand Rapids, MI: Baker Books, 1986–7; reissued 1995).

STUDIES AND ARTICLES ON JUDE

Richard Bauckham, *Jude and the Relatives of Jesus* (Edinburgh: T & T Clark, 1990), 459 pp. *This is a collection of original and previously published materials, building on the author's earlier commentary on Jude. Bauckham is one of the finest NT scholars working, and these specialized studies, focusing on Jude and the family of Jesus, are well worth reading.*

Lewis R. Doneslson, "Jude and 2 Peter" in *From Hebrews to Revelation: A Theological Introduction* (Louisville, KY: Westminster/John Knox Press, 2001), pp. 87–105. *A fine introduction to the basic issues in the study of the letter.*

Kenneth R. Lyle, Jr. *Ethical Admonition in the Epistle of Jude* (New York: Peter Lang, 1998), 152 pp. *This short dissertation (Southern Baptist Theological Seminary) in its original form, attempts to read Jude's moral discourse in light of a fixed model of moral decision-making evaluation (Stassen) and emphasizes the role of apocalyptic in Jude's worldview.*

Ruth Anne Reese, *Writing Jude: The Reader, the Text, and the Author in Constructs of Power and Desire* (Leiden, Netherlands: Brill, 2000), 182 pp. *While the popularity of reader-oriented criticism has faded, this volume shows that the insights that the method offers should not be forgotten. Mercifully short on jargon for a work from this discipline.*

J. Daryl Charles, "'Those' and 'These': The Use of the Old Testament in the Epistle of Jude" *Journal for the Study of the New Testament* 38 (1990): 109–24.

——— "Jude's Use of Pseudepigraphical Source-Material as Part of a Literary Strategy" *New Testament Studies* 37 (1991): 130–45.

Jarl Fossum, "Kyrios Jesus as the Angel of the Lord in Jude 5–7" *New Testament Studies* 33 (1987): 226–43.

John J. Gunther, "The Alexandrian Epistle of Jude" *New Testament Studies* 30 (1984): 459–62.

Stephan J. Joubert, "Persuasion in the Letter of Jude" *Journal for the Study of the New Testament* 58 (1995): 75–87.

——— "Facing the Past: Transtextual Relationships and Historical Understanding in the Letter of Jude" *Biblische Zeitschrift* 42 (1998): 56–70.

Carroll D. Osburn, "The Text of Jude 22–23" *Zeitschrift für die neutestamentliche Wissenschaft* 63 (1972): 139–44.

——— "The Christological Use of I Enoch I. 9 in Jude 14, 15" *New Testament Studies* 23 (1977): 334–41.

——— "The Text of Jude 5" *Biblia* 62 (1981): 107–15.

Robert L. Webb, "The Eschatology of the Epistle of Jude and Its Rhetorical and Social Functions" *Bulletin for Biblical Research* 6 (1996): 139–51.

Thomas Wolthuis, "Jude and Jewish Traditions" *Calvin Theological Journal* 1 (1987): 21–41.

SPECIAL STUDIES

Bede the Venerable, *Commentary on the Seven Catholic Epistles*, trans. David Hurst (Kalamazoo, MI: Cistercian Publications, 1985). *Written at the beginning of the eighth century, the selections in this volume shed a unique light on James and Jude. In a similar vein the* Ancient Christian Commentary on Scripture, vol. 11, ed. Gerald Bray (Downers Grove, IL: InterVarsity Press, 2000), *brings the insights of some of the most ancient Christian commentators, including Bede. Unfortunately the selections are so short that they provide little sense of the overall reception of either letter.*

Floyd V. Filson, "The Christian Teacher in the First Century" *Journal of Biblical Literature* 60 (1941): 317–28. *A short, outdated article on a topic begging for a fuller, modern treatment.*

John A. T. Robinson, *Redating the New Testament* (Philadelphia: Westminster Press, 1976). *This still-important volume includes a chapter on James (pp. 118–39) and a section on 2 Peter and Jude (pp. 169–99) that support the early dating of both James and Jude.*

Stanley K. Stowers, *Letter Writing in Greco-Roman Antiquity* (Philadelphia: Westminster Press, 1986), 188 pp. *This volume, while viewing Paul's letters as prescriptive for the genre and offering nothing on James and Jude, still provides useful general background on letter writing in antiquity.*

III. Commentary

JAMES 1:1–27 – THAT YOU MAY BE MATURE AND COMPLETE

*T*he first chapter of James serves in many ways as the *epitome*, or summary introduction, to the entire work. In it the author introduces the themes important to the rest of the letter – the challenge of temptations, the danger of riches, right speech, hearing and doing, concern for the exploited and oppressed – all under his desire that the readers be found to be "mature and complete, lacking in nothing." To understand the first chapter of James, then, is vital to understanding the letter of James.

JAMES 1:1

1 James, a servant of God and of the Lord Jesus Christ, To the twelve tribes in the Dispersion: Greetings.

INNER TEXTURE AND INTERTEXTURE

The first verse of the letter of James is elegant in its simplicity, an economy of expression characteristic of the entire letter. The author/sender begins with his name, James (Gk. *Iakōbos* in the nominative case from the Heb. *yaqôb*, Jacob), and describes himself not with reference to parentage (as, for example, "James the son of Zebedee"; Mk 1:19) nor patrimony (e.g., "a man of Tarsus named Saul"; Acts 9:11). Instead he uses a phrase that describes what must be taken to be the defining relationships of his life – "of God and of the Lord Jesus Christ." The phrasing in Greek is interesting, and capable of more than one translation. As we will see, James is as likely to use the word "Lord" (Gk. *kyrios*) in reference to Jesus as to God. Here the phrase "Lord Jesus Christ" seems to function as both a title and a proper name. Such use is common in the NT, and this particular form, in the genitive and without the article, is often found in greetings (e.g.,

Rom 1:9; 1 Cor 1:3; 2 Cor 1:2; Gal 1:3; Eph 1:2; Phi 1:2; 2 Th 1:2; Phm 3), although in these greetings the expression is part of the salutation ("Grace and peace to you from God our Father and the Lord Jesus Christ"; Rom 1:7).

The addressees are referred to as "the twelve tribes in the Dispersion," a reference again as remarkable for what it implies as for what it omits, lacking both geographical and clear sectarian purport. Significantly, James refers to himself as a servant/slave of God and of (the) Lord Jesus Christ and not as an apostle or brother, emphasizing subordination and subservience, not relationship. The simple word of salutation, "Greetings" (Gk. *chairen*), is common in letters throughout Hellenistic literature and serves two important purposes to which we will return on occasion throughout the commentary: it places the letter of James squarely within both an epistolary and a literary context.

The intertexture of 1:1 is rich in connections, and contradictions, when compared to NT and Hellenistic epistolary traditions. As we saw in the Introduction, the tendency to understand the form of the letters of Paul as determinative of the letter genre for all of the NT is a position that can no longer be sustained. Nor need James's metaphorical addressees, "the twelve tribes of the Dispersion," preclude his participation in a particular Christian community and his having in mind such a community and such believers as he wrote. To that extent, the letter is as real as any other in the NT.

SOCIOCULTURAL AND IDEOLOGICAL TEXTURES

The Introduction offered occasion to explore the question of James's identity. Of the many possibilities – one of the five or six Jameses named in the NT, an editor compiling the tradition identified with one of these James, or an author writing under the pseudonym of James – I have come to agree with the tradition. James is the brother of Jesus, the leader of the Jerusalem community identified in the Book of Acts and by Paul in Galatians and 1 Corinthians, who was also identified in the tradition as James "the Just" and James "of Jerusalem." According to Josephus (*Antiquities* 20.200-201[1]) and early Christian tradition he was executed in Jerusalem around 62 CE, giving us the *terminus ad quem* for this composition. In all likelihood, given the initial popularity of the letter reflected in the number of early citations and the fluid way in which James appropriated Jesus material,[2] it was most likely written a decade or more prior to his death, making it one of the earliest, if not the earliest, writing in the NT.

---

[1] Josephus, *Jewish Antiquities*, vol. 9, trans. L. H. Feldman, Loeb Classical Library (Cambridge, MA: Harvard University Press, 1969), pp. 495–7.

[2] By "fluid" I mean that James's method for using sources, insofar as it is discerned in the letter itself, did not distinguish between oral and written, traditional and contemporary, canonical and occasional. Contra the approach of Dean B. Deppe, *The Sayings of Jesus in the Epistle of James* (Chelsea, MI: Bookcrafters, 1989), I find that James moved easily – fluidly – between allusion and reference to traditional material (OT), and actual citation of that material. He simply never cited Jesus' material with a formula, suggestive of a period in early Christianity when that material was not fixed or understood as authoritative.

Such is my claim, and conclusion, about the composition of the letter of James, but beyond providing a ready point for discussion and debate, what is the significance of such a clear and specific claim for an understanding of the occasion of the letter? What does it *mean* to claim: the letter of James was written by James, the brother of Jesus, around the year 50 CE, in Jerusalem or its environs? I will mention five things.

First, the letter of James was written at a time and in a place of considerable social and political tumult and of considerable socioeconomic stratification. All roads may not have led to Rome, but all social and political realities emanated from and were effected by Rome. And Rome itself was a turbulent place. The relatively settled years and long reigns of Julius (101–44 BCE), Augustus (31 BCE–14 CE), and Tiberius (14–37 CE) were followed by the comparatively shorter and certainly more volatile reigns of Gaius ("Caligula"; 37–41 CE), Claudius (41–54 CE), and Nero (54–68 CE). Tumult at the top led to unsettled conditions elsewhere in the empire, allowing opportunists, careerists, and insurrectionists room to maneuver.[3] In Jerusalem and Judea, Samaria and Galilee this general climate was exacerbated by political and religious conflict between ruling parties and classes, and a fairly long list of very undistinguished appointments by Rome. The socioeconomic stratification was not limited to Palestine but was a reality throughout the ancient Mediterranean world and ancient economies in general. This will be discussed in some detail in chapters 2 and 5 of James. For now we need only mention that by contemporary standards there was an extreme concentration of wealth among the ruling elite (2%–3% of the population), a small class of retainers, a small merchant class, and the vast majority of the population surviving as peasants, peasant artisans, and slaves. Within Judea, Samaria, and Galilee the latter grouping may have accounted for 85% or more of the population, with most of the arable land controlled by only a few.[4]

Second, James was writing at a time and from and to a community of believers in which the distinction between Jew and Christian was not at all clear. We need to remind ourselves constantly that *all* the followers of the historical Jesus and all of the first believers in the resurrection of Jesus were Jews, thought of themselves as Jews, and understood their belief in Jesus within a Jewish matrix. Although it is possible to see evidence in the tradition of conflict between traditional Jews and Jewish believers in Jesus (e.g., Jn 9), and to see places in the tradition in which an emerging Gentile "church" begins to outnumber Jewish believers in the risen Jesus, these are a generation or so after the death of James. Debates about whether James was a Jewish Christian or a Christian Jew only confirm the point – James wrote at a time and from and to a community that was

---

[3] See Richard A. Horsley, *Jesus and the Spiral of Violence: Popular Jewish Resistance in Roman Palestine* (San Francisco: Harper and Row, 1987). See also, e.g., Josephus, *Antiquities* 18.4–10.

[4] See K. C. Hanson and Douglas E. Oakman, *Palestine in the Time of Jesus: Social Structures and Social Conflicts* (Minneapolis, MN: Fortress Press, 1998), pp. 101–29.

only beginning to see a distinction between traditional Judaism and emerging "Christianity."

Third, James wrote at a time when the emerging traditions of and about Jesus were anything but fixed. Little or nothing appears to have been written down, and so James is perhaps best understood as one of the first to gather a significant body of Jesus' sayings. Yet he was not aware, or did not especially care or at least was not especially careful to reflect this in his writing. Quotations of, references to, reflections on, and differences with material we now refer to as "Jesus material" or "sayings of Jesus" were all treated the same by James and always without citation formula or the NT Greek equivalent of modern quotation marks.

Fourth, James was writing from a position of no little prestige and authority within the small, growing community of believers, a position even recognized by Paul (Gal 2, though admittedly with a certain level of sarcasm). This status was conferred first by relationship, hence the appellation "the brother of the Lord." But it was not apparently limited to kinship (which was important in antiquity in ways often not appreciated today),[5] as the other appellations suggest – "the Just" an acknowledgment of the quality of his leadership, "of Jerusalem" a recognition of his status as leader of the Jerusalem church (although the later tradition that James was the first "bishop of Jerusalem" is anachronistic).

Fifth, nowhere in the letter does James claim such role or status. In a culture with a strong set of honor/shame values[6] this is not surprising. What is surprising, and what leads us to the next section, is the appellation James chose.

SACRED AND HOMILETICAL TEXTURES

"James, a servant [slave] of God and of the Lord Jesus Christ." A good author is able to say a lot in a few words. James was able to do so in one word, translated variously in the NRSV as "servant" and "slave" (Gk. *doulos*). In English we generally intend a single but all-important distinction between the terms servant and slave: volition. The servant hires him- or herself to an employer; a slave is owned by a master. In antiquity, while there were certainly classes of servants and slaves, the question of volition was one few could afford.

In reading James, we do well to explore the significance of both translations of *doulos*. To claim the status of servant was to make a social and an economic distinction, and to identify with those who constituted the greatest number but possessed the fewest goods. To claim the status of servant (while this was also true of slaves) was to choose to be identified not by parentage, birthplace, or

---

[5] See Bruce J. Malina, *The New Testament World*, rev. ed. (Louisville, KY: Westminster/John Knox Press, 1993), pp. 117–48.

[6] For a succinct summary, see John J. Pilch and Bruce J. Malina, eds., *Biblical Social Values and Their Meaning: A Handbook* (Peabody, MA: Hendrickson, 1993), pp. 95–104. This will be discussed in more detail in chapters 2 and 5 of James.

occupation, but by the one(s) in whose service one stood. But to claim the status of slave is to point beyond oneself to one's "master" in the truest sense.

In this way James fully partakes of what is called for in the "hymn" quoted by Paul in Phil 2:5–11.

> 5 Let the same mind be in you that was in Christ Jesus,
> 6 who, though he was in the form of God,
> did not regard equality with God
> as something to be exploited,
> 7 but emptied himself,
> taking the form of a slave,
> being born in human likeness.
> And being found in human form,
> 8 he humbled himself
> and became obedient
> to the point of death –
> even death on a cross.
> 9 Therefore God also highly exalted him
> and gave him the name that is above every name,
> 10 so that at the name of Jesus every knee should bend,
> in heaven and on earth and under the earth,
> 11 and every tongue should confess that
> Jesus Christ is Lord, to the glory of God the Father.

James announces in his self-introduction that he has emptied himself, not counting "equality" (fraternal kinship) as "something to be exploited" and claiming only the place of a slave. Tradition, as noted in the Introduction, records that he too was martyred, and while he is not, of course, confessed as Lord, he is revered as a saint. His example, however, is not so much in what little we know of his life but in what we find in his letter.[7]

JAMES 1:2–8

2 My brothers and sisters, whenever you face trials of any kind, consider it nothing but joy,
3 because you know that the testing of your faith produces endurance;
4 and let endurance have its full effect, so that you may be mature and complete, lacking in nothing.
5 If any of you is lacking in wisdom, ask God, who gives to all generously and ungrudgingly, and it will be given you.
6 But ask in faith, never doubting, for the one who doubts is like a wave of the sea, driven and tossed by the wind;

---

[7] In the next section, the versification in English translations collapse the Greek vv. 7–8 into one, a reflection of the significant difference in word order between Greek and English.

7, 8 for the doubter, being double-minded and unstable in every way, must not expect to receive anything from the Lord.

INNER TEXTURE AND INTERTEXTURE

There is no hiding from the abruptness of James 1:2. The very absence of transition, and in this instance of an extended greeting, prayer of thanksgiving, and so on, is both characteristic of James and cause for many scholars to classify the document as sermon, diatribe, epitome – anything but letter. As we saw in the Introduction, this argument often proceeds from a tacit or implicit determination that the core Pauline letters define the NT genre "letter," an argument clearly weighted against James. In this commentary, however, we will accept the witness of James itself and seek to discover what happens when we read the letter as a letter, abrupt (or missing) transitions and all.

The first chapter of James tells the reader much about the author, the author's perception of the reader, and the author's priorities. By beginning with trials (*peirasmos*), faith (*pistis*), maturity/completion (*teleios*), and doubt (*diakrinō*), James signals a number of his central concerns at the outset and, after reinforcing them throughout the first chapter, will return to them, one by one, in the rest of the letter. While some commentators (Dibelius, Wall) see a division between vv. 2–4 and 5–8, the inner textuality of the passage makes a strong case for rhetorical coherence (so Laws, Johnson, and others). Indeed, these verses offer some of the best evidence of the author's sophistication and skill in rhetoric.

A CLOSER LOOK – CLIMBING JAMES'S LADDER

The greeting (*chairein*) at the close of v. 1 is echoed by the joy (*charan*) with which the "brothers and sisters" are to consider or reckon "trials of any kind" (the phrase itself a marvelous example of alliteration, *peirasmois peripesēte poikilois*, lost in translation). There follows an instance of the rhetorical figure *gradatio* (climax), literally a ladder leading the reader from one rung to the next, in this case from the testing of faith to "endurance" and from endurance, when it has its "full effect" (*teleion*), to "mature and complete" (the two words in the NRSV rendering the Gk. *teleioi*), "lacking in nothing." Exactly where the figure ends is not clear, a fact that gives evidence of the rhetorical connection between vv. 4 and 5, for the "lacking" of v. 4 (*leipomenoi*) is followed by the "lacking" of v. 5 (*leipetai*). The reader who lacks wisdom is to "ask" (*aiteitō*) for it of God "who gives to all generously and ungrudgingly" and it will be "given" (cf. Mt. 7:7). But, we learn in v. 6, one must ask in faith without "doubting" (*diakrinomenos*) for the one who doubts (*diakrinomenos*) is like "a wave of the sea, driven and tossed by the wind." Such a person will receive nothing from the Lord, being "double-minded" (*dípsuchos*). To summarize this tight inner texture, James 1:2–8 looks something like this:

>   double-minded (v. 8)
>   *doubter* (v. 7)
>   *ask* in faith without *doubts* (v. 6)
>   one *lacking* wisdom should ask of God (v. 5)
>   *complete* (perfect), *lacking* in nothing (v. 4b)
>   *endurance completes* its *work* (v. 4a)
>   *testing* of faith *works endurance* (v. 3)
>   facing *trials* of any kind (v. 2)

Commentators largely agree and are technically correct to limit the *gradatio* to vv. 2–4. Yet the continuing progression through v. 8 cannot be ignored. That it has been ignored may be attributed to the those who, following Dibelius, have seen a break between vv. 4 and 5 and to the strong influence of the parallel passage in Rom 5.

Rom 5:3–4	James 1:2–4
And not only that, but we also boast in our sufferings, knowing that suffering produces endurance, 4 and endurance produces character, and character produces hope, 5 and hope does not disappoint us,	[W]henever you face trials of any kind, consider it nothing but joy, 3 because you know that the testing of your faith produces endurance; 4 and let endurance have its full effect, so that you may be mature and complete, lacking in nothing.

Such comparison, of course, leads us to the question of intertextuality, an especially rich field in these verses.

James uses the term "brothers" (Gk. vocative, *adelphoi*)[8] fifteen times in direct address, a frequency found in other NT letters (Paul, e.g., so uses the term fourteen times in the five chapters of 1 Thessalonians), and the usage is common in other Christian writings. Like the opening of 1 Peter, James speaks of trials and testing as a means of determining and strengthening faith, and 1 Peter has a slight *gradatio* of its own. Luke T. Johnson is surely correct, however, to argue that the "resemblance between the *gradatio* in James 1:2–4 and those in Rom 5:2–4 and 1 Pet 1:6–7 is more apparent than real."[9] There is certainly no literary

---

8   Following the NRSV, I will translate the Gk. ἀδελφοί/*adelphoi* as "brothers and sisters." That James, like other biblical and early Christian writers, did not intend the use of male nouns, pronouns, and endings to be taken in a gender-exclusive fashion is an arguable, and defensible, position. That one should make every effort to translate inclusively is paramount.
9   Luke T. Johnson, *The Letter of James*, Anchor Bible 37a (New York: Doubleday, 1995), p. 183.

dependence. Instead all three authors are using common *topoi* and figures in praise of the virtue of endurance.

More interesting, and promising, is the possible relationship of the saying about "asking" in v. 5 and the Synoptic saying on the same topic – "Ask and it shall be given to you" (Mt. 7:7/Lk 11:9) – and the possible provenance of the analogy comparing the doubter to a ship on a stormy sea. Also important is the introductory image of God as one "who gives to all generously and ungrudgingly." After having opportunity in the coming chapters to consider all of the possible parallels between Jesus sayings and passages in James, I will offer my own conclusions on this topic. But a few points, especially related to intertextuality, should be mentioned at the outset.

First, the congruence between James 1:5 and Mt 7:7/Lk 11:9 is considerable but not total. The same verbs – ask (*aiteō*) and give (*didōmi*) – are used in the Synoptics and James, the first verb in the active imperative, the second in the future passive. The only difference is in the person of the verb ask – second singular in the Synoptics and third singular in James – a reflection of the context (the Jesus saying is a part of the direct address of the Sermon on the Mount). Both passages are about prayer, but the Jesus saying is general, while the James passage is strikingly particular, both in the subject of the request and in the understanding of the God who hears and answers prayer. God is munificent, even prodigal, giving all things "generously." This term, *haplōs*, which allows multiple and complementary translations (e.g., "without hesitation" [Dibelius], "singly" [Moo], and "simply" [Johnson]),[10] contrasts with the person imagined in vv. 6b–8, whose lack of unity (*dipsuchos*) will undermine the request. The NRSV is guided by the participle (*didontos* "gives") in its translation, but "generously" may miss the rhetorical play at work in James's creative description of the Divine Giver who responds to all who ask. In this case, unlike the Synoptics, the asking is particular and particularly interesting for this letter and this early point in the letter. One who lacks "wisdom" (*sophia*) is to ask for it, a request that will be surely granted by God.

SOCIOCULTURAL AND IDEOLOGICAL TEXTURES

In the introduction I suggested that James is very much a Wisdom document, borrowing and building on a wealth of Wisdom traditions. Like Jesus, however, James offers his own version of that Wisdom, in what Borg and Witherington among others have referred to as "subversive" or "alternative" wisdom.[11] This

[10] Martin Dibelius, *The Letter of James*, rev. Heinrich Greeven, trans. M. A. Williams, Hermeneia (Philadelphia: Fortress Press, 1975), pp. 77–9; Douglas J. Moo, *The Letter of James* (Grand Rapids, MI: Eerdmans, 2000), pp. 58ff.; L. T. Johnson, *Letter of James* (1995), pp. 179–80.

[11] Marcus J. Borg, *Meeting Jesus Again for the First Time* (San Francisco: HarperCollins, 1994), esp. pp. 69–119, and Ben Witherington III, *Jesus the Sage* (Minneapolis, MN: Fortress Press,

alternative wisdom works within the forms and concerns of traditional, or conventional, Wisdom but subverts it by exploring the latter at and sometimes beyond its borders. That God is the giver of "every perfect gift" (James 1:17) is traditional. That God gives "all things" is also. That God gives "generously and ungrudgingly" pushes at the boundary, for elements of the tradition reflect a more exacting keeping of the accounts between Divine Giver and mortal recipient (e.g., Deut 8:1–20; Isa 1:10–20; Zech 1:1–6; but see also Psa 145). That God gives "to all" (*pasin*) has the potential to fall into the subversive, depending on whether one takes the referent of all to extend beyond the community of believers. I agree with Bauckham, Johnson, and others who see James as working well within the traditions of Wisdom literature, adapting Jesus material for his own message, or version, of the Gospel. As we will see, however, this subversive thrust is not absolute. What is suggested in v. 5 is modified in vv. 6–7: not everyone should expect to receive what they ask for from the Lord, only those who ask "in faith." Those who doubt (*diakrinomenos*) are compared to sea waves, tossed to and fro however the wind may blow. The expression is something of a commonplace, the waves (or the ship upon them in many instances) easily analogous to situations of indecision or rapidly changing opinions.[12] This image is then reinforced in a strong and unique expression. Building on the image of tossed and driven waves, James refers to the doubter as "unstable in every way," prefacing this comment by saying that the doubter is "double-minded" (*dipsuchos*), a word found here and at James 4:8 and nowhere else in the NT or LXX, but echoed in Christian literature "after and dependent on James."[13] This double-minded doubter is in sharp contrast to the person of faith, the person without doubts, to whom the one God gives in generous response.

We learn important things about author and audience in the opening lines of a work like James and about their perceptions of one another. That James moves from terse greeting to a celebration of "trials of any kind" hints of his own experiences and those of his implied readers, for while not unprecedented (1 Pet 1:6 is the nearest parallel) this is not the most obviously appealing start to a letter rhetorically imaginable. But it is the one James chose, so the interpreter needs to ask, if not "why?" – which presumes too much about what can be known – then at least, "what might we learn about author and audience from these opening concerns?"

First, we learn of the likely presence of trials and difficulties. Second, we learn the author's (and community's?) preferred response to such trials, in contrast to what we will soon learn about an inappropriate response (v. 13). Third, we

---

1994), esp. pp. 147–208 and on James, pp. 236–47, where the author, with whom I disagree on this point, reads James as an example of conventional wisdom. We do agree on the importance of Sirach for James.

[12] Demosthenes, Philo, etc. In our literature the hypocrite is compared to a "boat in a storm" (Sir 33:2).

[13] L. T. Johnson, *Letter of James* (1995), p. 181.

learn a fundamental component of the theology undergirding the work. Not accidentally, these three coincide respectively with the sociocultural, ideological, and sacred textures of this text.

While there are explicit references and clear hints about the social context of the author and audience of this letter, the early reference to "trials of any kind" and the "testing of your faith" must not go unnoticed. One cannot here draw specific conclusions about sometimes proposed persecutions or imagined antagonisms. One can suggest that the prominence of this theme in the letter reflects the prominence of the issue in the life of the community. This impression will be reinforced throughout the document; everyone involved, author and audience, has had more than passing contact with tough times. Not cataclysmic, apocalyptic disaster, but setback, disappointment, and challenge; the stuff of life. Faith, it seems, does not shield one from the often-challenging realities of everyday experience.

Faith does, in the ideology of the letter of James, provide one with the proper response to these realities: endurance. Endurance (*hupomonē*) is a character trait important to James (also evident in 5:11), the NT (e.g., Lk 8:15; Rom 5:5; 2 Cor 1:6, 6:4, 12:12; 2 Tim 3:10; Rev 1:9, 13:10, 14:12), and early Christian literature, not to mention generations of Christian preaching. Yet it is not an isolated virtue. Endurance, the growing capacity to experience disappointment and challenge with grace, courage, and resolve, is an outgrowth of faith, and itself yields maturity and completion, *telos* (perfection). Part of the subversive wisdom at the heart of James's ideology is the conviction that perfection is the goal, and trials are part of the journey toward it.[14] Such a conviction is itself not isolated but develops from James's understanding of God as the one "who gives to all generously and ungrudgingly." This understanding is expansive and contrasts with the natural, physical, and social limits that were part and parcel of the letter's context.

SACRED AND HOMILETICAL TEXTURES

Ask, but. That is on one level the impression given by these verses. God "gives to all generously and ungrudgingly," but. Does James understand God to be generous and ungrudging "to all" as long as all are "never doubting"? So it seems, but. The key is whether at this point in the letter James is focused on God or on potential petitioners. That is, should the reader and the preacher expect to learn primarily about James's understanding of the human condition or of the divine disposition? The emphasis here is decidedly on the human; James introduces a category of human character, *dipsuchos* (double-minded), at the conclusion of a short *gradatio* about the appropriate response to trials and temptations, from testing of faith to endurance to maturity, "complete, lacking

---

[14] See Patrick J. Hartin, *A Spirituality of Perfection* (Collegeville, MN: Liturgical Press, 1999).

in nothing." Then, should one be lacking in wisdom, one must ask in faith and it will be given. Ask in doubt, divided, or tossed about? Do not "expect to receive anything from the Lord." Is this a double standard? Yes, but a human one, not a divine one. God is consistent, giving wisdom to those who ask for it in faith and giving nothing to those who, by doubting, essentially do not ask.

The first point, then, is that double-mindedness is an exclusively human trait, as are double standards. God, "with whom there is no variation of shadows due to change" (v. 17), is one. It is not that God chooses to give to some and not to others; it is that some ask "in faith" while others ask with "doubts."

The second point comes from recognizing what is being asked for. James does not say, as Jesus does in Mt 7:7 and par., "Ask and it will be given you." James is completing his climax by speaking of wisdom, and in his understanding of wisdom (mature, stable, "quick to listen, slow to speak," expressed in faithful practice) it can only be asked for and given "in faith." Double-mindedness is the opposite of wisdom – immature, unstable, blessing and cursing from the same mouth, forgetting one's own appearance after turning from the mirror, and so on. It is not possible to grant wisdom to one with these traits. One must be tested, develop endurance, and come to maturity.

Third (three points, but no poem), what exactly is James referring to when he contrasts "in faith, never doubting" and "the doubter, being double-minded"? What, in practical terms, does it mean to ask "in doubt"? Is it to doubt that God can give, or to doubt that one wishes to receive? Big difference. Because the focus in the passage has been on the human side of things, so likely is the answer. Indeed, there is little in the ideological or sacred textures of the letter to suggest that God's capacity is ever called into question. That is a contemporary issue, not an ancient one. The image James has in mind here is one who is not sure he or she wishes to be in a mature and complete relationship with God. The "doubt" is whether one truly wants to ask and so receive, not doubt over God's capacity to give.

As suggested in the Introduction, the homiletical texture of this text suggests its own structure and focus. The preacher should consider creating her own *gradatio*, perhaps a series of parallel examples of one who asks "in faith" and how she got there, and of one who doubts, and how he is not yet able to receive wisdom from the Lord, being careful to distinguish human weakness from divine purpose and ending with an affirmation of the God who gives to all "generously and ungrudgingly" as they are able to receive.

JAMES 1:9–11

9 Let the believer who is lowly boast in being raised up,
10 and the rich in being brought low, because the rich will disappear like a flower in the field.

11 For the sun rises with its scorching heat and withers the field; its flower falls, and its beauty perishes. It is the same way with the rich; in the midst of a busy life, they will wither away.

INNER TEXTURE AND INTERTEXTURE

James 1:9–11 introduces one of the most significant themes of the letter, poverty and wealth. In characteristically subversive fashion James scorns conventional wisdom and calls for boasting not about status but about status reversal. This is in itself significant. James does not praise poverty per se but calls for "believers" (on the translation of the Gk. *adelphos* see note 8) who are poor or "lowly" (*ho tapeinos*) to boast in the change in their status, being raised up, action that can be understood only to be that of God. This reversal is paralleled by that of the rich (*ho plousios*), who are to boast in being "brought low" (*en tē tapeinōsei*).

Understanding the contrast between poor and rich, humbled and exalted, and the possible identities of each rests at the heart of any reading of the letter of James. In these verses the foundation for that contrast is first laid, and it is, interestingly enough, not about possessions as much as about status, which might even be called spiritual stature. The key is in the reversal, a reversal the author vividly and traditionally describes with analogy to the fleeting beauty of nature. The humbling of the wealthy lies in that they, like all things, will perish "like a flower in the field." Just as the rising sun will scorch and wither the field and the beauty of the flower fade, so will the rich (and the poor) wither away even "in the midst of a busy life."

The controlling image in this passage is doubly intertextual – the fading "flower of the field" (Gk. a*nthos chortou*) and the double reversal of poor and rich, which echoes Jesus' similar sayings (Lk 14:11, 18:14, and par.). The Greek, translated literally, means "flower of grass." Understood as an example of the rhetorical figure *synecdoche* (the use of the part to express the whole) the expression becomes "flower of the field." This figure becomes the key to the intertexture. The tradition is replete with references to fading flowers or grass, especially in analogy to the frailty of human existence (Pss 37:2, 90:5–6, 102:4–11, 103:15–16, 129:6; Isa 15:6, 51:12; Jer 12:4). There are also verses that speak of withering grass and the flower of the field, especially Psa 103:15–16 (LXX 102:15–16):

15 As for mortals, their days are like grass; they flourish like a flower of the field; 16 for the wind passes over it, and it is gone, and its place knows it no more.

The Greek of v. 15 is transliterated as follows: *anthrōpos hōsei chortos hai hēmerai autoû hōsei anthos tou agrou houtōs eksanthēsei*. The key phrase, *anthos tou agrou*, uses the literal term for field, *agros*. Jesus may have had this passage in mind in the Sermon on the Mount:

But if God so clothes the grass of the field, which is alive today and tomorrow is thrown into the oven, will he not much more clothe you – you of little faith? (Mt 6:30/par. Lk 12:28).

The key phrase here is *ton chorton tou agrou* (the grass of the field). James, as we have seen, uses the phrase *anthos chortou*, a synecdoche found in the Septuagint only in v. 6 of the ringing prophecy of Isa. 40:6–8 and also cited in 1 Pet 1:24.

6 A voice says, "Cry out!" And I said, "What shall I cry?" All people are grass, their constancy is like the flower of the field [Gk. *anthos chortou*]. 7 The grass withers, the flower fades, when the breath of the LORD blows upon it; surely the people are grass. 8 The grass withers, the flower fades; but the word of our God will stand forever.

This expression, which Laws refers to as a "unique mistranslation" of the Hebrew,[15] is the pivot for the reversal described in James 1:9–11. Be it a flower "of grass," a flower "of the field," or "the grass of the field," the force of the comparison is unchanged – the rich, even in the midst of the activities on which their wealth is based, will wither and fade as surely as a field and its flowers will under the scorching sun.

The analogy is clear, but the analogues are not. Who is the "believer" (*ho adelphos*) of v. 9? Who is the "rich" of v. 10? How shall we understand the force of the phrase "wither away" as it applies to the rich and the "raising up" of the lowly?

The options, actually, are fairly clear and may be summarized as follows:

1. The "believer" refers to all readers of the letter, of which there are two categories, the "lowly" and the "rich."
2. The "believer" refers to all readers of the letter, some of whom are "lowly." The "rich" are not believers but a group outside the community.
3. To "wither away" is to die a normal death without particular eschatological implications.
4. The exaltation of the lowly and the fading away of the rich should be understood in terms of apocalyptic eschatology.

To explore these options we must turn to the sociocultural and ideological textures.

SOCIOCULTURAL AND IDEOLOGICAL TEXTURES

The first step in examining these options is the longest step – consideration of the poor and the rich in James. In this section we will begin, but by no means complete, this examination (see especially the section on the sociocultural texture of 2:1–13). James 1:9–11 does not specifically mention the poor but instead

---

[15] Sophie Laws, *The Epistle of James* (Peabody, MA: Hendrickson, 1980), p. 64.

uses the term "lowly" (*ho tapeinos*) in counterpoint to the "rich" (*ho plousios*). Vv. 9–10a create a simple *chiasmus*:

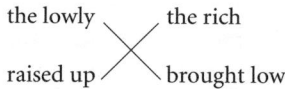

But although "raised up" and "brought low" stand in neat opposition, "the lowly" and "the rich" do not. In choosing to use *ho tapeinos* instead of *ho ptōchos* (the poor), as in 2:2 ff., James introduces an added element of uncertainty. The interpreter must attend to questions not only of economic poverty but of the spiritual poverty possibly implied by the use of "lowly," a word that is frequently rendered as "humble" (Mt 11:29; 2 Cor 10:1) and juxtaposed with or against "the proud" (e.g., James 4:6, "God opposes the proud, but gives grace to the humble"). Here, of course, the division is far from complete. Poverty has many dimensions, and economic/physical poverty is neither a precondition for nor exclusive of spiritual poverty (see any and all considerations of the first Matthean beatitude). But the mixture of lowliness, boasting, and exaltation in James 1:9 ff. is particularly evocative. We will see in Chapters 2 and 5 that there is good reason to understand the community to which James writes as having economically impoverished as well as prosperous members, but that "the rich" is likely used as an epithet principally in reference to those *outside* the community. So the first analogue in v. 9 is not to all members of the community but to those who are economically and/or spiritually impoverished at the time of writing, just as the references in v. 2 to those who face times of trials and in v. 12 to those who endure temptation are not to all but to those coping with particular challenges at the time. Eventually this will no doubt include every reader at some time in his or her life, but the words of encouragement are for the times of trial.

The contrast, then, is not limited to those within the community but likely points the "lowly believer" to someone outside, someone not only prosperous but visibly noteworthy in that prosperity. That prosperity and that person will surely wither and fade. The description echoes Isa. 40:6–7 and anticipates James 4:13 ff. ("Come now, you who say, 'Today or tomorrow we will go to such and such a town and spend a year there, doing business and making money'"). Busyness is no more an inoculation against mortality than prosperity (Lk 12:16–20). The call on the rich to "boast" (implied) in being brought low is ironic and the necessary correlate to the boasting of the lowly. My position, then, is that neither of the prevailing options (options 1 and 2) for understanding the rich and the poor in James is sufficient; the distinctions are too restrictive.

But what about the significance of the inevitable withering and fading of the rich? Is James referring to the inevitability of death or to a particular judgment on the rich? Further, how does one's answers to these questions reflect or impact on one's understanding of James's eschatology? Once again, as is almost always the case in dealing with this chapter – because of the way James later expands on ideas and concerns introduced in Chapter 1 – we must anticipate conclusions to be developed more fully later in this volume. To use contemporary phrasing, James certainly has a sharpened eschatological consciousness. He actively and patiently awaits the "coming of the Lord" (5:7ff.), and he expects a particular and telling judgment on the rich (4:13–5:6). Neither of these, however, is especially at work in this passage. The images of the fading flower and the scorching heat of the sun are both natural, and their force is not apocalyptical. Instead James is bringing to bear the natural rhythms of life and death (cf. 3:6), rhythms from which, to judge by the teaching of James and Jesus, the rich often imagined themselves exempt. How little things change.

SACRED AND HOMILETICAL TEXTURES

Does James (and for that matter, Jesus) despise the rich? Yes, at least the ones he depicts in his letter. Most any other conclusion avoids the textual evidence. Ideologically James sits comfortably with those who speak of God's "preferential option for the poor." His is a theology of liberation, a conclusion I find, after teaching and preaching James in Nicaragua, to be fairly obvious, but not widely held.[16] The challenge is to discern from what and for what James espouses liberation. On that he will have much more to say, and so we have more work to do.

Here one needs to reiterate that boasting is not about status or standing but about the very process of reversal, a reversal for which neither the believer nor the rich is responsible. It is God who exalts the lowly and humbles the rich, as Mary sings in the Magnificat:

> 51 He has shown strength with his arm,
> he has scattered the proud in the imagination of their hearts,
> 52 he has put down the mighty from their thrones,
> and exalted those of low degree [*tapeinous*];
> 53 he has filled the hungry with good things,
> and the rich [*ploutountas*] he has sent empty away. (Lk 1:51–3, RSV)

How we proclaim these words and what implications we draw from them for our own actions are crucial. What it means to join with God in the preferential option for the poor is by no means apparent or obvious. There are here, and not just in the next verses, temptations to be avoided. One temptation is to conclude that we are responsible for bringing about the reversal. Another is to conclude that no action expressing and embodying our solidarity with God and the poor is required. James will correct both views. The force of vv. 9–11 is to remind all, especially those whose good fortune in life may serve as a shield

---

[16] See especially Elsa Tamez, *The Scandalous Message of James: Faith without Works Is Dead*, trans. John Eagleson (New York: Crossroad, 1990) and Pedrito U. Maynard-Reid, *Poverty and Wealth in James* (Maryknoll, NY: Orbis Books, 1987).

from the harshness experienced by most, that life is fragile. And precious. The homiletical challenge is to enable hearers to examine their lives in view of the reality of their eventual deaths and to explore the choices they make each day not as meaningless but as filled with life and death significance.

JAMES 1:12–18

12 Blessed is anyone who endures temptation. Such a one has stood the test and will receive the crown of life that the Lord has promised to those who love him.
13 No one, when tempted, should say, "I am being tempted by God"; for God cannot be tempted by evil and he himself tempts no one.
14 But one is tempted by one's own desire, being lured and enticed by it;
15 then, when that desire has conceived, it gives birth to sin, and that sin, when it is fully grown, gives birth to death.
16 Do not be deceived, my beloved.
17 Every generous act of giving, with every perfect gift, is from above, coming down from the Father of lights, with whom there is no variation or shadow due to change.
18 In fulfillment of his own purpose he gave us birth by the word of truth, so that we would become a kind of first fruits of his creatures.

INNER TEXTURE AND INTERTEXTURE

The first issue confronting interpreters concerns the limits of the pericope. Johnson includes v. 12 with vv. 9–11 and vv. 13–16 with vv. 17–21. Moo and Dibelius treat v. 12 as an "isolated saying" and consider vv. 13–18 as a unit. Wall divides the verses in half, 12–15, 16–18, while Reicke and Laws treat 12–18 as a single pericope, a conclusion with which I concur for the following reasons: (1) the "Blessed" (*makarios*) at the beginning of v. 12 signifies an important shift; (2) the repetition, "temptation/tempted" (*peirasmon/periazomenos*) strongly connects vv. 12–13; (3) the theme of temptation unites the first half of the passage; and (4) the warning against deception in v. 16 bridges the discussion of a wrong understanding of God in vv. 13–15 with its correction in vv. 17–18.

In many respects the passage echoes in parallel fashion the opening verses of the chapter: the blessing on the one who endures temptations recalls the "consider it nothing but joy" in the face of "trials of any kind" in v. 2. The "doubter" of vv. 6–8 anticipates the wrong understanding of temptation in vv. 13–15. The "perfecting of faith" climax in vv. 3–4 is mirrored in reverse by the elaborate climax, from temptation to death, in vv. 14–15. The giving of wisdom from the God "who gives to all generously and ungrudgingly" anticipates giving of "every perfect gift" in v. 17.

The passage is also among the most challenging for textual critics and translators, containing as it does a number of variants and *hapax legomena*. For example, in v. 12 the NRSV reads, "the crown of life that the *Lord* has promised" and notes "Gk *he*; other ancient authorities read *God*." (The "crown of life" is also promised in the Apocalypse to those poor yet rich in the church at Smyrna, who are "faithful until death"; Rev 2:9–10.) The Gk. *epēggeilato* offers neither noun nor pronoun, emphasizing the promise more than the promiser, and was often "corrected" in later manuscripts with the insertion of "God" or "the Lord."

Translators have wrestled with the meaning of *apeirastos* in v. 13. Laws notes, "The adjective *apeirastos* is virtually without precedent in biblical or secular Greek, and its meaning is therefore uncertain."[17] The various translations offered over the years by commentators surely evidences the truth of the phrase "all translation is interpretation,"[18] and they will be, along with my own reading, discussed more fully and appropriately in the next two sections.

The most intriguing inner textual and intertextual issue in the passage may be the incredible climax found in vv. 14–15. The "progression" from desire to death may be rendered as follows:

one is tempted by one's own desire,
   being lured and enticed by it;
     then, when that desire has conceived,
        it gives birth to sin, and that sin,
           when it is fully grown,
               gives birth to death.

The climax begins with a link to the theme of temptation (*peirazei*), which is the result of "one's own desire" (*epithumias*), and this evocative language of desire continues in the participles "lured" and "enticed." Then there is a rhetorical ladder within the ladder, from conception (*sullabousa*) to birth (*tíktei*) to growth (*apotelestheîsa*) to death (*thánaton*), the last phrase, "give birth to death," completing the climax in an especially powerful way.

A number of other evocative terms or phrases in this passage should also be noted. The admonition of v. 16, "Do not be deceived," is also found in Paul (1 Cor 15:33; Gal 6:7). The Pauline usage introduces quotations, and that may well be the case here. "Every generous act of giving, with every perfect gift," for example, has a memorable, rhythmic quality, and while Johnson is correct to discount efforts to identify the verse as a quotation when we have no hint of a source, the enduring popularity of the verse, as well as its frequent citation, has certainly established it as one within Christian tradition.[19] The pleonasm of the verse is not a problem – except for translators, who have difficulty rendering the elegance of the Greek.

---

[17] S. Laws, *Epistle of James* (1980), p. 70.
[18] The truth of this phrase, and the phrase itself, was taught me by the late David J. Wilmot of the Univ. of Chicago.
[19] L. T. Johnson, *Letter of James* (1995), p. 195.

The source of these gifts is referred to in a unique expression as the "father of lights" (*tou patros tōn phōtōn*), who is further described as one "in whom there is no variation or shadow due to change." The text itself is by no means secure, and as Metzger notes, "The obscurity of the passage has led to the emergence of a variety of readings."[20] Johnson examines the five main variants before concluding, "the basic meaning remains clear despite all the variations. The text opposes the steadfastness of God to the changeableness of creation."[21] Yet the interpreter should not pass too quickly over this extraordinary reference to God. The "lights" of which God is the Father are presumably heavenly ones – twinkling stars, whirling planets, waxing and waning moon, circled and circling sun, itself sometimes eclipsed by the shadow of moon or planet – all both fixed in their courses and constantly changing. The textual and translation possibilities that contrast God with such changeableness are many, as Metzger and Johnson note. God, however, is One, fixed and steadfast.

James is not done with extraordinary images for God, however. In v. 18 God, because of a desire or wish (the NRSV reads "in fulfillment of his own purpose," an emphasis on the Gk. *boulētheis* ["plan" or "counsel"], which is an overtranslation), "gave us birth by the word of truth." This understanding of the creation of humanity by the word of truth (dative of means) calls to mind Genesis 1, John 1, Proverbs 8, and a fairly conventional Wisdom view of creation by the divine word. What is surely unconventional is first to refer to God as "Father" and then immediately to refer to God "giving birth." Before turning to look at the sociocultural and ideological aspects of this and other ideas in the passage, we should also note the expression "a kind of first fruits of his creatures." The "first fruits" (Gk. *aparchēn*) recalls animals and produce offered in sacrifice according to the Torah and was a favorite expression of Paul, especially in Rom (8:23, 11:16, 16:5) and 1 Cor (15:20, 23, 16:15), and is similarly found in the Apocalypse (Rev 14:4).

SOCIOCULTURAL AND IDEOLOGICAL TEXTURES

"The general theme of this section is of what may or may not be said to come from God, in terms of future reward or destiny, present experience, and formative past events."[22] The basic dynamic of the passage is clear: (1) the experience of testing naturally calls one to ask about its source; (2) do not think it comes from God, for God is not tempted and tempts not; (3) instead we are tempted by our desires, which if followed lead to death; (4) the unchanging God, on the contrary, gives good things, above all, gives us birth. The interplay of question and answer, temptation and blessing, human desire and divine purpose, birth and death

---

[20] Bruce M. Metzger, *A Textual Commentary on the Greek New Testament*, 2d ed. (Stuttgart, Germany: German Bible Society, 1994), p. 608.
[21] L. T. Johnson, *Letter of James* (1995), p. 197.
[22] S. Laws, *Epistle of James* (1980), p. 66.

make this a lively and complex passage. Yet two themes, one sociocultural and one ideological, seem to stand out.

The sociocultural issue is the quick return of the themes of temptation and endurance. While there is as yet in the letter no evidence of specific persecution or oppression, the reader is confirmed in the suspicion raised in vv. 3–4 and 9–10 that James is writing to a community whose experience is challenging and difficult, at least from time to time, a fact of life for most people in antiquity.

The ideological issue is how James believes the readers are internalizing and interpreting their experiences. It is only natural to ask, "why?" and "why me?" James does not deny this but cautions that if one goes on to ask, "why God?" and to conclude that one is tempted by God and not by one's own desires, one is not just going too far – one is entirely deceived.

This self-deception is countered with an emphatic affirmation of the goodness and immutability of God and a reverse climax, from desire to death. In as poetic a passage as one finds in the letter, God is praised as "the Father of lights, with whom there is no variation or shadow due to change," who gives "every perfect gift." It would seem we have moved into the sacred texture of the text.

SACRED AND HOMILETICAL TEXTURES

"Do not say, 'It was the Lord's doing that I fell away'; for he does not do what he hates. Do not say, 'It was he who led me astray'; for he has no need of the sinful" (Sir 15:11–12). The tendency, biblically, is as old as the Garden.

11 "Have you eaten from the tree of which I commanded you not to eat?" 12 The man said, "The woman whom you gave to be with me, she gave me fruit from the tree, and I ate it." 13 Then the LORD God said to the woman, "What is this that you have done?" The woman said, "The serpent tricked me, and I ate." (Gen 3:11–13)

If God had asked, the serpent would have had a good excuse too.

The road of self-excuse, the tendency to always blame others, finally leads one to blame God. Few join Job in saying, "Shall we receive good at the hand of God and not receive the bad?" (Job 2:10). Without attempting to solve the problem of theodicy, one can still join in recognition of the problem that "the blame game" can become. James's response to the questions perhaps arising among his readers in the face of difficulties and challenge is entirely in keeping with his theology and his emphasis on the practice of faith.

Homiletical texture abounds in the passage. The problem may be to choose where to focus. How, in an age when people sue the restaurant for serving fattening food and the teacher for their poor grades, but excuse themselves for not choosing salads over french fries or for not studying for the test, can we help but not finally blame God for any and every circumstance not of our liking? And if we do, how shall we understand true evil and develop the endurance to handle real temptation?

Finally, the compelling, and unusual, understanding of God as giver of gifts, Father of lights, and the one who "gives us birth by the word of truth" also merits homiletical attention, for the juxtaposition of "Father" and "giving birth" is uncommon, to put it mildly. The opportunity to use Scripture to challenge gender-specific stereotypes can be liberating in and of itself. And in a letter best known for its uncompromising call to faithful Christian practice, verses that emphasize God's goodness and gifts should themselves be emphasized.

JAMES 1:19–27

19 You must understand this, my beloved: let everyone be quick to listen, slow to speak, slow to anger;
20 for your anger does not produce God's righteousness.
21 Therefore rid yourselves of all sordidness and rank growth of wickedness, and welcome with meekness the implanted word that has the power to save your souls.
22 But be doers of the word, and not merely hearers who deceive themselves.
23 For if any are hearers of the word and not doers, they are like those who look at themselves in a mirror;
24 for they look at themselves and, on going away, immediately forget what they were like.
25 But those who look into the perfect law, the law of liberty, and persevere, being not hearers who forget but doers who act – they will be blessed in their doing.
26 If any think they are religious, and do not bridle their tongues but deceive their hearts, their religion is worthless.
27 Religion that is pure and undefiled before God, the Father, is this: to care for orphans and widows in their distress, and to keep oneself unstained by the world.

The last nine verses of chapter 1 form a coherent unit,[23] with a unifying theme: actions speak louder than words. Within this unit, however, some see divisions – vv. 19–21, on listening and speaking; vv. 22–5, on listening and acting; and vv. 26–8, on restrained speech and unrestrained charity – while other interpreters variously group the verses. We will treat them as a unit (as Laws does).

INNER TEXTURE AND INTERTEXTURE

19–21. A textual issue arises with the first word of this passage. The *textus receptus*, and thus the King James Version (KJV), take the first word to be *hōste* (therefore), perhaps based on the need to provide a stronger connection with the previous verses. This explains why a copyist might change the text from

---

[23] A position held by virtually all commentators, even M. Dibelius, *Letter of James* (1975), p. 108, whose tendency is to see fragments where others do not.

iste (NRSV "you must understand this") as found in the best textual evidence, but it is difficult indeed to imagine a copying error in the reverse.[24] In fact the imperative *iste* better connects vv. 19–21 with the preceding verses, for the emphatic "you must understand" parallels the "do not be deceived" of v. 16.[25] But the link is more formal than substantive, because James here introduces a new emphasis, away from correcting errant theologies and anthropologies and on to perhaps the most persistent theme in the letter, the call for right behavior.

The rest of v. 19 is a carefully balanced exhortation, the third person singular imperative (*estō*) followed twice by *eis* plus the infinitive (*akoûsai, lalēsai*) and once by *eis* and the noun (*orgēn*). The balance is also found in the sequence "quick, slow, slow," thus, let every person be

> quick to listen,
>> slow to speak,
>> slow to anger.

Wall considers this verse to be the thesis statement of the body of the letter, 1:22–5:6, dividing the body into three "essays": quick to hear (1:22–2:26), "slow to speak" (3:1–18), and "slow to anger" (4:1–5:6). The suggestion is interesting but flawed, for any reading of James that does not emphasize the persistent call to faithful practice, or doing, is inadequate. As we will see, a better candidate for the thesis statement of the letter is 1:22.

Like much wisdom the saying, "be quick to listen, slow to speak, slow to anger" is better attested than it is followed, and although the exact form of the saying is unique to James, there are close parallels within the biblical Wisdom tradition, and one phrase or another of the triad is quite common in a variety of traditions, from ancient Egypt to Greek philosophers (e.g., Lucian) and the *Pirke Aboth*. Sir 5:11 offers the closest parallel, "Be quick to hear, but deliberate in answering." The wording, however, only agrees on "quick" (*tachus*). Also common is the juxtaposition of speech and anger – "A fool gives full vent to anger, but the wise quietly holds it back" (Prov 29:11).

Anger (*orgē*) is the pivot of v. 20, and while the verse lacks the rhythm and balance of v. 19, it also has a certain proverbial quality. The verse is notable for two additional reasons: it is the first of many uses by James of the terms "righteousness" and "righteous" (*dikaiosunē, dikaios*; 2:23, 24; 3:18; 5:6, 16), and James here chooses to use the term for man/male (*andros*) rather than his preferred term for human beings, *anthrōpos* (1:7, 19; 2:20, 24; 3:7, 8, 9; 5:17). The use of *andros*, here and at 1:23, seems merely stylistic; research demonstrating that males are more prone to anger because of testosterone levels comes some 1,900 years after the writing of the letter, and as far as I know the only evidence that males are more likely to forget what they see in a mirror is anecdotal.

---

[24] B. M. Metzger, *Textual Commentary on the Greek NT* (1994), p. 609.
[25] See Robert W. Wall, *The Community of the Wise* (Valley Forge, PA: Trinity Press International, 1997), p. 71, among others.

> A CLOSER LOOK — GOD AND RIGHTEOUSNESS
>
> The verse is problematic for an important grammatical and semantic reason: how shall we understand the use of the genitive in the phrase, "God's righteousness," literally "righteousness of God"? Is it subjective and thus to be understood as a quality or character of the deity, thereby adding to our understanding of God's nature as the one "with whom there is no variation or shadow due to change" (1:17b)? Or is the genitive objective detailing God's requirements for people of faith, thus building on v. 19? Finally, should "righteousness of God" be understood as a genitive of origin, "that which God gives, his justification, the verdict of acquittal or acceptance"?[26]
>
> The discussion, as often happens, frequently turns on how interpreters take Paul's use of the expression, which seems an unnecessary detour. Laws is correct to identify the objective genitive as the grammatical answer, especially given the force of the verb *ergazomai* ("work" or "produce"), which is something humans do, not God. However, this also seems to be an example of a meaning not limited to either/or. The richness of the Greek allows for both/and. God's righteousness — the righteousness characteristic of God, which may also touch humanity and which the believer is called to emulate — is contrasted with the outworking of anger, which whatever it may accomplish will not accomplish righteousness.

V. 21 offers a further contrast, between "all sordidness and rank growth of wickedness" and "the implanted word that has the power to save your souls," which is to be welcomed with "meekness," a contrast paralleling that between human anger and divine righteousness. Meekness (*prautēti*) recalls the "lowly" (*tapeinos*) of v. 9 and is an important component of virtue lists (e.g., Gal 5:22–3) and Matthew's depiction of Jesus' self-description in the well-loved call to the "weary and heavy-laden" in Mt 11:28–30. NRSV "sordidness" is an overreading of *ruparian*, also found in 2:2 to describe "filthy" clothes. The verb *apotithemi* can mean simply to remove clothes but in our literature almost always is used metaphorically for the removal of sin of one kind or another (e.g., Heb 12:1; 1 Pet 2:1). The usage tends to have overtones of baptism and the symbolic removal of an old garment and "putting on" (*enduō*; Rom 13:14; Eph 4:24) a new garment, a usage explicit in 1 Pet 3:21: "baptism, which this prefigured, now saves you — not as a removal of dirt [*apothesis rupou*] from the body, but as an appeal to God for a good conscience, through the resurrection of Jesus Christ."

Commentators have been most interested, however, in the "implanted word" (*ton emphuton logon*) that is able to "save souls." What is the word that the

---

[26] S. Laws, *Epistle of James* (1980), p. 81.

reader is to receive – Wisdom, the Gospel, the kerygma, the word Incarnate? And if this word is "implanted" in some yet to be understood sense, why does the reader need to "receive" it? Dibelius was wise to seek "simpler explanations for the passage than the hypothesis of complex trains of thought."[27] Neither Pauline theology nor Stoic philosophy convincingly lies within the passage, and while we have no other biblical examples of "implanted word" we have James's own use of *logos* elsewhere in this chapter, and the inner dynamic of his rhetoric to guide us. We are to put off one thing – "all sordidness and rank growth of wickedness" – and welcome/receive the other – "the implanted word that has the power to save." What we put off is unnatural; what we receive is natural. We are moving to ideology, and our discussion must wait for the next section.

22–5. "But be(come) doers of the word [*poiētai logou*], and not merely hearers, who deceive themselves." Here, I will argue in considering the ideological and sacred textures of the passage, is the thesis statement of the letter of James. When all is said, all is not done. The remainder of the letter is largely devoted to exploration and application of this thesis. In the immediate verses James explains what it means to be a "hearer only"; it is to be self-deceiving, having a "religion" that is empty and foolish. From 1:27 on James details what it means to practice the faith. Johnson is correct to choose "become" to translate the opening *ginomai* over the NRSV "be." James considers the practice of faith to be ongoing, something to be worked for and worked on, rather than something achieved and accomplished.[28]

A CLOSER LOOK – THROUGH A GLASS DARKLY?

The image used to elaborate what James means by the self-deceit of "hearing only" is, frankly, a bit of a mess. Johnson has argued persuasively that the basic dynamic and contrast would have been well understood in James's day.[29] In a general sense the same is true for the contemporary reader: hearing without doing is like looking at one's reflected image and forgetting what you look like; that is, hearing without doing is ridiculous. Where the metaphor breaks down, and where Johnson is helpful, is in the specifics. Two points are particularly useful: (1) in antiquity comparisons to looking in a mirror pointed toward moral improvement; (2) the idea of looking into the Law as into a mirror was

---

[27] M. Dibelius, *Letter of James* (1975), p. 114.
[28] The verb translated as "deceive" is also noteworthy, *paralogizomai* having at its center the word/*logos* we are called to do. Its only other NT use is an interesting turn of phrase in Col 2:4, *paralogizētai en pithanologia*, "deceive with plausible arguments" (another word containing "word").
[29] Luke T. Johnson, "The Mirror of Remembrance (James 1:22–25)" *Catholic Biblical Quarterly* 50 (1988): 632–45.

something of a commonplace in Second Temple and Hellenistic Judaisms.[30] Unfortunately this does not explain the inconsistencies in James's image.

Those who are hearers only (Gk. is masculine singular throughout) look at themselves in the mirror, "themselves" a translation of a difficult phrase in Greek, *to prosōpon tēs geneseōs*, which means literally "the face of (their) birth" and is usually translated as "natural face." (James will use *genesis* in an equally difficult way in 3:6.) These go away and immediately forget what they were like. The doers do not look into a mirror but into "the perfect law, the law of liberty" (*nomon teleion ton tēs eleutherias*), a phrase we will discuss when considering the ideological texture of the passage. The verb for "look" is different. Rather than the typical *katavoeō* we find *parakuptō*, otherwise used in the NT to describe Peter and the beloved disciple "stooping" to look (*blepō* is added) in Lk 24:12 and Jn 20:5, and to describe "things into which angels long to look!" (*parakupsai*; 1 Pet 1:12). Nor do these go away; they "persevere" (NRSV), *paramenō*, which generally means "remain" (e.g., 1 Cor 16:6) and so are "not hearers who forget but doers who act – they will be blessed in their doing" (v. 25). This is not comparing apples and oranges, this is comparing apples with gold and diamonds! Nevertheless, the meaning remains obvious: be a hearer/doer, not a hearer only.

26–7. The language of appearance, self-deception, and inadequate faith is continued in v. 26, while the language of "filth and abounding evil" in v. 21 is countered with "religion that is pure and undefiled" in v. 27. James also introduces two themes he will later return to, the "tongue" and the "world."

Three of the five NT uses of "religion" and "religious" (*thrēskeia, thrēskos*) are found in these verses. James creates another hypothetical situation, this one easier to follow: if some "think" (*dokei*, a common word for think, suppose, or imagine) themselves to be religious "and do not bridle their tongue" (*mē chalinayōgōn glōssan autou*; cf. 3:3), that is, are "slow to speak," two things result. They "deceive" (Heb 3:13 uses the noun *apatē* to describe the "deceitfulness" of sin) their heart (James uses *kardia* here and at 3:14, 4:8, and 5:5, 8 for the emotional/spiritual center), and their "religion" is proven foolish and/or futile (*mataios*; Mk 7:7 uses the adverb *matēn*, "in vain do they worship me").

Yet "religion that is pure and undefiled before God" is to "do" two things: care for widows and orphans, a biblical principle of long standing and witness (Ex 22:22; Deut 26:12; Isa 1:17; Jer 22:3; Zech 7:10; Tob 1:8; Sir 35:16; 4 Esd 2:19), and "keep oneself unstained [*aspilon*] by the world [*tou kosmou*]." As noted, "unstained" likely keys off v. 21, while the world to which one is to keep unstained

---

[30] Ibid., pp. 636–41, cites Plutarch and Seneca, Wisdom of Solomon 7:26, and Philo, *The Contemplative Life* before concluding, "Neither for Philo nor for James was there anything particularly mystical about imaging God's law as a mirror for moral instruction. It was [a] literary convention of prosaic and predictable use" (p. 641).

James 1:1–27 – That You May Be Mature and Complete 53

by is later depicted as the opposite of God (4:4) (friend of God vs. friend of the world), once again moving us to other textures.

SOCIOCULTURAL AND IDEOLOGICAL TEXTURES

An important sociocultural and ideological question in 1:19–27 deals with what James meant by "word" (*logos*) and "law" (*nomos*). While a complete discussion of law in James will be found in the second chapter, we can anticipate that discussion in this look at the use of "word." The term is used five times in the letter. The last use in 3:2, "if someone makes no mistakes in speaking [*en logō*]," is not important for this discussion. The others are gathered here:

1:18   "he gave us birth by the word of truth" [*logō alētheias*]"
1:21   "welcome with meekness the implanted word [*ton emphuton logon*] that has the power to save your souls [*sōsai tas psuchas humōn*]"
1:22   "become doers of the word [*ginesthe de poiētai logou*]"
1:23   "if any are hearers of the word [*akroatēs logou*]"

Thus we find all the uses clustered in six verses of the first chapter, thereafter dropped entirely except the one time in chapter 3, where the meaning is entirely different. What happened? It appears that as James's argument unfolds, *logos* is replaced by *nomos* (law), which is first found at 1:25, and that for James the two terms are in many ways synonymous and summarized this in the citation of Lev 19:18, found in 2:8, as "the royal law according to the Scripture" – *nomon... basilikon kata tēn graphēn* ("You shall love your neighbor as yourself") – and thereby extending from word to law to Scripture. The words are of course not entirely synonymous, or there would be no reason to change terms. But it is in keeping with James's overall style to use them loosely, if not interchangeably.

The most intriguing use of "word" is in 1:21: "the implanted word that has the power to save your souls" (*ton emphuton logon ton dunamenon sōsai tas psuchas humōn*). The "power to save" is "implanted" in us. Yet we must receive it if it is to do its work. In fact we must "welcome with meekness" (*en prautēti*), the way in chapter 3 that we are to show our wisdom. As we saw, to search for evidence of "elemental spirits" or other philosophical principles is to miss the mark, for there is little in James (1:17, 21; 3:6) that suggests a sophisticated philosophical background or that invites much speculation. Rather, the juxtaposition of meekness and power, that which is implanted as that which must also be received, is born of the natural creative tension between hearing and doing, faith and practice, which is at the heart of James's anthropology and theology.

A second juxtaposition in this passage is also suggestive: human anger/divine righteousness, "for your [Gk. *andros*] anger [*orgē*] does not produce [Gk. *ergazetai*] God's righteousness. James never speaks of God's anger or wrath, nor of "righteous anger." Anger is antithetical to the divine and so must be put off with every other sordid wickedness.

SACRED AND HOMILETICAL TEXTURES

Interestingly, the main admonitions in this passage – be quick to listen, slow to speak, slow to anger; be doers of the word and not merely hearers; care for orphans and widows; keep oneself unstained from the world – are fairly commonplace. As we have seen, sources as varied as Sirach, Proverbs, the prophets, and Jesus, with all of whose teachings James would have been familiar, anticipate much of James's instruction in this passage. Moreover, from Philo to Plato, with multiple sources in between, the philosophers and teachers of the ancient Mediterranean world offered comparable wisdom. Even an ancient Near Eastern source, the "Instruction of Ani," offers something similar: "Do not talk a lot. Be silent and thou wilt be happy" (4.1. *ANET*, p. 240). This does not mean, however (and contra Dibelius among others), that the letter of James is merely a compendium of conventional wisdom.

It is interesting that a word, "religion," so much a part of most discussions of faith, is used so infrequently in Scripture. Apparently the place to look for "religionless Christianity" (Bonhoeffer) is in the NT. James, of course, was no more interested in the term than any other NT writer. He was interested in the phenomenon and in sharing with his community a right understanding of religion.

While we might offer any number of guesses if asked for the sine qua non of the truly religious before coming up with bridling the tongue, James seems to have meant it. Almost the whole of chapter 3 is devoted to the power and danger of speech, and it comes up again in 4:11–12. Presumably this concern also carries over into the positive definition of religion, the "pure and undefiled" variety, in v. 27 – to care for orphans and widows in their distress and to keep "unstained" by the world. Later in the letter James has more to say about "the world," juxtaposing "God" and "world" as opposites.

BRIDGING THE HORIZONS – OUT OF SILENCE

The homiletical issue in this passage is how to lift up the moral exhortation to help those in distress, to which contemporary listeners are likely to be well disposed, and the language of purity, to which they likely will not be. James does not allow us to pick and choose, weaving social ethics and moral purity together throughout the letter.

One clue can be taken from the third chapter, where James writes of the impossibility of holding conflicting opposites (bless and curse, salt and fresh water) together (3:10–12), a passage that ends with a call to righteousness and peace, which pairs virtues, in contrast to the conflicting anger and righteousness in 1:20. Implicit in James's worldview and explicit in the teaching of the letter is that moral purity (as opposed to ritual purity, I think) and ethical practice must go together. So when preaching James they must be proclaimed together, whether the listeners like it or not.

Ironically, the best homiletical suggestion is found in 1:19 – "let every *preacher* be quick to listen, slow to speak." The sermon begins in silence. We must hear the Gospel before we proclaim the Gospel, and we must hear it in silence. Frederick Buechner spoke of this truth in his incomparable Beecher Lectures.

> The preacher pulls the little cord that turns on the lectern light and deals out his note cards like a riverboat gambler. The stakes have never been higher. Two minutes from now he may have lost his listeners completely to their own thoughts, but at this minute he has them in the palm of his hand. . . . Everybody knows the kind of things he has told them before and not told them, but who knows what this time, out of silence, he will tell them?
>
> Let him tell them the truth. Before the Gospel is a word, it is silence. . . .
>
> Out of the silence let the only real news come. . . . The preacher is not brave enough to be literally silent for long, and since it is his calling to speak the truth with love, even if he were brave enough, he would not be silent for long because we are none of us very good at silence. It says too much.[31]

We have so much to say, and James gives us so much to do, who has time for silence? True enough, but the practice of faith and the responsibility of the pulpit demands that the preacher makes time for silence. It really does not matter how well you say it if you have nothing to say, and the "something" comes to us in silence (1 Kg 19:12).

Be still, and know that I am God (Psa 46:10).

JAMES 2:1–26 – I BY MY WORKS WILL SHOW YOU MY FAITH

The shift in scope and rhetoric between the first chapter of James and the chapters to follow is apparent in the first verses of chapter 2. Arguments and perspectives introduced in the previous chapter – true wisdom, the nature of faith, God's concern for the poor, and so on – now begin to be developed in detail and example. That the first example has to do with a contrast between rich and poor, and the reaction of the community to each, is hardly unimportant. What was only hinted at is now fully articulated. Faith, of Christ and in Christ, must be lived out in faithful daily practice if it is to have any meaning at all.

Therefore, the division of chapter 2 is second in importance to the rhetorical and semantic unity of the chapter. In as an effective argument as one can find in

---

[31] Frederick Buechner, *Telling the Truth: The Gospel as Tragedy, Comedy, and Fairy Tale* (New York: Harper and Row, 1977), p. 23.

Scripture, James makes his case for the importance of Christian *practice* in any account of Christian *faith*. As we have begun to see already, James understands faith to mean belief *and* practice. In chapter 2 James works out much of the meaning of this conviction for how the community is to live and what priorities it is to hold. While most commentators emphasize the unity of chapter 2, they do not agree on the chapter's literary divisions. Johnson and Walls see breaks between vv. 1–7, 8–13, and 14–26; Laws between vv. 1–9, 10–13, and 14–26; Ropes between vv. 1–7, 8–11, 12–13, and 14–26; Dibelius, interestingly, makes the strongest case for the unity of the chapter and divides the argument into two "treatises," the first on "partiality" (2:1–13) and the second on "faith and works" (2:14–26; he sees a third, and related, treatise on the tongue at 3:1–12).[32]

JAMES 2:1–13

1 My brothers and sisters, do you with your acts of favoritism really believe in our glorious Lord Jesus Christ?
2 For if a person with gold rings and in fine clothes comes into your assembly, and if a poor person in dirty clothes also comes in,
3 and if you take notice of the one wearing the fine clothes and say, "Have a seat here, please," while to the one who is poor you say, "Stand there," or, "Sit at my feet,"
4 have you not made distinctions among yourselves, and become judges with evil thoughts?
5 Listen, my beloved brothers and sisters. Has not God chosen the poor in the world to be rich in faith and to be heirs of the kingdom that he has promised to those who love him?
6 But you have dishonored the poor. Is it not the rich who oppress you? Is it not they who drag you into court?
7 Is it not they who blaspheme the excellent name that was invoked over you?
8 You do well if you really fulfill the royal law according to the scripture, "You shall love your neighbor as yourself."
9 But if you show partiality, you commit sin and are convicted by the law as transgressors.
10 For whoever keeps the whole law but fails in one point has become accountable for all of it.
11 For the one who said, "You shall not commit adultery," also said, "You shall not murder." Now if you do not commit adultery but if you murder, you have become a transgressor of the law.
12 So speak and so act as those who are to be judged by the law of liberty.

---

[32] L. T. Johnson, *Letter of James* (1995); Robert W. Wall, *Community of the Wise* (Valley Forge, PA: Trinity Press International, 1997); S. Laws, *Epistle of James* (1980); James H. Ropes, *A Critical and Exegetical Commentary on the Epistle of St. James*, ICC (New York: Charles Scribener's Sons, 1916); M. Dibelius, *Letter of James* (1975).

13 For judgment will be without mercy to anyone who has shown no mercy; mercy triumphs over judgment.

INNER TEXTURE AND INTERTEXTURE

1. 2:1 is the fifth time James addresses the reader as "brothers and sisters" (*adelphoi*), two times as my beloved brothers (and sisters) and now for the third time without the affectionate modifier. At some point one begins to become suspicious, for the familiar address is again followed by sharp words. 2:1 also presents something of the same challenge found at 1:1, for only in these two places do we find specific reference to "Jesus Christ." This second reference is the more problematic, for the entire phrase in which the reference is found is composed in Greek as a string of loosely related expressions in the genitive case – *tou kuriou hēmōn Iēsou Christou tēs doxēs* – which could be literally, awkwardly, and unsatisfactorily translated as "of the Lord our Jesus Christ of the glory."

First, though, the reader must attend to the expression translated by the NRSV as "with your acts of favoritism" (*en prosōpolēmpsiais*). This evocative expression is found in its verbal form later in the argument (2:9), as a noun in the oft-cited and climactic realization of Peter in Acts 10:34 and in Paul in Rom 2:11, as well as Eph 6:9 and Col 3:25. The word is a compound, built of a noun, "face" or "appearance" (*prosōpon*) and a verb, "receive" (*lambanein*), and is doubly significant because it is found in the LXX at Lev 19:15, "You shall not render an unjust judgment; you shall not be partial (*lēmpsēi prosōpon*) to the poor or defer to the great: with justice you shall judge your neighbor," a verse and passage central to James's viewpoint. The challenge is not in understanding the meaning of the phrase, something made clear in the example in 2:2–4. The challenge is in the juxtaposition of "your acts of favoritism" and "really believe in our glorious Lord Jesus Christ?" It is a juxtaposition that I take to be crucial for understanding James and that returns us to the phrase "our glorious Lord Jesus Christ."

This long string of genitive phrases has been variously rendered over years of translation. KJV, RSV, TEV, and others agree on "our Lord Jesus Christ, the Lord of Glory," assuming a second *kyrios* ("Lord") to make sense of the phrase. Laws and others suggest a more literal "our Lord Jesus Christ, the Glory" but then must rather laboriously account for the additional title by way of the Hebrew *kabōd* and the *Shekinah*. Attempts to construe "glory" with "faith" (*pistis*) are undermined by their relative distance in the expression and differences in case; so also the suggestion of "faith in the glory of our Lord Jesus Christ." Interestingly, the very awkwardness of the expression argues in favor of its originality, for an interpolator would likely have provided a smoother phrasing less apt to call attention to itself.[33]

---

[33] So M. Dibelius, *Letter of James* (1975), p. 127. The awkwardness of the phrase has implications for the original "Christianity" of the letter, for just as an editor would be expected to have smoothed out the phrase, an interpolator would be expected to have inserted something more felicitous.

However the phrase is finally rendered, the meaning of the verse has more to do with how one understands the words that precede it, *echete tēn pistin*, literally "have the faith" (NRSV "really believe"), and the juxtaposition of this phrase with "acts of favoritism." First, is the force of the genitive objective or subjective? That is, is James talking about having faith *in* Jesus Christ or having (sharing) the faith *of* Jesus Christ? NRSV decides the question for the reader by translating the expression "believe in our glorious Lord Jesus Christ." This rendering, like much else in majority readings of James, seems overly dependent on readings of Paul. It also provides a question that is not present in the Greek. A more neutral translation is preferred, allowing the reader to weigh the juxtaposition of faith and partiality before and while attending to the christological implications: *My brothers and sisters, in acts of favoritism you do not have the faith of Jesus Christ, our Lord of glory.*

2-4. The example in 2:2-4 is based on a relatively straightforward contrast between the receptions afforded two persons who visit "your assembly" (*sunagōgēn humōn*). What this "assembly" is, however, is not at all clear. The term is elsewhere translated in the NRSV as "synagogue" and used in reference to a place of worship. James is familiar with the early Christian equivalent, *ekklēsia*, and uses it at 5:14. Does James intend a distinction between the assembly imagined in chapters 2 and 5? It seems unnecessary to so argue, because the emphasis is not on the type of gathering (worship, formal or informal adjudication of disputes, fellowship) but on the treatment of visitors no matter what the gathering.

Further consideration of the nature of this assembly, along with more thorough analysis of the characters in the drama depicted in 2:2-4, will follow in the next section. Here the first character is not said to be rich but is described as appearing so. The "gold rings," whether or not meant to depict a Roman citizen of equestrian rank,[34] speak of a marked social status. The "fine clothes" resonate more deeply, and interestingly, in the biblical tradition. Luke uses the words to describe the robe Herod places on Jesus before sending him back to Pilate (Lk 23:11) and, in Acts, to describe the appearance of the angel who appeared to Cornelius (Acts 10:30). In the Apocalypse the adjective is fairly common (Rev 15:16, 18:14, 19:8, 22:1, 16).

The contrast with the description of the other person who enters the assembly is sharp. The second person is described as poor (*ptōchos*), and the clothes as dirty (*rupara*). While discussion of the implications for our reading of James's understanding of social class must wait, the impression is of a beggar.

That they are visitors to the assembly/synagogue/gathering is evident because both are directed to their assigned seats. The first visitor (1) is directed to a fine seat over here or (2) is invited to "please" sit over here, depending on how the reader construes the use of the term *kalōs*. In either case, the effect is to contrast

---

[34] S. Laws, *Epistle of James* (1980), p. 98.

an exaggerated courtesy in greeting the first visitor with a dismissive "Stand there" in greeting the second. James's own judgment is as swift as his example is brief: you are making judgments about and distinctions among those who come to your assembly/synagogue/gathering, thereby not only making judges of yourselves but judges with questionable, even evil, motives.

5–13. In quick succession there follows in vv. 5–7 demonstration of why such judgments and distinctions are wrong in the apparent understanding both of the poor and of the rich. In v. 5, James reminds the reader that God has "chosen the poor in the world to be rich in faith and to be heirs of the kingdom that he has promised to those who love him." The echo of, if not reference to, Mt 5:3 (= Lk 6:20) is unmistakable. In fact, James's phrasing acts as an interpretation of the beatitude. Pointedly, in the Synoptic tradition we have one reference to those who will "inherit the kingdom" (Mt 25:34–5), where those who do not distinguish between the hungry or thirsty, the stranger (who was welcomed – *sunēgagete*!), the naked, the sick, or the imprisoned are invited to "inherit the kingdom prepared for you since the foundation of the world."[35] God's choice is contrasted with the reader's propensity to dishonor the poor in preference for the rich, now mentioned by name (*plousioi*; see 1:10–11). The ridiculousness of dishonoring the poor in order to honor the rich is spelled out in two proofs, the first in two parts, resulting in three charges: (1) the rich oppress you, (2) the rich drag you into court, and (3) the rich blaspheme the excellent name invoked over the reader.

Oppression (*katadunasteuō*) should not be confused with persecution (*diōkō*), but the reference to "blaspheme the excellent name" makes it impossible to ignore the religious implications of the actions recalled or anticipated. Nor is "drag you into court" a subtle expression. As we will see in the next section, it is not necessary to envision either widescale religious persecution or more particular Jewish Christian antagonism to understand the passage. At root are a contrast between rich and poor and a compelling depiction of why favoring the former over the latter is senseless.

It is also sinful, which ties the passage together and leads to a shift in emphasis at vv. 8–9. "You do well if you really fulfill the royal law according to the scripture, 'You shall love your neighbor as yourself.' But if you show partiality, you commit sin and are convicted by the law as transgressors." Showing partiality (the verbal form of the expression used in 2:1) is now linked to the "royal law," which is expressed in "scripture" as "You shall love your neighbor as yourself" (Lev 19:18; also Mk 12:31; Lk 10:27, in answer to a question about *inheriting* eternal life; Rom 13:9; Gal 5:14). The move here is significant and will be the subject of reflection when we consider the sacred and homiletical textures. Showing partiality to the rich and dishonoring the poor are not a question

---

[35] Paul also speaks of inheriting the kingdom, but in the negative, listing those who cannot do so in 1 Cor 6:9–10, 1 Cor 15:50 (flesh and blood), Gal 5:21, and Eph 5:5.

of bad manners, they are violations of the law as summarized (by Jesus) in the command to love the neighbor. The final move in this section hammers the point home: to violate the law in one point is to violate the whole of the law.

Johnson is correct not to link James's argument here with that of Paul in Gal 5:3; as Laws points out, "His statement that the law must be kept in every particular or it is not kept at all, finds ample parallel within all branches of Judaism."[36] James, like Jesus (Mt 5:21ff.; Mk 10:19ff.) and Paul (Rom 13:9ff.), turns to the ethical portion of the decalogue for his examples, speaking of adultery and murder in the order found in LXX. The "one who said," that is, God, spoke both commandments (all commandments are understood), making no distinction between them or between those who violate one as opposed to another.

"Thus" the argument requires, for having set out the consequences James now sets out the alternative, "So speak and so act as those who are to be judged by the law of liberty." Again, we will defer discussion of "law" to the next section. Here we find James inviting the reader to reject partiality for mercy, because "judgment will be without mercy to anyone who has shown no mercy" and "mercy triumphs over judgment."

SOCIOCULTURAL AND IDEOLOGICAL TEXTURES

James 2:1–13 is especially rich for interpreters interested in its sociocultural and ideological textures. We are afforded a glimpse into a gathering of the community, a glimpse offering considerable detail. We meet the clearest expression of James's ideological position on poor and rich, and his most extended reflection on "the law" (*ho nomos*). Any reading of James will be well rewarded by attention to these topics, and we will consider them in turn.

James 2:2–4 relates one of the more memorable examples[37] among the many in the letter. The language is colorful, with James's vivid depictions and sharp contrasts calling to mind the examples of Jesus – certainly the "rich man and Lazarus" (Lk 16:19–31) and the "guest without a garment" (Mt 22:11–13) come to mind, as does the following passage from Luke:

7 When he noticed how the guests chose the places of honor, he told them a parable. 8 "When you are invited by someone to a wedding banquet, do not sit down at the place of honor, in case someone more distinguished than you has been invited by your host; 9 and the host who invited both of you may come and say to you, 'Give this person your

---

[36] L. T. Johnson, *Letter of James* (1995), p. 232; S. Laws, *Epistle of James* (1980), p. 111. See especially the excursus by M. Dibelius, *Letter of James* (1975), "Whoever Is Guilty of One Is Guilty of All," pp. 144–6.

[37] The term "example" is chosen for the sake of neutrality. The nature of this and other examples in James – metaphor, parable, analogy, illustration from community life, etc. – is the subject of the paragraphs to follow.

place,' and then in disgrace you would start to take the lowest place. 10 But when you are invited, go and sit down at the lowest place, so that when your host comes, he may say to you, 'Friend, move up higher'; then you will be honored in the presence of all who sit at the table with you. 11 For all who exalt themselves will be humbled, and those who humble themselves will be exalted." 12 He said also to the one who had invited him, "When you give a luncheon or a dinner, do not invite your friends or your brothers or your relatives or rich neighbors, in case they may invite you in return, and you would be repaid. 13 But when you give a banquet, invite the poor, the crippled, the lame, and the blind. 14 And you will be blessed, because they cannot repay you, for you will be repaid at the resurrection of the righteous." (Lk 14:7–14)

The passage is quoted at length for a number of reasons. First, there is similarity in dynamics and terms – seats are chosen, and distinctions are made between rich and poor. Second, we are at a gathering of some sort, presumably still "at the house of a leader of the Pharisees to have a meal on the sabbath" (Lk 14:1), a gathering that provides Jesus with both pretext and occasion for teaching about hospitality, priorities, and practice. Third, and this is the point of emphasis in the present discussion, while Luke tells us that Jesus "told them a parable" (*parabolē*), the line between situation, story, and application is fluid, typically fluid for the Synoptic Gospels, which leads to our question about James 2:2–4. Is this a "real" situation from the life of the community or a "metaphor or simile, drawn from nature or common life, arresting the hearer by its vividness or strangeness" (to draw on the parable definition of C. H. Dodd)?[38] In other words, before we draw too many conclusions from this glimpse of a gathered community provided by James we must decide whether we are glimpsing a *Sitz im Leben Jakobus* or a parable of James?

A CLOSER LOOK – SYNAGOGUE, STORY, AND SETTING

Wall argues forcefully that "the select details of conflict in 2:1–7 suggest an actual incident, a real crisis familiar to ancient and modern readers alike: those who have money and power oppress those without money and power, threatening to divide the community along socioeconomic lines."[39] He then constructs an elaborate juridical setting in which the poor person's attempt to seek justice is undercut by the community's bias in favor of the rich one.[40] Aside from a questionable privileging of the supposedly real over the parabolic, efforts to see an incident of a legal nature in the life of the community to which James

---

[38] C. H. Dodd, *The Parables of the Kingdom*, rev. ed. (New York: Charles Scribner's Sons, 1961), p. 5.
[39] R. W. Wall, *Community of the Wise* (1997), p. 103.
[40] R. W. Wall cites the work of Maynard-Reid, who is in turn dependent on that of R. B. Ward, "Partiality in the Assembly: James 2:2–4," *Harvard Theological Review* 62 (1969): 87–97. Determinative for many efforts like Wall's is an attempt to relate the assembly in v. 2 with the actions of the rich alleged in v. 6, if not in v. 7.

writes in 2:2–4 are undone by three problems: (1) the opening *ean gar* in v. 2, (2) the reference to "your synagogue" and the uses of *sunagōgē* in the NT, and (3) James's love and use of the metaphorical.

First, the grammatical construction (*ean* plus the aorist subjunctive) is generally used for a hypothetical situation and reads "If there *should* come," not "when a person came/comes," which supposes a historical rather than hypothetical situation.[41]

Second, reference is to *sunagōgēn humōn*, "your synagogue."[42] The word synagogue is used fifty-three times in the NT outside of this reference in James (omitting the two references in the Apocalypse), all in the Gospels and Acts, and all designating a place of Jewish worship, study, and prayer. While there is certainly evidence that community decisions were made in such places[43] and that disputes were brought for resolution,[44] the evidence is extrabiblical and entirely unnecessary to a reading of James. The point is not why these two are visiting the synagogue but how they are treated no matter why they are visiting. Only the determination that James is offering comment on an incident in the life of the community requires the interpreter to develop a possible scenario requiring movement so completely outside the text.

Third, while I maintain that this letter is as particular as any other in the NT, its author having a particular, historical, audience clearly in mind, this does not require us to understand the example to be rooted in a particular experience of this particular community, any more than it requires us to determine which particular member of the community was being referred to in 2:11 as not being guilty of adultery while nonetheless a murderer. The letter of James is full of comparison, analogy, metaphor, and the like. The narrative quality of 2:2–4 suggests the category of parable/allegory at least as much as suggests an example from the life of the community.

The simplest conclusion (to anticipate a bit) is that "synagogue" is used in the letter of James much as it is in the rest of the NT, to designate a gathering place/occasion for Jewish and/or Jewish Christian worship. The scene, characters, and incident were (re)created by James to represent a problem in the life of the community, not as report but as story.

The comments in this closer look, however, do not mean that we have nothing to learn from these verses about the background out of which and the

---

[41] S. Laws, *Epistle of James* (1980), p. 93, my emphasis.
[42] It is not clear to me why Maynard-Reid, *Poverty and Wealth* (1987), p. 4, translates the pronoun in the first person plural, "our synagogue."
[43] R. W. Wall, *Community of the Wise* (1997), pp. 111–12.
[44] Josephus, *Vita*, 277 ff. is often cited, but strictly speaking Josephus writes of "gathering" (*sunagontai*) in the "prayer house" (*proseuchēn*), not praying (*proseuchontai*) in the synagogue (*sunagōgē*).

community to which James wrote. In fact, we can learn not so much what happened as what mattered. After all, which is more revealing: that a particular incident of preferential treatment of a rich person occurred at a community gathering or that James considered favoritism against the poor such an actual or potential problem that he used a compelling illustration of it prominently in the argument of his letter? The terms and details are chosen by the author for the reader's attention, and reflection makes them, if anything, even more revealing than they would be if understood as simple reportage.

We start by returning to the significance of James's use of the phrase "your synagogue" (*sunagōgēn humōn*). Both words are important. The term synagogue certainly but not exclusively roots the gathering in Jewish experience and is a part of the argument for the early dating of James. It is not, of course, the author's only term for a gathering or gathering place of the community, because (and this admittedly adds to the argument against an early date for the letter) in 5:14 leaders of the community are referred to as "the elders of the church" (*tous presbyterous tēs ekklēsias*).[45] That the gathering is referred to as a synagogue certainly suggests a *religious* gathering, but this need not be limited, as our contemporary usage suggests, to worship. Nor, and this may be more to the point, does it exclude worship. The term remains imprecise as to what may have taken place after everyone was settled into position, and there we must leave it. The possessive pronoun "your" is also interesting, demanding that the interpreter consider whose synagogue this was. "Your" synagogue implies there may be an "our" synagogue and even a "their" synagogue. Yet little or no attention has been given to the pronoun by commentators. Three possibilities present themselves: that James is emphasizing that it is a distinctively Christian or Jewish Christian gathering as opposed to the Jewish gathering traditionally assumed by the term synagogue; that James is emphasizing what may happen in the intended audience's particular community as opposed to what is possible in others; or that James is emphasizing the responsibility the community has for what takes place in their gathering.

As interested as the interpreter is in what James intended to indicate in the reference, James himself seemed most interested in what he was suggesting might happen in "your synagogue," thus bringing the argument home for the readers. As noted before, the two persons, the first described as prosperous and the second both described and designated as poor (*ptōchos*) in v. 2, were each in turn directed to a place from which to participate or observe the gathering. Because they need to be directed to their seats or stations, both are presumably visitors, which argues against understanding this as a juridical

---

[45] The use of both terms in the letter suggests a period when most everything about the life of the Christian community was far from fixed. See the excellent entry by Wolfgang Schrage, "συναγωγή," in *Theological Dictionary of the New Testament*, vol. 7 (Grand Rapids, MI: Eerdmans, 1971), pp. 798–852.

proceeding – why would someone not a member of the community come to the community seeking justice? A series of verbs follows, in the aorist subjunctive indicating hypothetical condition and in the second person plural serving to indict the entire community, not a particular community leader or the single "usher" responsible for seating. In the indictment that follows the description of the scene (vv. 5–6) the group or class represented by the second visitor is termed again as the poor (*tous ptōchous*), and the term introduced in 1:9–11 is recalled to describe the class represented by the first visitor, the rich (*hoi plousioi*). To this distinction, and its central importance for James, we now turn.

The literature on social classes in the NT world has grown voluminously in the last generation, literature rarely reflected in interpretations of James. There is opportunity here only to highlight what is available elsewhere in greater detail,[46] before examining the implications of this literature for our reading of James's letter.

To oversimplify, contemporary scholars, from both social-scientific and ideological interpretive perspectives, have largely recast the terms of discussion by replacing long-prevailing understandings of the poor along the lines of late-OT/early rabbinic *anawim* (poverty) with an understanding grounded in the material poverty, honor/shame, and patronage categories of Mediterranean culture. To oversimplify the oversimplification, poverty was not (just) a matter of spirit, these folk were hungry.

Dibelius is a classic and influential example of what happens when a traditional spiritualization of poverty is applied to the letter of James. The interpretation attempts to trace both a historical-biblical and a social-cultural arc,[47] moving from a time in Israel's history and interpretation when poverty was viewed as a sign of divine repudiation (the "friends" of Job?) to a time, after national collapse and exile, when all were poor and in need of encouragement. The "'poor' and 'pious' appear as parallel concepts (Pss 86:1 f., 132:15 f.), and the enemy of the poor is also the enemy of God (Psa 109:31)." Dibelius's reading postulates the emergence of a "special religious community" that sided with the Maccabees in the second century BCE and later, "in an archaicizing manner, the name and character of the pious of an earlier period are transferred to the Pharisees, who now appear as the poor.... The pious thought of themselves as the poor because *poverty had become a religious concept.*"[48] It is not necessary to continue to follow the arc by which Dibelius traced application of the concept of the poor from Pharisees to the Synoptic "sinners"/Talmudic "people of the land" (*'am ha'aretz*) and the messianic pietists of Jesus' day. Suffice to say it is a literary arc, notable in light of contemporary research and opinion

---

[46] See the section on "Sociocultural Texture" in Suggested Reading.
[47] M. Dibelius, *Letter of James* (1975), pp. 39–45.
[48] Ibid., p. 40, his emphasis.

for its ideology more than for its insight, and our consideration of ideology must wait.

Social-scientific critics have sought to correct the literary readings of form and redaction critics with a heavy dose of sociohistorical anthropology. While their insights have been widely and helpfully applied to readings of the Synoptic Gospels, little has made its way into readings of James. In James 2 such insights are especially helpful.

The first point to make is the extreme social stratification that characterized the ancient world, including the world of our text. Various hierarchical pyramids have been drawn, with the emperor and his retainers on top (at most one percent), and a small retinue of officials and landholders below (the equestrian class some think the first visitor's ring signifies, at most three percent). At this point there is an extreme drop in wealth and increase in numbers, to an emerging merchant class (perhaps as much as five to ten percent), a peasant class with small family/clan holdings of land (here the percentages dividing the last four "classes," as well as the lines of division, are imprecise), craftworkers/shopkeepers (who did not own land and probably included the family of Joseph the carpenter and Mary his wife), and the day laborers, slaves, and "expendables," the *ptōchos* of James 2. Where the lines are drawn between the eighty to ninety percent of those who make up the base of the pyramid is far from clear, but the appropriateness of a pyramid is strong, for the wealth of those at the top was only available through the deprivation of those at the bottom – the rich prospered on the backs of the poor, slave or free. And often it might be the slaves who were better off, for owners had a vested interest in the well-being and productivity of their slaves that they did not have in those who were hired for day labor (more on this when we consider chapter 5).

Mention of productivity brings us to the second major insight to be learned from social-scientific critics: the world of our text was what economists and anthropologists call "zero sum." There was a fixed amount of wealth to be had, and the only way to have more than one could produce in a day with one's own wit and work was to take it away from someone else through taxes, interest, or conquest. Today we take two things for granted simply unknown to the biblical world: the very possibility of excess capacity/productivity and the use of tools/technology to increase continually the productivity of workers, resulting in more output (wealth) for the same amount of labor. Today we think the "pie" will always expand so the rich can have more pie without having to take it from the poor. In a zero-sum society the pie always stays the same. If I want seconds, you will have to go without. And the people at the top of the social pyramid wanted a lot more than seconds.

They took it by force – force of arms, force of law (enforcing usurious loans resulting in the confiscation and consolidation of landholdings), and force of taxation at rates that often exceeded fifty percent, when, for example, Roman and Jewish Temple taxes were combined and the fees of tax collectors added in. And they took it at a great cost to society, whether Roman or conquered territory.⁴⁹

This leads to the third, and for this section, final insight from social-scientific criticism: for the vast majority of those living in the first-century Mediterranean world, life was unimaginably precarious and fragile. The daily challenge was not to climb another rung up the ladder of success but simply to find or earn enough to eat to survive (Mt 6:11). What was true for the majority in society was true of the followers of Jesus and of the community to which James wrote. The great disparity in wealth and the desperate circumstances of the poor led naturally to animosity and often to revolt. Animosity could not be directed toward the richest one percent – they were out of reach – and so was often directed to the religious leaders and official servants who perpetuated (and exploited) the system for their own survival and gain.

All of this is part of the background of the parables, healing, controversies, arrest, and execution of Jesus. And it is in the foreground of the letter of James, especially chapter 2. James contrasts the status of the poor in the eyes of the world (reading the dative in v. 5 as a dative of respect) with God's election of them as heirs, then contrasts God's favoritism for the poor with the community's apparent favoritism against them ("You have dishonored the poor"). We have moved from description to ideology.

James, it seems, writes out of an ideological bias in favor of the poor, not the spiritualized poor or the pious poor but the poor who struggle each day for their daily bread. Despite the parallels with Matthew's gospel, this ideology is more typically Lukan, again suggesting a fluidity in the tradition best assigned to its earlier stages. James calls for the community to join with God's bias, not only in attitude (2:1–6) but in practice (1:17; 2:14–26). Hence the call is really not for impartiality (which as we shall see is often quite partial in favor of the elite) but for partiality and action on behalf of the poor. And all of this, for James, is how one keeps the law. But how does James understand the "law" he wants kept and fulfilled?

A CLOSER LOOK – JAMES'S USE OF LAW

Discussion of the "law" in the letter of James has long been held almost entirely in dialogue with the letters of Paul. As suggested in the Introduction, this ideological shaping of the discussion has failed to do justice to either apostles or their writings. In this section I will offer my ideological reading of James's ideology of the law, both ideologies (mine and James's) influenced much more by the

---

⁴⁹ The encounter of Jesus and Zaccheus in Lk 19 provides the best biblical evidence. See K. C. Hanson and D. E. Oakman, *Palestine* (1998), pp. 99–129.

teachings of Jesus as found in the Synoptics than by the writings of Paul. And this is, I think, the key point: if James is read in conversation with the teachings of Jesus as found in the Synoptic Gospels, one's conclusions are dramatically different than if one reads James primarily in conversation with Paul.

In the Greek text James uses the term and makes reference to *nomos* a total of ten times, plus a reference to the one "lawgiver" (*nomothetēs*).[50] Clearly law is an important concept for James, one he lifts up to the community in three places in the letter. The verses are given below for ease of reference.

James 1:25. But those who look into the perfect *law*, the *law* of liberty, and persevere, being not hearers who forget but doers who act – they will be blessed in their doing.

James 2:8–12. You do well if you really fulfill the *royal law* according to the scripture, "You shall love your neighbor as yourself." 9 But if you show partiality, you commit sin and are convicted by the *law* as transgressors. 10 For whoever keeps the *whole law* but fails in one point has become accountable for all of it. 11 For the one who said, "You shall not commit adultery," also said, "You shall not murder." Now if you do not commit adultery but if you murder, you have become a transgressor of the *law*. 12 So speak and so act as those who are to be judged by the *law of liberty*.

James 4:11–12. Do not speak evil against one another, brothers and sisters. Whoever speaks evil against another or judges another, speaks evil against the *law* and judges the *law*; but if you judge the *law*, you are not a doer of the law but a judge. 12 There is one *lawgiver* and judge who is able to save and to destroy. So who, then, are you to judge your neighbor?

Before moving to questions and comparisons, it is worth attending to how James himself seems to use the concept.

"Perfect law of liberty" (*nomon teleion ton tēs eleutherias*) once (1:25)
"Royal law" (*nomon Basilikon*) once (2:8)
"Law of liberty" (*nomou eleutherias*) once (2:12)
"Whole law" (*holon ton nomon*) once (2:10)
"Law" (*nomos*) six times (2:9, 11; 4:11)

More than a distinction between the modified and absolute uses of the term is noteworthy, namely, the *contexts* in which James uses the term.

In 1:25 law is mentioned in the explanation of the metaphor of the one who forgets his or her image in a mirror, supporting the dictum in 1:23, "be doers of the word [*tou logou*] and not merely hearers who deceive themselves." To "look into the perfect law, the law of liberty [Gk. *nomon teleion ton tēs eleutherias*] and persevere [*parameinas*]" is to be "not hearers who forget but doers who act – they will be blessed in their doing." While *nomos* is mentioned, it is doing the word (*ton logon*) that is the focus of the verses.

---

[50] By way of comparison, Paul uses the term twenty-eight times in the six chapters of Galatians.

> In our present passage, 2:1–13, law is mentioned repeatedly in vv. 8–12. In an interesting turn of phrase James writes in v. 9, "You do well if you really fulfill the royal law [*nomon Basilikon*] according to the scripture [*tēn graphēn*], 'You shall love your neighbor as yourself.'" James cites Lev 19:18 as "scripture," the citation meant to be a summary, a representative example, or the essential element of the royal law. Complicating matters for the interpreter are the reference in v. 10 to the "whole law" (*holon ton nomon*) and the examples from the Decalogue (adultery and murder) of what a transgression of part of the law might be. This is contrasted with an admonition to "so speak and so act as those who are to be judged by the law of liberty" (*nomou eleutherias*), a law whose principal element seems to be mercy (*eleos*; 2:12–13).
>
> In the third passage, 4:11–12, the focus is on speech and actions – practices – that are important for the community. The law (*nomos*) is mentioned four times, without a modifier, but once again for the purpose of comparison. To speak evil against or judge someone is to speak evil against the law and thus to become a judge rather than a doer of the law. The analogy continues with a reminder that the one lawgiver is also the (one) judge.

The point of this closer look is, I hope, clear. While James uses the term "law" a significant number of times, his use must be qualified by recognition that it is never considered alone, and the very usage qualifies the significance of the term. Instead of independent usage James writes of word and law, law according to Scripture, and law and two commands from the Decalogue, speaking evil/judging of another and speaking evil/judging the law. In each case, James's use of law is subordinate – in support of – a point he is trying to make.

A second point follows: James's use of law is much more like that of the understanding attributed to Jesus in the Gospels than to that of Paul in Romans and Galatians. James does seem to "assume" the law, but so did Jesus (Mt 5:17–48), and one of the areas in which James and Jesus sound alike is their views on the law (cf. Mt. 22:34–40 and par.). Indeed, it is far from clear that James and Paul *mean* the same thing in their use of the term *nomos*. While, for example, Wall writes an impressive treatise on the law in James, it is arguable that his repeated references to "Torah" are inappropriate for a discussion of James, although they surely are appropriate for Paul.[51]

Both points, of course, appear to run counter to the depiction of James in Acts and Galatians, our primary "historical" sources. According to the chronology guiding this commentary, Acts is considerably later in date than James, and Galatians roughly synchronous. Moreover, Paul's admittedly harsh words are somewhat ameliorated by the fact that the one(s) who influenced Peter to draw back from table fellowship with Gentiles was not James himself, but "from

---

[51] R. W. Wall, *Community of the Wise* (1997), pp. 83–98.

James" (*tinas apo Jakōbou*; Gal 2:13), while Paul a few verses earlier reports himself and his teachings to be accepted by James, Cephas, and John (Gal 2:9). Further, the one stipulation Paul acknowledges being made by the three was to "remember the poor" (Gal 2:10), which certainly fits the picture of James we have been drawing. This leaves only the so-called Jerusalem council, as reported in Acts 15:22–9. Here Luke attributes to James insistence on two aspects of ritual/moral purity (abstaining from that which was sacrificed, contained blood, or was strangled; fornication), and while one could hardly call these stipulations the "whole law" the emphasis also seems to "assume" the keeping of other commandments, for example, the Decalogue. In any case Luke's clear literary intent was to depict James as a mediator and his decision as a wise and healing one, whatever later commentators (beginning with Paul) conclude. And, I think, it shows James having a somewhat fluid understanding of the law.

To summarize, it seems best to allow James his own use, understanding, and application of the term *nomos* before reading and comparing James with Paul, the rabbis, Jesus, or other literary and historical sources. His use of modifiers serve not to designate (the "royal" law as opposed to some other law, e.g.) but to intensify. His understanding of law, as of the teaching of Jesus, was fluid, not fixed, making it a difficult target for praise or critique. "Law," above all, is what members of the community are to "do."

SACRED AND HOMILETICAL TEXTURES

One of the problems with the letter of James is that in the final analysis the author leaves the interpreter nowhere to hide from the demands of the letter. Insight and understanding are fine, and comparison with other aspects of the tradition have their place, but James is essentially a "what have you *done* for me lately" letter. So having considered James's understanding of partiality, having grappled with the insights of scholarship into poor and rich in James, and having considered and compared his use of law, we are prepared for the real interpretive burden for people of faith that this passage presents: how does it speak to us and our communities, to the poor and rich in our world, and to our understanding of "love your neighbor as yourself"?

The Latina scholar Elsa Tamez offers words of wisdom and caution for readers of this passage, particularly for our social reconstruction and application,

> I do not mean that the poor are not pious, but only that if we make the poor and the pious synonymous then real economic oppression and God's concern for this very class of people are lost. The rich become the pious poor and the poor rich in piety, and the economic order and the unjust power stay as they are. Thus the rich always come out ahead: they are rich in real life and piously poor before God and thus the heirs of God's reign.[52]

[52] E. Tamez, *Scandalous Message of James* (1990), pp. 44–5.

This is an ideological claim: God has a special preference and concern for the materially poor, disadvantaged, and deprived. The challenge for the reader is multiplied by the fact that while Tamez obviously holds this ideology, so does James, so does Jesus, and so, finally, does the Church.

James, however, will not be satisfied with getting a rhetorical "Amen." James wants to know what we have done. By turning the terms of the discussion onto the law James is also indicating a willingness to continue the discussion on his readers' terms and not just his own. The homiletical challenge of 2:1–13 is not to run screaming in fear from the pulpit. Favoritism? Poverty and wealth? Keeping the whole law? Loving our neighbor? How can we preach about this? How can we not?

A final crucial point is informed by sociocultural texture as much as the sacred and homiletical. What is a stake in the encounter with the brother and sister who will be depicted as hungry and exposed in 2:15–16 is similar to what was at stake in 2:2–4. Yes, there is an opportunity to show patronage by providing for physical needs, but in a culture grounded in the importance of honor and shame, there was also an opportunity to restore and bestow honor by removing the marks of their shame.

That is still true today and is often missing in even the best efforts of charitable churches and Christians. To make it simple, when we bestow patronage (give food, clothes, shelter, money, etc. to those in need) we must find ways to do it that do not bring shame. Instead we need do it in ways that restore and bestow honor. It can be harder, but enough is at stake that the effort is truly worthwhile.

JAMES 2:14–26

14 What good is it, my brothers and sisters, if you say you have faith but do not have works? Can faith save you?
15 If a brother or sister is naked and lacks daily food,
16 and one of you says to them, "Go in peace; keep warm and eat your fill," and yet you do not supply their bodily needs, what is the good of that?
17 So faith by itself, if it has no works, is dead.
18 But someone will say, "You have faith and I have works." Show me your faith apart from your works, and I by my works will show you my faith.
19 You believe that God is one; you do well. Even the demons believe – and shudder.
20 Do you want to be shown, you senseless person, that faith apart from works is barren?
21 Was not our ancestor Abraham justified by works when he offered his son Isaac on the altar?
22 You see that faith was active along with his works, and faith was brought to completion by the works.
23 Thus the scripture was fulfilled that says, "Abraham believed God, and it was reckoned to him as righteousness," and he was called the friend of God.

24 You see that a person is justified by works and not by faith alone.
25 Likewise, was not Rahab the prostitute also justified by works when she welcomed the messengers and sent them out by another road?
26 For just as the body without the spirit is dead, so faith without works is also dead.

James 2:14–26 contains the best known, and most controversial, verses in the letter. Continuing in the style discussed in 2:1–13, James expands, develops, and demonstrates a central idea introduced in chapter 1: faith is inseparable from practice. In the first half of chapter 2 James considers those who claim "to have faith in our glorious Lord Jesus Christ" but show partiality to the rich rather than embrace God's favor for the poor, and finds such faith claims wanting. In the present passage James considers those who claim faith, perhaps as expressed in v. 19, "You believe that God is one," but fail to meet their own community members' most fundamental human needs for food and clothing. For James such faith is "dead" (*nekros*) – no faith.

No doubt the greatest challenge in reading this passage is to read it on its own terms. Once again, the shadow of Paul and of centuries of reading James with Paul, rather than with Jesus, as the interpretive partner, looms large. As discussed in the Introduction the present commentary seeks to read against this tradition and understands the shadow of Jesus, not of Paul, as the one beneath which James abides. We will, however, offer some account for how and why such apparently (or, at least, traditionally) Pauline terms and emphasis found their way into the interpretation of the letter of James. To anticipate what will be developed in the discussion of sociocultural and ideological textures (as opposed to inner texture and intertexture), once again I maintain that similar terms have quite different meanings for James and Paul (see the discussion of law/*nomos* in 2:1–13) and that their roughly contemporaneous treatments represent the working through and working out of how followers of Jesus will live and practice as the community of faith.

INNER TEXTURE AND INTERTEXTURE

The structure of 2:14–26 is similar to that of 2:1–13. James states his theme in the first verse (v. 14), offers a vivid and compelling example concluding with an emphatic restatement of his theme (vv. 15–17), and develops his argument with logic (presented through an interlocutory dialogue, vv. 18–19) and proofs from Scripture, restating his theme at the beginning and end of his proofs (vv. 20–6).[53] This similarity in structure, along with James's continuing development of the understanding of faith begun in 2:1–13, causes one to wonder at the insistence

---

[53] James's persistent repetition reminds one of the hoary homiletical advice, "Tell them what you are going to tell them, tell them, tell them what you told them."

of Dibelius that "A connection between this treatise and the proceeding one cannot be established."[54]

14–17. As in 2:1–13, James begins his argument with a negative, in this case with a question requiring a negative answer. In 2:1 it is not possible to "have faith" and show favoritism. In 2:14 it is not possible to "say you have faith" but have no works (*ergos*). Why? Because, in another question demanding a negative answer, "Is faith able to save you?" (*mē dunatai hē pistis sōsai auton?*).

Immediately three terms demand attention, faith (*pistis*), works (*ergos*), and save (*sōzō*). How does James use and intend the reader to understand these critical words? Nine of the twenty uses of "faith" (noun and verb forms) found in James are in the current passage (2:14–26), as are twelve of fifteen uses of "works" (noun) and one of the five uses of "save." This is probably the best place to consider their meaning for James.

As is predominantly the case in much of the letter, James rather casually uses terms that later take on fixed, precise meanings. Interpreters must be careful not to expect James to write more theologically than he does. For example, James has a clear but unemphatic eschatology and soteriology. Humanity needs to be saved, and this saving is finally something that takes place at the end of the present age (to express this in a phrase James admittedly does not use). But we learn nothing of heaven, paradise, or eternal bliss, and certainly encounter no apocalyptic details, just a reference to a coming reversal (1:9 f.) and a reminder that the good gifts "come down" from "the father of lights" (1:16–17). James is waiting for the coming of the Lord and urges his readers to do patiently the same (5:7), for "the coming of the Lord is near" (5:8). He also waits for a time of judgment, a time that is also near, for "the Judge is standing at the doors" (5:9). It is from this judgment that the reader must seek to be "saved." We saw in chapter 1 that the "implanted word" is able to "save your souls" (1:25) and will learn in chapter 4 that "there is one lawgiver and judge who is able to save and destroy" (4:12). Saving, then, seems to have for James an implicit eschatological and soteriological connotation, although he also uses the term in its root sense as physical healing in chapter 5.[55] But how are we "saved"? This brings us to the crux of the question – faith and works.

There will be much more to say about this beyond the lexical, but the terms themselves are interesting and revealing. Our passage in Greek has 217 words. Twenty-five (twelve percent) of them are either "faith" or "works," a truly notable

---

[54] M. Dibelius, *Letter of James* (1975), p. 149. Compare L. T. Johnson, *Letter of James* (1995), p. 246: "The essential connection between this section and the first part of chapter two is also fairly obvious."

[55] "The prayer of faith will save the sick, and the Lord will raise them up...." This also has a soteriological overtone, however, for the verse concludes, "and anyone who has committed sins will be forgiven" (5:15).

James 2:1–26 – I by My Works Will Show You My Faith

incidence, but more important for James is the juxtaposition. James cannot talk about faith without talking about works. Faith/belief, understood as faith/belief in (the Lord) or the faith/belief of (the Lord), is inextricably connected with works, deeds, actions, and practices. This section is about unpacking these connections.

James continues the pattern he established in 2:1 and followed in 2:14 by moving from negative question to negative example (first 2:2–4, now 2:15–16), again using *ean* plus the subjunctive to express a hypothetical condition. The conditions have some similarity, and certainly both "little parables" (Martin) are vividly described, but there are also notable differences. Rather than visitors to the community who needed to be directed to their positions in the gathering, here we are dealing with "a brother or sister" (*adelphos hē adelphē*). "Brother or sister" is not rooted in the translator's attempt to best reflect the force of the Greek in contemporary English but is one of the few occasions in the NT outside Gospel references to the family of Jesus and epistolary greetings when the word "sister" (*hē adelphē*) is used. The crucial point is that the ones described are designated as members of the community. And they are in need, naked (*gymnoi*) and lacking their daily bread. The phrase, *tēs ephēmerou trophēs*, differs from the familiar petition in the Lord's Prayer (Mt 6:11: "Give us this day our daily bread" (*ton arton hēmōn ton epiousion doe hēmin sēmeron*); Lk 11:3: "Give us each day our daily bread" (*ton arton hēmōn ton epiousion didou hēmin to kath' hēmeran*). So it is another Synoptic passage, Mt 25:34ff., that is apropos, where among others in need we read of the hungry and the naked (this latter term need not mean completely unclothed but rather inadequately or immodestly covered).[56]

Whatever the parallels, we are given a clear depiction of someone in the community in obvious physical need, for which the hypothetical faith-without-works reader offers only a prayer of blessing and good wishes, without giving the one in need "what they need for their body." James closes this phase of the argument with another emphatic question – what good (*ophelos*) is it? – the same rhetorical question with which he began v. 14, and with the same answer – no good at all. "Thus," bringing matters to their first conclusion with an emphatic, memorable, and soon-to-be-repeated phrase, "faith, by itself [*kath' heautēn*] unless it has works, is dead."

18–20. These verses have proven to be most perplexing to interpreters. Not that James's basic meaning is hard to grasp. The problem, and it is really only v. 18 that is problematic, is finding a way to construe the Greek to say what most everyone agrees it says. The challenge with v. 19 is intertextual: is James referring to the *Shema*, and what kind of demons does he have in mind?

---

[56] *Theological Dictionary of the New Testament*, vol. 1 (Grand Rapids, MI: Eerdmans, 1964), 773–5.

A CLOSER LOOK – A CONFUSING VERSE

V. 18 serves as an argument from reason and, in keeping with rhetorical (diatribe) and homiletical practice, anticipates possible objections through an imagined interlocutor. Such is the force of the opening, "But someone will say" (*All' erei tis*), the "but" standing as a strong adversative indicating that what follows is to be taken as an objection. The problems are many after this clear point, so much so that one path seeks to undo this one bit of clarity by positing a lost verse fragment that would have preceded the objection. One need only highlight, not rehearse, the history of interpretation.[57]

The problems are compounded by the absence of quotation marks in Greek, making it difficult to know when the objection ends and James's response begins, and by the almost shorthand way in which James presents the imagined conversation. As noted, the opening adversative cues the reader to expect a strong objection. But the words that follow sound like what James himself would say, not an opponent, whom we would expect to say, "*I* have faith."[58] Hence some suggest that our interlocutor is an ally of our author, which again runs smack into our one clear point, the opening adversative. Moreover, those who seek a solution through text emendation have no textual basis in manuscript tradition for suggesting a change. Most recently Wall has argued for a reading based on the *textus receptus* (which he refers to as the "majority reading"), which replaces the "apart from" (*chōris*) in v. 18b with "by" (*ek*), producing a lovely chiasmus (faith/from works – from works/faith) but running completely against the sense most interpreters recognize as James's meaning and completely without support in the earliest manuscripts.[59]

Frankly, there is no acceptable solution to the problems of v. 18. Wall is incorrect, however, to seek a solution in the second half of the verse. These words are clear, if somewhat sarcastic, anticipating the sharper sarcasm of v. 19. When James says (and this seems to be where his voice returns), "Show me your faith apart from your works, and I by my works will show you my faith," he understands himself to be asking the impossible: no one can "show" faith except through works. Thus the opening adversative is clear, as is the sarcastic response. The words in between, "You have faith and I have works," unless emended by the translator, must remain a point of confusion. Fortunately the confusion does not obscure the author's argument.

---

[57] M. Dibelius, *Letter of James* (1975), who refers to the verse as "one of the most difficult New Testament passages in general," offers a clear explanation, with excellent notes (pp. 154–8).

[58] The suggestion of J. H. Ropes, *Critical and Exegetical Commentary* (1916), p. 209ff., based on an extract from Teles (whom he dates to "c. 230 B.C."), that the pronouns be read as "one says ... another says" has not convinced later interpreters. *Su, kagō* clearly mean "you" "and I."

[59] R.W. Wall, *Community of the Wise* (1997), pp. 139–40.

James 2:1–26 – I by My Works Will Show You My Faith

Vv. 19–20 brush close to being ad hominem, comparing the "faith" (*pistis*, the same Gk. word translated in the rest of the passage by the NRSV as "faith" but in v. 19 as "belief") of the interlocutor to the faith of "demons" (*daimonia*) and referring to the person as *hō anthrōpe kene* (you senseless person). In the NT *daimonia* are almost exclusively found in the Gospels and seem always to be there as a foil for Jesus, either to be exorcised (e.g., Mk 1:39, where his activity is summarized as "preaching in their synagogues and casting out demons") or for Jesus himself to be accused of being possessed by (e.g., Mk 3:22, where the scribes say, "He has Beelzebul, and by the ruler of demons he casts out demons"). Commentators have been more interested in the "shuddering" than the "faith" of the demons, whose knowledge of Jesus' true identity comes early in Mark ("I know who you are, the holy one of God"; 1:24). The evil spirits who rout the seven sons of Sceva know (*ginōskō*) Jesus and know (*epistamai*) Paul (Acts 19:15), but the idea that demons have faith seems original to James.

What faith is it, however, that the senseless person and the demons are said to share? "You have faith that God is one" (*su pisteueis hoti heis estin ho Theos*). Is this a reference to the *Shema* in Deut 6:4 and Jewish tradition (Heb. *Shema Israel Adonai Elohim, Adonai ehad*; LXX *akoue Israēl kyrios ho theos hēmōn kyrios heis estin*)? Probably it is,[60] and it is perhaps also a reference to Jesus' references to Deut 6:4–5 (Mk 12:28 and par.). The irony and sarcasm underneath James's own use of the tradition is sharp. "You do well" to have faith in God and to recite your faith in a traditional confession. But you do not do enough. In fact you do no more than the demons unless you practice the faith you confess, because "faith apart from works is barren (*argē*), a shift in terms (from "dead" to barren) and a play on words (*argē, ergōn*) that both widen the semantic field of our understanding of what it means to be without works and anticipates the biblical proof to come.

21–6. James concludes his argument with two proofs from Scripture. There is no break between vv. 20 and 21, and rhetorically v. 20 serves to introduce the biblical proofs at least as much as it summarizes vv. 18–19. The choice of figures from the tradition is laden with significance. Abraham seems obvious, although the choice of the "sacrifice of Isaac" (traditionally designated the *Akedah*, or "binding") as an exemplum is not. The choice of Rahab, the prostitute (*hē pornē*), strikes a reader today, unaware of the treatment of Rahab in later traditions (convert, wife of Joshua, mother of priests, etc.), as odd. Both the oddity and

---

[60] M. Dibelius, *Letter of James* (1975), among others, p. 159; S. Laws, *Epistle of James* (1980), p. 125, notes minor textual problems, the presence or absence of the article before *theos* and the word order, while B. M. Metzger, *Textual Commentary of the Greek NT* (1994) concludes that the order *heis estin ho Theos* "is in conformity with the prevailing formula of Jewish orthodoxy" (p. 610).

the significance must await the following sections, as must our abbreviated discussion of Paul. Here our interest is in how James uses these biblical examples to forward his own argument.

James has already said in this passage that faith without works is not able to save (2:14), is dead (2:17), and is barren (2:20). Now he introduces "our ancestor Abraham" (*Abraam ho patēr*), who with his wife Sarah were the prototypical barren ancestors, asking in a question formed to require a positive answer, "Was not our ancestor Abraham justified by works when he offered his son Isaac on the altar?" The reader is intended to say "yes," but the reader familiar with the Abraham cycle in Gen 12–23 probably says, "wait a minute!" Abraham "believed the Lord and the Lord reckoned it to him as righteousness" in Gen 15:6, while the offering of Isaac comes half a lifetime later in Gen 22. How can James use Abraham as a proof that "faith apart from works is dead" when human faith and divine approval seem to take place detached from any action on Abraham's part other than a little stargazing? Here the reader needs to be careful not to press the advantage of readily available copies of biblical texts, not to mention searchable databases. Nor should we confine the meaning of "Abraham" to Gen 15:6 and 22:1–18, any more than the meaning of "Rahab" is confined by the epithet "harlot" and the act of "hospitality" by which she and her family were saved (Josh 2, 6:17–25; Heb 11:31). Both characters serve for the tradition and for James as rich symbols of faith. Other than Jehoshaphat (2 Chron 20:12), no one else tells us that Abraham was known as God's "friend" (LXX, however, uses a different term based on *agapē* rather than *philos*), but the reader understands what James means.

Abraham was so close to God that he was called friend, so trusting in God that he offered up the very promise that overcame his and Sarah's barrenness. Thus the "scripture was fulfilled" (2:23) because "faith was active along with his works, and faith was brought to completion by the works" (2:22). This bringing to completion (*eteleiōthē*) recalls the one who does well to "really fulfill [*teleite*] the royal law according to the scripture, 'You shall love your neighbor as yourself'" (2:8). In this sense, for James the "righteousness" (*dikaiosunēn*) and faith of Abraham was latent, barren, unless and until it came to fruition in his actions, which were not limited to but exemplified in the offering of Isaac (thus the plural, works). "You see that a person is justified (*dikaioutai*) by works and not by faith alone" (v. 24).

Abraham and righteousness form a ready and obvious pair in many readers' recollection of the biblical world. But Rahab? That is another matter altogether. Space does not permit adequate explanation of the roots and significance of this reference, nor will we be able to explore the sociocultural and ideological meanings of James's choice of such a marginalized figure (non-Israelite, female, sex worker, etc.) in testimony to his understanding of righteous faith. Suffice to say that over time Jewish tradition developed a rich understanding of Rahab as a proselyte and exemplar, not unlike Ruth. Johnson writes, "In Jewish tradition, Rahab was celebrated as a proselyte and as a model of hospitality."⁶¹ To James, Rahab, like Abraham, was justified by her actions.

James will hammer the point home one last time in v. 26, comparing faith without works to a body without spirit (*pneuma*, a term used only one other time by James, 4:5): both are dead. We have now seen James repeatedly claim and persuasively demonstrate that there is no faith apart from works; such faith is dead, barren, it is no faith. James never says anything about "works without faith" – that is Paul's problem, to which we must soon turn.

SOCIOCULTURAL AND IDEOLOGICAL TEXTURES

Not surprisingly, given the history of interpretation of James 2:14–26, the interest in this section will have much more to do with its ideological texture than its sociocultural texture. We have seen that the choice of biblical proofs was popular and current, if not necessarily obvious to modern readers. But we learn nothing about prostitution in the ancient Mediterranean and can draw no conclusions about James's view since the epithet applied to Rahab is his only mention of the word. His view of demons seems consistent with that of the Evangelists.

We may learn more about the community from which and for which James wrote from his second hypothetical situation in 2:15–16. Recalling what was discussed in 2:1–13 about honor and shame, we are reminded that while "bodily needs" were presented for attention, more was at stake than a meal and a coat. Responding to these needs gives the community an opportunity to restore a person or persons to honor. While the visitor in 2:2–4 was depicted as dressed in rags, the rags of the "brother or sister" in v. 15 had fallen to shreds, leaving them exposed, if not necessarily nude.

That James considered such a depiction of need plausibly attributed to a member of the community is revealing. As he did the condemnation of the other hypothetical member who offers only a traditional blessing (the expression is found throughout the biblical tradition; see Gen 15:15; Ex 4:18; Judg 16:6; 1 Sam 20:42; Tob. 10:12; Jth 9:35; Jesus offers the blessing after healing and forgiving, e.g., Mk 5:34; Lk 7:50). This one could only be condemned if he or she presumably had the means or access to the means from the community to relieve the want. We learn then that the community from which and/or to which James wrote was somewhat disparate in social and economic status. Again to return to material shared earlier in the chapter, given the fragile hold on life of those at the bottom of the socioeconomic pyramid and the day-to-day existence implicit in James's depiction, failure to respond to the need for food and clothing was life threatening for the person in need.

---

⁶¹ L. T. Johnson, *Letter of James* (1995), p. 245. He goes on to cite an impressive list of rabbinic texts. *1 Clement* 10 tells us of Abraham and 12 of Rahab. In the summary about the latter we find, "You see, beloved, that the woman is an instance of not only faith (*pistis*), but also of prophecy." *Apostolic Fathers*, vol. 1, trans. Kirsopp Lake, LCL (Cambridge, MA: Harvard University Press, 1912–77), *1 Clement* 12.7.

A CLOSER LOOK – PAUL AND JAMES

We know they met, and we know that they did not see eye to eye. We do not know the depth of the disagreements or the extent of their interaction. We do not know who, if either of them, wrote specifically in response to the other. It is not that scholarship has not tried to find the answers. The problem, as I argued in the Introduction and since, is that Paul so dominated the development of Christianity and the history of interpretation that it is hard for James to get a word in edgewise. Moreover, one is tempted to share the conclusion of Johnson, who commented that the "steady stream of works trying to adjudicate the theological differences between James and Paul ... do not much improve on the earlier discussions in the history of interpretation." The paragraph concludes with a caution worth noting:

That the topic continues to generate such constant, if not obsessive, attention suggests something about the angle from which James has been approached within the historical-critical paradigm, as well as the theological preoccupations that have dominated a purportedly "scientific" study of the Bible.[62]

Johnson may have had Dibelius in mind, for the latter's excursus on "Faith and Works in Paul and James" clearly reveals his own ideological commitments, as he consistently denigrates James as one who "writes as a Christian who obviously found his God without [the] shaking of his soul" and his audience as "other such Christians." Paul and James finally cannot be compared, according to Dibelius, because only Paul "proposed an original view of the importance of faith which is grand and audacious."[63]

Other interpreters are more generous to James (which probably reveals another set of ideological convictions), especially Johnson, who offers a convincing argument that the points of convergence between James and Paul, even in Romans and Galatians, far outweigh the points of divergence, points that invariably seem to center on this passage and Rom 4.[64] While I do not maintain that James and Paul were of one mind on all topics, Sharon Dowd's reminder that "James is using Paul's vocabulary but not his dictionary" is helpful.[65] This seems especially true of "righteousness," less so of "faith," and, ironically enough, not at all true of "works." Instead of another rehearsal of all the points of agreement and disagreement between James and Paul, or a comparison of their respective theologies, I will briefly outline an understanding of James and Paul as fellow interpreters of an emerging tradition, with more careful attention to righteousness, faith, and works.

---

[62] L. T. Johnson, *Letter of James* (1995), p. 156.
[63] M. Dibelius, *Letter of James* (1975), pp. 174–80.
[64] L. T. Johnson, *Letter of James* (1995), pp. 58–64.
[65] Sharon Dowd, "Faith That Works" *Review and Expositor* 97 (2000): 202.

As developed in the Introduction, the present commentary is based on a very early dating of the composition of James's letter, sometime in the mid- to late fifties of our era, prior to the death of James in 62 CE, which makes the letter of James contemporaneous with the letters of Paul and makes them together the earliest documents of the NT. It also makes for problematic decisions about who knew whom and who was writing against whom. Of course they were acquainted, as Acts and Galatians agree if not in the details then at least in the broadest ways: they had met, more than once, exchanged views, and went for the most part their separate ways, or rather Paul went and James stayed in Jerusalem.

As far as we know Paul never wrote a letter to Jerusalem, although correspondence of some sort is imaginable. We cannot determine with any certainty how Pauline letters were copied, collected, and circulated to secondary communities beyond the initial addressees. However, if we assume even a short period of a few years for such activity to take place, it is reasonable to claim that *James never read a letter of Paul and that Paul never read the letter of James.* The only basis for reaction or response would have been their limited personal contacts and what they were hearing about the other. That they were hearing things is evidenced by Gal 2:12, for the "certain people" who "came from James" were surely coming to confirm reports that had arrived from Antioch. Without pressing the point too finely, it seems reasonable to claim that to the extent James and Paul may have been reacting and responding to one another (something I am not entirely convinced they ever did in writing), it was on the basis of hearsay and recollection, not always the most reliable.

The tendency of Paul and James to "talk past each other" is therefore understandable. One also must wonder at the degree to which NT interpreters have unknowingly exaggerated the level of disagreement between Paul and James because it is something interesting about which to write. Every journal that devotes an issue to the letter of James is guaranteed to have at least one article on the topic. It is also undeniable that Paul and James, while sharing the same macrohistorical milieu, could still be said to live in "different worlds." They obviously did not have the same priorities or share the same outlook on every issue.[66] But perhaps more importantly, because they were writing from and to community and because those communities themselves differed in profound ways, they were often not concerned about the same topics. Finally, to conclude in this spirit of speculation, it is probably true that Paul and James did not think or worry about each other nearly as much as interpreters of James think and worry about Paul but about as much as interpreters of Paul worry and think about James.

---

[66] Any parish pastor who has visited an international mission site or hosted an international missionary has experienced something of this divergence, described by one such pastor as "One Lord, one faith, one baptism, and two really different ways of doing church."

Before looking at the three terms mentioned for consideration, a more credible, sociocultural insight should be added to this ideological reflection. James and Paul were writing at a time when the Jesus tradition was anything but fixed, institutionally, politically, and textually. Christianity was still Jewish and would remain so for decades. Outside of Jerusalem, Paul shaped a church and a tradition, but it was, as far as the testimony of biblical evidence, a tradition largely unformed by the traditions about Jesus now common to us from the Gospels. In Jerusalem James was shaped by and, at least in his letter, shaping, the Jesus tradition. The large number of references, allusions, and echoes, as well as the occasional but unattributed quotation of a Jesus saying, is remarkable in James and in strong relief to the comparatively small amount of anything comparable in the letters of Paul. That is why it is fair to insist on reading James in light of Jesus and not in light of Paul. As I have argued in and since the Introduction, the history of interpreting James using Paul as the measuring rod always inhibits appreciation of James.

The seven undisputed letters of Paul contain ninety-five uses of one form or another of the Greek *dikaiosunē* (righteousness). Maybe that is why Luther stopped his theses at ninety-five. James uses the term eight times, half of them in the discussion of Abraham's righteousness in 2:21–5. By contrast, James will mention "works" eighteen times, Paul a little more than fifty in the seven letters. Clearly there is a difference in priority. Where the priorities seem to merge, at least lexically, is in the importance of faith. Both writers use one or another form of *pistis* considerably more than they do various forms "works" or "righteousness," Paul more than he uses the latter two words combined, James almost so. This bit of computer-assisted word counting suggests that the starting point for a meaningful discussion about James and Paul is faith, not works or righteousness. It is faith they share and a matter about which they agree much more than they disagree.

The letter of James assumes the faith of its readers from the beginning and seeks to shape how that faith is understood and practiced. The first mention of faith is as something that is tested, yielding endurance (1:3). Those who ask in faith receive (1:6), and the prayer of faith saves (5:15). Other than these three verses, mentions of faith are confined to James 2. As we have seen, the structure and style of James 2 is argumentative, as Watson notes an example of deliberative rhetoric,[67] a mode that by its very nature produces sharp and polarizing images. (That this is also true of Galatians, for example, explains why James and Paul may seem more at odds than they really are. They were having passionate, pointed, discussions. But not with each other.)[68] Once again a certain understanding of faith is assumed, and the practice of the community is considered and found

---

[67] Duane Watson, "James 2 in Light of Greco-Roman Schemes of Argumentation" *New Testament Studies* 39 (1993): 94–121.

[68] See Hans Dieter Betz, *Galatians*, Hermeneia (Philadelphia: Fortress Press, 1979).

wanting in light of it. What is that understanding? Faith, for James, is of and in Jesus Christ (2:1) and in God (2:19, 23), is like every good thing a gift from God (1:16), and is fundamentally and inextricably linked to the practices by which it is made known (2:17, 26). The absence of practice (works/*erga*) is the absence of faith and will mean eschatological judgment (2:13) not saving (2:14).

I do not think that Paul would disagree with this. He would modify it and certainly expand on it and add points of emphasis, but he would not repudiate it.[69] If we look beyond Romans and Galatians, we find Paul writing of faith in ways that we have come to think of as Jamesian. In Phi 1, Paul, after reflecting on his situation and choosing to continue to live "for your progress and joy in faith" (1:25),[70] exhorts the readers to "live your life in a manner worthy of the gospel of Christ, so that, whether I come and see you or am absent and hear about you, I will know that you are standing firm in one spirit, striving side by side with one mind for the faith of the gospel" (1:27). Faith is known in the "manner of life" (*politeuō*), a manner that must be "worthy of the gospel." Writing to Philemon, Paul offers a prayer "that the sharing of your faith may become effective (*energēs*) when you perceive all the good that we may do for Christ" (Phm 6), hinting at both the request he is about to make of this patron and the link of faith and action. Paul prays that the God will make the Thessalonians (2 Th 1:11) "worthy of his call and will fulfill by his power every good resolve and work of faith [*ergon pisteōs*]." One can include Romans and Galatians, where repeated arguments that "a person is justified by faith apart from works prescribed by the law" (Rom 3:28) and that "a person is justified not by the works of the law but through faith in Jesus Christ" (Gal 2:16), while prominent, are no more prominent than the chapters of exhortation presenting in detail what manner of life the reader must have to demonstrate "faith working in love" (Gal 5:6; also Rom 12–15 and Gal 5–6).

These examples also serve to make another important point, long noted but nonetheless worth noting again: when Paul speaks of being justified by faith "apart from works," it is always "apart from works of law" (*ergōn nomou*). *James and Paul simply do not mean the same thing when they write of "works," and interpreters who write as if they did distort the thought of both.* Further, Paul is clearly (and James perhaps is) writing in Galatians and again in Romans in the midst of internal discussions over how and on what basis Gentiles will be welcomed into full participation in the life of the early community. Previous

---

[69] A discussion of *pistis* in Paul is beyond the scope of this volume. See, among the host of possibilities, Ben Witherington III, *Paul's Narrative Thought World: The Tapestry of Tragedy and Triumph* (Louisville, KY: Westminster/John Knox Press, 1994) and James D. G. Dunn, *The Theology of Paul the Apostle* (Grand Rapids, MI: Eerdmans, 1998), pp. 334–89.

[70] See A. Droge, "To Die Is Gain" in *A Noble Death: Suicide and Martyrdom among Christians and Jews in Antiquity*, ed. Arthur Droge and James Tabor (San Francisco: HarperCollins, 1992), pp. 113–28.

debates, it seems to me, often failed to account for the fact that Paul, especially in Galatians and Romans, writes much more about how one receives faith or comes to faith, and James writes almost exclusively about what one is or is not doing in the life of the community of faith – the difference, one might say, between a missionary and a pastor.

SACRED AND HOMILETICAL TEXTURES

Comparing the understanding of faith, works, and righteousness in Paul and James is finally an academic and ideological exercise. One wants, after all, to get it right. But if James would remind us of one thing in all this discussion, it is that getting it right is in and of itself insufficient. Apt and accurate theology is only a basis upon which practice may unfold. It is practice of faith that counts. Perkins reminds us that "'faith without works' spares individuals the embarrassment of radical disruptions in their lives and relationships."[71] James is big on radical disruptions. The Church, unfortunately, has usually been big on continuity. Hence the historic problems with James are not in spite of its powerful content but precisely because of its content.

James challenges the reader with an understanding of faith intimately and intricately connected with the whole of human life. Faith is not so much "known" by its works, like the tree by its fruit, as it *is* its work, root and branch as well as fruit. Excellent preacher that he was, James maintains this point relentlessly in 2:14–26 and presents the reader with a stark choice, not between faith or works but between living or dead faith, that is, between faith (and salvation) or death. With vivid example, biting sarcasm, and biblical proofs, James clearly disturbed his readers. That the letter of James rarely occurs in the lectionaries of the Christian churches suggests that he continues to do so.

BRIDGING THE HORIZONS – FAITH IS ALL ABOUT THE PRACTICE

As we have already seen in a number of passages, the sacred texture of James reveals more about Christian life and practice than it does about the author's theology. James was more interested in what God wants of the community than in what the community thinks about God. Three points are worth noting.

First, *practice is essential to faith*. It does not grow out of faith, complement faith, or serve as an alternative to faith. Practice and faith are one. I have tried to use the term "practice" consistently for a number of reasons, including the obvious fact that "practice" is not as charged a term as "works." I am also informed by the recent literature on faith practices.[72] This literature, while not

---

[71] Pheme Perkins, *First and Second Peter, James, and Jude* (Louisville, KY: John Knox Press, 1995), p. 113.

[72] Dorothy Bass and Craig Dykstra, eds., *Practicing Our Faith* (San Francisco: Josey Bass, 1997).

intentionally grounded in James, shares James's understanding of Christian practice as essential to Christian faith. Remove the practice (prayer, Bible study, hospitality, worship, witness, etc.), and you are left not with some sort of inert, potential faith but with an insipid philosophy. Dorothy Bass and Craig Dykstra explain the nature of Christian practice in the introduction to *Practicing Our Faith* as follows:

> Practices address fundamental human needs and conditions through concrete human acts.
> Practices are done together and over time.
> Practices possess standards of excellence.

When we see some of our ordinary activities as Christian practices, we come to perceive how our daily lives are all tangled up with the things God is doing in the world.[73]

The tangled texture of life was well understood by James, and he resisted simplistic efforts to divide or compartmentalize it into sacred or secular, church or world, faith or works. The Vietnamese Buddhist monk Thich Nhat Hanh is also insightful here, reminding us that we practice in a twofold sense – like a team preparing for the big game and like a doctor or attorney practicing medicine or law. Practices are preparation and fulfillment at one and the same time, training for and doing, anticipating and fulfilling.[74] Most of all, practicing is embodying in the truest Jamesian sense of "giving life to."

Second, *physical needs matter*. James is sensitive to the tendency to disparage the importance of "the needs of the body" (*ta epitēdeia tou sōmatos* – only here in the NT) in comparison with presumably nobler work of the spirit (Acts 6:1–4). He is also keen to the human tendency to "offer" a prayer instead of an offering, rather than alongside one. The community member who blesses the one who is hungry and naked but offers no scrap of food or clothing profits them nothing. In churches around the so-called first world each week prayers will be offered in impressive numbers for the "needs of the world." If we take James seriously, we must acknowledge that the prayers are not enough, and since the poor will always be with us we will always have the opportunity to do what we can do to alleviate their suffering and desperation. By referring to the one in need as a "brother or sister" James may or may not have intended to signal the extent of the community's responsibility to human need. He was certainly not trying to build a gate around the Church for the comfort and convenience of those who do not want to be bothered by the needs of others.

This brings us to the third point: *in practicing hospitality and charity it is **our faith**, and not just the body of the brother or sister in need, that is made alive.*

---

[73] Ibid., pp. 6–8.
[74] Thich Nhat Hanh, *Peace Is Every Step* (New York: Bantam Books, 1991) and *Living Buddha, Living Christ* (New York: Riverhead Books, 1995).

> James 2:14–26 successfully subverts the reader's sense of privilege in deciding whether or not to help the one in need. We are conditioned to think that we have been given the capacity to save a life, and in a sense we have. But it is our own lives that are saved, not the other's. If we turn aside from the other's need or fool ourselves into thinking that a well-phrased blessing will suffice, it is our faith, not their faith, that dies. So the decision about helping is a decision about us not them, and to the extent we understand this, we understand that for the community and people of faith there is no "them," everyone is "us," the body of Christ.

The final challenge of James 2:14–26 is homiletical. How does one preach such a daunting text without either stripping it of all its vividness, irony, and impact or alienating one's audience? One helpful clue from the text itself can be found by considering again the form and structure of the text. While I do not concur with Dibelius and others that James can be seen in total as a diatribe, there is diatribe in the text and chapter 2 is a classic example. Duane Watson mentions the features of the diatribe prominent in the chapter.

[T]urning from the audience to introduce dialogue with imaginary interlocutors in the second person and simulate direct address (vv. 18–23);
objections and false conclusions of the interlocutor (vv. 18a, 19);
series of questions and answers to the interlocutor, often using the Socratic method (vv. 20–3);
material posed in question form to the interlocutor, often made to force him or her to reject it (cf. v. 20);
harsh censure of the auditors for their behavior (vv. 2–6, 8–13, 14–17, 18–20);
illustration of vices (vv. 2–4, 15–16);
censorious rhetorical questions which characterize the interlocutor's vice and include a harsh term of address like "fool" (v. 20 ἄνθρωπε κενέ);
maxims and quotations of poets and philosophers (vv. 8, 10, 11, 23);
examples, comparisons, and antitheses (vv. 2–4, 8–9, 15–16, 21–3, 25);
irony and sarcasm (vv. 18–20);
personification (v. 13, 17, 26);
special moral and philosophical topics like word *versus* deed (vv. 1–26);
stock formulas.[75]

The list is quoted in its entirety to make two points. First, with such length of parallels there is no escaping the conclusion that James 2 is a diatribe, a form of argumentation popular in antiquity and well practiced by Paul. Second, in the rehearsal of the parallels we find material for the preacher, suggesting the following conclusion: to preach this text faithfully, the preacher will need to keep faith with the form of the text.

---

[75] D. Watson, "James 2 in Light of Greco-Roman Schemes" *NTS* (1993): 119.

Form serves content, and in this instance the form can serve to ease communication of the content (which is why the form was created and passed on in the first place). But a prior decision must be made by the individual preacher: do I have the courage and confidence in my audience to truly do this text justice? This is not, by the way, an invitation to "blast" the congregation. It is a decision about whether or not at this time in one's ministry and in the life of the congregation both pastor and people are ready to give James a full hearing.

If the answer is yes, then the homiletical texture of 2:14–26 is rich indeed. The movement of the text is dynamic, dialogical, and inductive, inviting the audience/reader to participate, reach conclusions, and make decisions actively. Should a sermon based on such a dynamic text settle for less? James, and so the preacher of James, does not underestimate what is at stake, for to the community of believers, a living faith is life itself.

Note the elements of James 2:14–26:

v. 14	Proposition in the form of a question: can faith without works save?
vv. 15–16	Example from the life of the community that uses humor and sarcasm.
v. 17	Restatement of the proposition as a declaration: faith by itself without works is dead.
v. 18	Objection by imagined interlocutor; proposition restated as impossible hypothetical.
v. 19	Sarcastic "affirmation" of interlocutor's faith claim.
v. 20	Restatement of proposition as a challenge to the interlocutor.
vv. 22–5	Two proofs from Scripture incorporating two restatements of the proposition.
v. 26	Concluding statement of the proposition in the form of an analogy.

By my count James has held up the proposition "faith without works is dead" six times in one form or another; repetition for the sake of emphasis, yes, but also repetition with variety, allowing different opportunities to convince the hearer/reader of the truth of the argument. One is persuaded by analogy, another by reason, a third by humor and sarcasm, a fourth by compelling illustration from the life of the community. In this diatribe and in a sermon based on it all might be persuaded, not the least because James never loses sight of the proposition.

For many communities a sermon that insists on faithful Christian practice will be disquieting, for such faith is, to recall Perkins, radically disrupting. The hungry mouth and naked body before us need more than our lunch money and the extra coat in our closet, and more than our prayers, but they certainly need those. It is crucial for the preacher to communicate two truths: first, that the human needs we meet matter to God and must matter to us; and second, that our response is at least as much about our need to practice our faith as it is about the importance of compassionate response to human need.

How should the preacher do so? If we follow James's example, we will begin with a clearly stated and often restated proposition. We will include a compelling example from the life of the community. We will anticipate the responses and possible objections of our listeners, and will respond to each one in turn with wit and humor (if not sarcasm), showing the theological inconsistency and inadequacy of those responses. And we will remind them of the wonderful tradition, biblical and historical, that witnesses to the truth of the proposition: faith without works is dead.

JAMES 3:1–18 – TEACHERS, TONGUES, AND RIGHTEOUSNESS

Wall has argued persuasively, if not finally convincing in every detail, that the heart of the letter of James, 2:1–5:7, is a midrash on the wisdom saying found at 1:19, "let everyone be quick to listen, slow to speak, slow to anger."[76] He is certainly correct that chapter 2 develops the theme "quick to listen" as "doing, not just hearing" and that in chapter 3 attention turns to "slow to speak," considering the power, danger, and destructive potential of speaking in rich and evocative detail. With its opening warning to teachers, its familiar analogies, and its strong criticism of the double-tongued and divisive, James 3 is at one and the same time familiar and disconcerting for many readers.

3:1–12 is clearly a unit, although Dibelius and others argue that the passage is made up entirely of traditional material loosely assembled by the author or editor. A few have sought to separate v. 1 from the rest of the chapter, arguing that the focus on teachers is sufficiently different from the more general discussion of the power and danger of speech to merit separate treatment, but the distinction is at the level of interpretation, not composition. More significant are the claims of those who make a strong division between vv. 12 and 13, seeing v. 13 as the beginning of a separate literary unit. There is a broad consensus over the division between 3:1–12 and 3:13ff. The same cannot be said about the length of the literary unit that follows. Johnson and Dibelius treat 3:13–4:12 as a unit, while Moo sees a break at 4:3. While there is certainly continuity of thought and theme between 3:18 and chapter 4, I concur with Ropes, Laws, Martin, Wall, and Davids that 3:13–18 constitutes a separate rhetorical unit, and so the examination here will contain one division.[77]

JAMES 3:1–12

1 Not many of you should become teachers, my brothers and sisters, for you know that we who teach will be judged with greater strictness.

---

[76] R. W. Wall, *Community of the Wise* (1997), p. 75.
[77] L. T. Johnson, *Letter of James* (1995); M. Dibelius, *Letter of James* (1975); D. J. Moo, *Letter of James* (2000); J. H. Ropes, *Critical and Exegetical Commentary* (1916); S. Laws, *Epistle of James* (1980); Ralph Martin, *James*, Word Biblical Commentary (Waco, TX: Word Books, 1988); Peter H. Davids, *The Epistle of James* (Grand Rapids, MI: Eerdmans, 1982).

2 For all of us make many mistakes. Anyone who makes no mistakes in speaking is perfect, able to keep the whole body in check with a bridle.
3 If we put bits into the mouths of horses to make them obey us, we guide their whole bodies.
4 Or look at ships: though they are so large that it takes strong winds to drive them, yet they are guided by a very small rudder wherever the will of the pilot directs.
5 So also the tongue is a small member, yet it boasts of great exploits. How great a forest is set ablaze by a small fire!
6 And the tongue is a fire. The tongue is placed among our members as a world of iniquity; it stains the whole body, sets on fire the cycle of nature, and is itself set on fire by hell.
7 For every species of beast and bird, of reptile and sea creature, can be tamed and has been tamed by the human species,
8 but no one can tame the tongue – a restless evil, full of deadly poison.
9 With it we bless the Lord and Father, and with it we curse those who are made in the likeness of God.
10 From the same mouth come blessing and cursing. My brothers and sisters, this ought not to be so.
11 Does a spring pour forth from the same opening both fresh and brackish water?
12 Can a fig tree, my brothers and sisters, yield olives, or a grapevine figs? No more can salt water yield fresh.

INNER TEXTURE AND INTERTEXTURE

Reading James 3:1–12 may cause some to recall the short "Block that metaphor!" fillers in the *New Yorker* magazine of years past. Bits and horses, rudders and ships, fires and forests, and on and on. There is so much figure one loses sight of the ground, for the "tongue" itself is figure for human speech, tongue and body as synecdoche for speech and conduct. As is generally the case with James, his meaning is painfully clear: make every effort to keep control of the tongue (be "slow to speak"), for no member of the body has a greater capacity for doing harm, in spite of its capacity for doing good.

1. The first verse signals a shift from the preceding verses in the exhortative "my brothers and sisters" (*adelphoi mou*), just as it rounds off the rhetorical unit in v. 12. Of special interest is the reference for "teachers" and the shift from second person plural to first person plural in the second half of the verse, "we who teach will be judged with greater strictness" (*meizon krima lēmpsometha*). Discussion of the role, if not office, of teacher (*didaskalos*) will be found in the section to follow. That James includes himself among the teachers is significant, at once claiming an important role in the life of the community (see 1 Cor 12:28) and accepting the "greater strictness" in judgment. But which judgment? The judgment of the community or that of the eschaton (last days)? Presumably both (see the discussion of James's eschatology in chapter 5).

2–6a. James continues in the first person plural, writing that "all of us" make mistakes. The verb here, *ptaiomen*, meaning to trip or stumble, is not a particularly strong metaphor for moral or religious transgression, nor is it common in the NT (here, 2:10; 2 Pet 1:10; Rom 11:11). Wisdom tradition before James frequently singled out speech as a place of weakness and failing, Sir 19:6b ("Who has not sinned with his tongue?") being closest to 3:2, but many examples may be found in the canon (Prov 12:13, 13:3, 21:23; Sir 14:1, 20:18, 22:27), and James may have owed these traditions a debt. The wisdom was conventional and commonplace.

V. 2 also introduces a note of metaphorical ambiguity that persists throughout the passage. How is it, after two chapters of emphasizing deeds over words, that suddenly the one who is "perfect" is said to be so in *speech*? Moreover, we "all stumble," yet one could presumably not stumble, someone who does not stumble in speaking (lit. "in word"/*en logō*). Is James suggesting an impossible possibility, or a possible impossibility? This ambiguity is inherent to the juxtaposition of the metaphors themselves, two of which (bit, rudder) suggest control, the third (fire) the lack or impossibility of control. Which is it?

The one who does not stumble in speech is "perfect" (*teleios anēr*), able to control (bridle) the whole body. Here James picks up a term unusual in the NT, "bridle" (*chalinagōgeō*), recalling the metaphor introduced at 1:26, "If any think they are religious, and do not bridle their tongues but deceive their hearts, their religion is worthless." There follows the first of three familiar metaphors, each based on the rhetorical trope comparing lesser and greater.

But first there is a text-critical problem, described by Johnson as "severe,"[78] text critically, if not semantically, true. As we will see, vv. 4 and 5b introduce the second and third metaphors with the Greek expression *Idou*, often translated "Look!" or "Behold." In a significant portion of the manuscript tradition v. 3 begins in similar fashion, but in a more important set of texts the opening expression in v. 3 is *ei de*, introducing a hypothetical "if." Metzger and most commentators choose the more difficult reading, "if," more difficult because it is harder to explain why *ei de* would have been miscopied from an original *ide* than vice versa.[79] In any case the meaning is clear. Note should also be taken of Martin's emphasis on the importance of the term "body" (*sōma*), introduced in v. 2 and used again in vv. 3 and 6, which he sees as evidence of the author's concern with the "body of Christ." Attention will be given to his suggestion when considering the sacred and homiletical textures of the passage, for the inner texture of the passage works well without the additional referent and does not intrinsically suggest the analogy.

---

[78] L. T. Johnson, *Letter of James* (1995), p. 257.
[79] The likely explanation is a copying confusion known as *itacism*, the mishearing by copyists of *ei* and *i* when read aloud, the mode in which copying was done. εἰ δέ is found in B³ L Ψ and many uncials, ει δε in ℵ A B* C K P, ἴδε in many uncials and minuscules, and ἰδού in *textus receptus*. B. M. Metzger, *Textual Commentary on the Greek NT* (1994), p. 611.

Three comparisons follow in rapid succession, each comparing the place of the tongue in the body to the effect a small instrument (bit, rudder, fire) has on a much larger corpus (horse, ship, forest). All of the comparisons were common in antiquity. Dibelius cites parallels in Sophocles (bit), Aristotle (rudder), and Philo (helmsman, charioteer, fire), among many others, and concludes, wrongly I think, that James was dependent on such sources.[80] Instead, as was argued in the Introduction, it is probably more appropriate to say that James used Wisdom and other familiar comparisons in a way analogous to his use of what we now identify as Jesus' sayings, with ease and effortlessness, without recourse to citation formulas – intertextuality as second nature if you will.

While the central analogy is clear, from the lesser to the greater, each individual comparison has its own difficulties, and cumulatively there is significant tension between the first two and the third. In the first comparison we cannot be sure if James intends the bit and bridle for a chariot or a single rider. Either is possible, but the chariot is perhaps more likely (see Acts 8:28–9; Rev 9:9, 18:13).[81] The problem here, as with the rudder, helmsman, and ship, is that the tongue does not "control" the body, while the emphasis being sought is on "control" of the tongue. Moreover, in a manner more explicit in the example of rudder, ship, and helmsman, wherein the great ship is "guided by a very small rudder *wherever the will of the pilot directs,*" there is an outside force providing control.[82]

In this sense the fire/forest comparison is the closest analogy. Prior to this comparison James reiterates the figure of the tongue, "a small member" (*mikron melos*) that "boasts of great exploits" (*megala auxei*). The latter expression is difficult, because the term for boast (*aucheō*) is not otherwise attested in the NT (the synonyms *kauchaomai* and *katakauchaomai* are found four times in James itself, and throughout the NT, usually in a negative sense), and the modifier (*megala*) can be taken to mean "great boasts," "boasts a lot" (Laws), or with most commentators, "great things." The force of the analogy argues for the last: the small member boasts of great things.

V. 5b starts with exhortative *Idou* (Look!), as in v. 4, and the source of text-critical difficulties in v. 3. A nicely balanced expression follows, lost in the NRSV "How great a forest is set ablaze by a small fire." James emphasizes the fire by placing it first in the sentence and uses the comparative in perfect alliterative parallel (the term, but not the usage, common in the NT), *hēlikon pur helikēn hulēn anaptei,* to nice rhetorical effect – perhaps "How small a flame ignites how great a forest" (*hulē,* "forest," only here in NT). Comparing the effects of speech to those of fire is well attested (e.g., Prov 16:27: "Scoundrels concoct evil, and

---

[80] M. Dibelius, *Letter of James* (1975), pp. 184–93.
[81] So L. T. Johnson, *Letter of James* (1995), p. 257, who notes the widespread use of the image following Plato, *Phaedrus,* 246B–247C.
[82] S. Laws, *Epistle of James* (1980), p. 145, reminds us that this analogy is ancient indeed. "Steer not with thy tongue (alone). If the tongue of a man (be) the rudder of a boat, the All-Lord is its pilot" (Amen-em-Opet 8; *ANET* p. 423 f.).

their speech is like a scorching fire"), as are analogies about fire spreading in a forest (Isa 9:18: "wickedness burned like a fire, consuming briers and thorns; it kindled the thickets of the forest"; see esp. Philo, *Decal.* 173), but the precise analogy, tongue-fire-forest, seems unique to James.

"And the tongue is a fire." And that is the problem, because the fire, in James's analogy and in human experience, is not easy to control, while the first two comparisons, bit/horse, rudder/ship, are about control. The tension will be explored more completely in the sections to follow, but the inner-textual significance must again be noted. James has constructed a series of images whose net effect is ambiguous, much like the ambiguity of the impossible possibility in v. 2. No one can control the tongue, for it is like a fire. If one could control the tongue (or is it, *when* one succeeds in controlling the tongue?), it is analogous to the way a rudder guides a ship and a bit a horse – what seems like no great achievement is in fact momentous indeed.

6–8. Dibelius describes v. 6 as "among the most controversial in the New Testament.... In fact there are few verses in the New Testament which suggest the hypothesis of a textual corruption as much as this one does."[83] It is certainly among the most difficult to translate if not to understand. Our efforts to understand it may be helped by a restatement and transliteration.

And the tongue is a fire.	*kai hē glōssa pur.*
The tongue is placed among our members as a world of iniquity	*ho kosmos tēs adikias hē glōssa kathistatai en tois melesin hēmōn,*
it stains the whole body,	*hē spilousa holon to sōma*
sets on fire the cycle of nature,	*kai phlogizousa ton trochon tēs geneseōs*
and is itself set on fire by hell.	*kai phlogizomenē hupo tēs geennēs*

The problems are numerous: punctuation in manuscripts is neither clear nor consistent, terminology and usage is unusual, and hypotheses about sources, emendations, and the like abound. In all, though, I find that both James's hand and his intent are clear. In Greek the style, while idiosyncratic, seems Jacobean; alliteration, repetition, and wordplay are frequent. The style is connected by term and theme with what precedes, and it leads to what follows. It seems, then, unnecessary and unhelpful to posit major corruption and emendation. As long as the meaning and thought flow are clear, it is better to wrestle as best we can with what we have.

"The tongue is a fire" restates the theme, much as James restated again and again the theme of chapter 2 ("faith without works is dead"). The most contentious issue interpreters face is how to understand the nouns (*ho kosmos tēs adikias hē glōssa*) and verb (*kathistēmi*) that follow, and the participles (*spilousa, phlogizousa, phlogizomenē*) that conclude the verse. The first key is found in the verb, which James also uses in 4:4 and which in the middle/passive voice

---

[83] M. Dibelius, *Letter of James* (1975), pp. 193–4.

carries the sense of "to be" or, more strongly, "is established."[84] So the "tongue is" or "is established as" what? A world of unrighteousness in our members? Perhaps, James pushing the small/great distinction to the edges of language, suggesting that this small member "stains (pollutes, corrupts) the whole body" while "boasting of great things" by saying the tongue "sets on fire the cycle of nature, and is itself set on fire by hell" (*kai phlogizousa ton trochon tēs geneseōs/kai phlogizomenē hupo tēs geennēs*). Interpreters should be careful here not to miss the rhetor at work, for James may have been more interested in the turn of the phrase, while his interpreters are searching for the philosophical and theological underpinnings of his thought. Dibelius devotes an excursus ("The Cycle of Becoming") in search of what is likely not to be found,[85] the origin of James's expressions found here, and we need not repeat the search. The use is most likely of a piece with his use of other sources, natural, free and naively adaptive. What it does accomplish is to push the limits of the tongue's capacity to the beginning (the "cycle of nature") and end ("on fire by hell") of creation.

Vv. 7–8 are a comparative breeze, with James extending the analogy from creation to talk about creatures and their susceptibility to being "tamed by the human species," perhaps with Gen 1:28 in view. The restless wickedness of the tongue, by comparison, can be tamed by no one (*tēn de glōssan oudeis damasai dunatai anthrōpōn*). James concludes this phase of his assault on the tongue by referring to it as "a restless [*akatastaton*] evil," recalling the one who is "double-minded, unstable [*akatastatos*] in every way" (1:8) and "full of deadly poison," perhaps with the poison of the reptiles (*herpeton*) in v. 7, although the word *ion* can also mean "rust," as it does in 5:3.

The cumulative rhetorical effect of 3:2–8 is an emphatic, if confusing, warning and denouncement of the tongue – human speech. The presumption, which we will explore, seems to be that more harm than good comes from speech. This is not surprising in light of the emphasis throughout James on actions beyond words alone, but the sharpness of the denunciation, despite the attempt in the examples of bit and rudder to suggest that the tongue might be controlled, is remarkable. This is, in the verses to follow, somewhat ameliorated.

9–12. In these verses James shifts attention to a different kind of impossibility. In vv. 2–8 the reader is impressed with the impossibility of controlling the tongue. In vv. 9–12 James argues from example that it is impossible, or at least a contradiction of his own natural theology, for those in the community to do anything less. Whereas in vv. 2–8 one gathers that James believes that the "default setting" of the tongue, to borrow a term from technology, is to cause harm, in vv. 9–12 he argues the opposite: because the default setting is praise of the Creator, cursing the creature is a contradiction and thus impossible.

---

[84] L. T. Johnson, *Letter of James* (1995), p. 259.
[85] M. Dibelius, *Letter of James* (1975), pp. 196–8.

The shift from the problems to the possibilities of the tongue in v. 9 is important. After so many verses of denunciation (a fire, a world of unrighteousness, staining the whole body, a deadly poison, etc.), James now offers a different possibility: "With it we bless the Lord and Father. . . . " This phrase, *eulogoumen ton kurion kai patera*, not otherwise attested in the NT or Hebrew Bible, is a pleonasm and not a reference to Jesus (*ton kurion*) and God (*patera*), as is from time to time suggested. While the idea of blessing God is deeply rooted in Torah ("blessed be God Most High"; Gen 14:20) and no doubt in the Jewish/Christian worship of James's day ("Blessed be the Lord, the God of Israel"; Psa 41:13), this does not mean that James was dependent on the formula of another, and suggestions of emendation are unhelpful.[86] Nor is James likely to have been influenced by the Pauline "Blessed be the God and Father of our Lord Jesus Christ" (2 Cor 1:3).

James is stating what is for him a central truth about human nature and purpose, the praise and blessing of God the Creator. Again hearkening back to Gen 1:26–8, James speaks of human beings as those "made in the likeness of God." Can we bless God and curse those made in God's image? No! Jesus' instruction to make peace with the brother or sister before placing a gift before God is called to mind (Mt 5:23–4), as is the admonition of 1 Jn 4:20–21 – "Those who say, 'I love God,' and hate their brothers or sisters, are liars; for those who do not love a brother or sister whom they have seen, cannot love God whom they have not seen. The commandment we have from him is this: those who love God must love their brothers and sisters also."

The verbs for bless and curse in James 3:9 are in the first person plural, returning to the usage in vv. 1 and 2 – "all of us make many mistakes." We will see later that attempts to ground such statements in the particular teaching or worship experiences of the community probably overreach, but we cannot fail to note James's willingness to include himself again among those whose practice seems to fall short of their profession of faith.

Yet, in a return to the kind of rhetorical confusion we found in vv. 2–8, James goes on to argue that such doublespeak is (or is it, *should be?*) impossible. Four examples follow in quick succession, following the pattern of v. 3: (1) springs do not give two kinds of water, fresh and brackish; (2) fig trees do not give olives; (3) grapevines do not yield figs; and (4) salt water does not make fresh water. These common examples, basically observations of nature's order, with more parallels outside than within biblical tradition – although Jesus' sayings about trees and fruits (Mt 7:17–19, 12:33; Lk 6:43–4) may lie behind two of the examples – are used to make a claim about community practice. As the community members should not be double-minded, so their speech should be singular. In fact the force of the examples suggests that doublespeak is as impossible for the person

---

[86] Ibid., pp. 201–3.

of faith as are a spring with both sweet and bitter water, a fig tree with olives, and so on.

The cumulative impact of 3:1–12 is substantial and chastening. But to fully appreciate its depth the interpreter must consider its sociocultural, ideological, and sacred textures.

SOCIOCULTURAL AND IDEOLOGICAL TEXTURES

James 3:1–12 raises any number of interesting social, historical, and ideological issues. In this section the following will be treated: (1) What was meant by "teacher" (*didaskalos*)? (2) What do we learn about James from the use of the first person plural, the author including himself among the "teachers"? (3) What do we learn about the community from the admonition that "not many among you should become teachers"? (4) What is the ideological background for James's strong diatribe against the "tongue"? One other issue of significance for this section, James's understanding of judgment ("we who teach will be judged with greater strictness") will be postponed to chapter 5, when James's eschatology is considered.

Teachers in the NT and Early Church

The chapter begins with a warning for teachers and a word of discouragement for those who might want to "become teachers" (*didaskaloi ginesthe*). Whom did James have in mind? Was this an office within the community or simply a role in community life? There is surprisingly little literature on this question, so interpreters must be cautious in their conclusions.

The evidence for a formal office of teacher, in comparison, for example, to elder (see 5:14), is scant. The term *didaskalos* is found prominently in Paul (Rom 12:7; 1 Cor 12:28–9; also Eph 4:11), in the pastoral epistles (among the author's self-designation in 1 Tim 2:7 and 2 Tim 1:11), and in Heb 5:12 ("by this time you ought to be teachers"). But far and away the most frequent use is in the Gospels, specifically, in reference and address to Jesus. Matthew uses the term ten times, Mark twelve, Luke seventeen, and John seven (eight counting Jn 8:4). In the Synoptics the use is distributed between Jesus' disciples ("[T]hey woke him up and said to him, 'Teacher, do you not care that we are perishing?'"; Mk 4:38), opponents ("Then some of the scribes and Pharisees said to him, 'Teacher, we wish to see a sign from you'"; Mt 12:38), and more friendly inquirers ("A certain ruler asked him, 'Good Teacher, what must I do to inherit eternal life?'"; Lk 18:18). Jesus also uses the term in reference to himself, for example, at Lk 22:11, "[S]ay to the owner of the house, 'The teacher asks you, "Where is the guest room, where I may eat the Passover with my disciples?"'"

So far, so good, but not far enough. Two Gospel sayings complicate the discussion greatly. In Jn 13:13 Jesus says, "You call me Teacher [*ho didaskalos*] and Lord, and you are right for that is what I am." Here Jesus emphatically accepts the designation others have given him as teacher. In contrast is Jesus' rejection in Matthew of the use of that term for others. In Mt 23 Jesus condemns the "scribes and Pharisees" because, among other things, they "love to be greeted with respect in the marketplaces, and to have people call them rabbi."[87] Jesus continues, "But you are not to be called rabbi, for you have one teacher, and you are all students. . . . Nor are you to be called instructors, for you have one instructor [*kathēgētēs*, only here in the NT], the Messiah" (Mt 23:8, 10). While the context suggests a broad repudiation of the love of honorific titles, teacher/rabbi seems to have a level of meaning for Matthew not found in the rest of the NT (and also, presumably, the term instructor [*kathēgētēs*]). Perhaps familiarity with the force, if not the content, of these verses underlay James's caution to those who would "become teachers" and recognition that those who are teachers "will be judged with greater strictness." If so, and the suggestion is admittedly speculative (and should only be read in line with this commentary's general approach to the casual relation of James and the teaching of Jesus), our author did not completely share the concern of Jesus in Matthew's gospel. After all, "teacher" is a designation the author accepted for himself.

This does not say that James was unconcerned about the designation. Unfortunately our evidence is too slight to form strong conclusions about the precise focus of that concern. It is simply not clear who or what a teacher was or did. First, to hold "teacher" and "rabbi" as synonyms tells us more lexically than it does semantically, for what was meant by rabbi in the first century of our era is also far from clear,[88] and the use of the title in the NT is likely anachronistic.[89] Second, while almost all commentators agree with Laws that teachers were accorded "enormous respect" within Judaism[90] and with Wall that this respect was "congruent with the values of the larger Greco-Roman world,"[91] as noted previously there is little agreement or literature about the duties and responsibilities of a "teacher."[92] Did 11–13 discusses responses to "anyone coming to you" and first mentions "the one teaching [*ho didaskōn*, a substantive participle] all these things," followed by apostles and prophets (Did 11:1–2; reversing Paul's order in 1 Cor 12:28). Did 13:2 maintains that a "true teacher" (*didaskalos alēthinos*) is "worthy, like the worker, of bread/sustenance." But we are given no further insight into the duties of the teacher, no more than we are in *Pirke Aboth* ("Let

---

[87] Jn 1:38 and 20:16 tell us that "Rabbi" means "Teacher" (*didaskalos*).
[88] See Hayim Lapin, "Rabbi" in *Anchor Bible Dictionary* (New York: Doubleday, 1992), vol.5, pp. 600–2.
[89] See the lively debate between H. Shanks and S. Zeitlin in *Jewish Quarterly Review* 53: 337–45 (Shanks); 345–9 (Zeitlin); 59:152–7 (Shanks); 158–60 (Zeitlin).
[90] S. Laws, *Epistle of James* (1980), p. 141, citing Joachim Jeremias, *Jerusalem in the Time of Jesus* (London: S.C.M. Press, 1969).
[91] R. W. Wall, *Community of the Wise* (1997), p. 162.
[92] See Floyd V. Filson, "The Christian Teacher in the First Century" *Journal of Biblical Literature* 60 (1941): 317–28.

the fear of thy teacher be as the fear of heaven"; 4.12) or *The Shepherd of Hermas* (9.22.2), among other frequently cited sources. Instead, it is the "teaching" (*hē didaskalia*) that is of interest to sources roughly contemporary to and soon after James (so, for example, the pastoral epistles).

As we will see, that James claims the designation "teacher" for himself is not insignificant. Other than "servant," it is the only claim he makes for himself and, of equal significance, as a teacher he makes no claims on his students. This suggests a contrast between the sort of claims an "apostle" (Paul?) might make on his "children" (the Corinthians?). James reproves, instructs, admonishes, and chastens, but makes no demands and puts forward no prerogative. At best this is only suggestive of the role and understanding of teacher in the community of James and in the NT world. Perhaps more than anything it speaks of the need for more detailed and nuanced study of the subject "teacher."

James as Teacher

The shift from second to first person plural in v. 1 has been noted. The shift remains in v. 2 (all stumble) and v. 3 (bit and horse), and changes to third person in vv. 4–8, returning to first person plural in v. 9 (blessing and curse from the same tongue). The cumulative effect of these first person plural usages, despite the bit and horse analogy, is negative. *We* shall be more strictly judged, *we* stumble, *we* bless and curse from the same mouth. What does it mean for James, the teacher, to keep such company? There are two issues here: James's self-identification as a teacher and his identification with those who sin in speech.

First person verbs are noticeably infrequent in James and apart from hypothetical quotations used in argumentation (1:13; 2:18; 4:13, 15) are found only here and at 5:11, "Indeed we call blessed [*makarizomen*] those who show endurance." The use of the first person therefore stands out, and it is natural for interpreters to seek as much insight as possible from the few clues available. But as we have seen, the role of teacher is ill-defined in the early community, and we learn as little from James's discouragement of those who would seek to become one as we do from any other source.

As in 1:1, it is what James does not claim for himself that often interests us more. He does not claim to be an apostle or a prophet, but a teacher. If apostles are known by the one on whose behalf they are sent, and prophets by the fulfillment of their words, teachers are known by the content of their teaching. This may be exactly what James intended, claiming a significant role that nonetheless turned attention away from himself to his message while accepting the responsibility that comes with presuming to instruct others.[93]

This understanding carries over into the self-identification among those who "stumble." While there are certainly occasions in the letter when James seems

---

[93] The contrast here with the "Apostle" (1 Cor 9:1!) Paul could not be any greater.

to distance himself from the reader (e.g., 4:13 ff.), on this central topic – be slow to speak – his identification here is strong indeed. "All of us make many mistakes" (3:2).

The Community and Its Practice

Most prominently among interpreters, Ralph Martin has argued that the setting of chapter 3 is the worship life of James's community. He understands the three references to the body (vv. 2, 3, 6) to be references to the "body of Christ," the community of faith, and the discussion of tongue and speech to be about right conduct in worship, so that "'Poisoning the whole body' (vv 6, 8) is a sad verdict passed on the consequences of wrongful teaching in the Jacobean congregations."[94] In this Martin has little support, other than from Reicke, and for good reason: it is likely an overly historicized reading of the intertexture, making too much of the *Pauline* metaphor of the body (1 Cor 12, etc.) and of *Pauline* concerns for order in worship (1 Cor 14). The inner texture, or poetics, of the uses of *sōma* suggests otherwise, so that the admittedly frequent use of the term finds referent within the text, not beyond it. The opening metaphor, sinning as "stumbling" (v. 2) gives rise to a series of other physical images making reference to the body, the relative frequency having to do with coherence and emphasis through repetition, not with the desire to push the reader beyond the text to find meaning. The naturalness of this reading is supported by the repeated references to the natural order in 3:1–12 (horse, winds, fire, forest, beast and bird, reptile, sea creature, springs, fig tree, vine, olives, salt and fresh water, not to mention "the cycle of nature" in v. 6). The body references are much more at home in this company than understood as a reference to the (Pauline) body of Christ. Moreover, while the community surely "blessed" God in its worship, is the interpreter to understand, by limiting 3:1–12 to the worship and catechetical life of the community, that this is also the setting for cursing those "made in the likeness of God" (v. 9)?

What we learn about the community is not specific to teachers or to worship, but to community speech in general: as far as James was concerned this speech was not consistent or faithful, certainly beginning with the teachers but just as certainly not stopping there.

The Tongue

The ideological interest here is the tension already noted between the emphasis on actions over against or instead of speech found in chapters 1 and 2 and the emphasis here on speech itself. Which is it? For the "perfect" person of faith, it is both, because speech is itself an action – blessing and cursing, for example. The

---

[94] R. Martin, *James* (1988), pp. 103–7, 122–4 (quote from p. 123).

one who controls the tongue, the one slow to speak, *acts* wisely. Double speech, angry speech, and empty speech are also actions, actions that belie faith. There is nothing peculiar or unique in this ideology. It is part of the Wisdom that James inherited and part of the philosophies by which his community was surrounded.

Does the emphasis James puts on speech indicate that it was a particular problem for his community? That conclusion goes farther than the evidence and human experience permit.

BRIDGING THE HORIZONS — SACRED AND HOMILETICAL TEXTURES

"In the beginning was the Word [*ho logos*], and the Word was with God, and the Word was God" (Jn 1:1). "Anyone who makes no mistakes in speaking [*en logō*] is perfect" (James 3:2).

Christianity is a religion of the word, oral and scribal. In speech and in writing believers have opportunity to witness to faith or to failings. What we write, however, can often be erased (with the exception of the accidentally sent e-mail). When we have spoken, the word is out. Learning to control the tongue was, and is, a vital part of Christian practice.

James makes a strong case for both the importance and the difficulty of taming the tongue. Having spent two chapters arguing that right speech in and of itself is insufficient, he corrects any misimpression that speech does not matter. He also seems to insist that the reader attempt the impossible. We saw earlier that the metaphors of 3:1–12 stand in significant tension with one another, suggesting how the tiny tongue controls the large body (bit, rudder) and claiming that the tongue is out of control (fire, etc.). Moreover, as important as taming the tongue may be, "no one can" (v. 8). Yet an untamed tongue is depicted as contrary to nature: "From the same mouth come blessing and cursing. . . . this ought not to be so" (v. 10), anymore than fig trees yield olives or springs pour forth bitter and sweet water (vv. 11–12). This may well be exaggeration for effect, a hyperbolic impossibility meant to convince the reader of both the importance and the difficulty of the task. It also suggests another possibility. At least it did to the late Henri Nouwen.

The most frequent argument for silence is simply that words lead to sin. Not speaking, therefore, is the most obvious way to stay away from sin. This connection is clearly expressed by the apostle James: ". . . every one of us does something wrong, over and over again; the only man who could reach perfection would be someone who never said anything wrong – he would be able to control every part of himself" (James 3:2).

James leaves little doubt that speaking without sinning is difficult and that, if we want to remain untouched by the sins of the world on our journey to the eternal home, silence is the safest way. Thus, silence became one of the central disciplines of the spiritual life.[95]

---

[95] Henri Nouwen, *The Way of the Heart* (New York: Ballantine, 1981), pp. 35–6.

One response to the impossible possibilities James finds in human speech is silence. It is a response that would make for very brief sermons. Yet it should not be discounted all together and certainly not from worship. Silence is the very ground on which the Spirit of God may walk among us.

Be "slow to speak," James wrote. A popular aphorism holds, "It is better to keep silent and be thought a fool than to speak and remove all doubt."[96] Wisdom traditions, Scripture, the rabbis, and the desert ammas and abbas concurred. Many people in our day, however, are convinced that every person's every thought is worthy of being voiced or at least of being "blogged" to the world on the Internet.

The practice of the discipline of silence for a time or a season enriches the Christian life in many ways. And just as fasting can increase one's appreciation for food, so can silence aid our understanding of speech. Homiletical exhortation to control the tongue is likely to prove fruitless. Everyone knows and has felt the danger and powerful sting of the tongue yet has failed to keep it in check. A more encouraging word can be offered for the practice of silence. While James did not specifically call for silence, the logic of his argument suggests it. The practice of silence will likely further our appreciation for it.

The caution to teachers in 3:1 applies to preachers as well, for we too will be judged with greater strictness.

JAMES 3:13–18

13 Who is wise and understanding among you? Show by your good life that your works are done with gentleness born of wisdom.
14 But if you have bitter envy and selfish ambition in your hearts, do not be boastful and false to the truth.
15 Such wisdom does not come down from above, but is earthly, unspiritual, devilish.
16 For where there is envy and selfish ambition, there will also be disorder and wickedness of every kind.
17 But the wisdom from above is first pure, then peaceable, gentle, willing to yield, full of mercy and good fruits, without a trace of partiality or hypocrisy.
18 And a harvest of righteousness is sown in peace for those who make peace.

After two chapters emphasizing the necessity of actions and not just words, chapter 3 begins with a thorough, and largely negative, consideration of the (potential) impact of words on the life of the community. At the end of these

---

[96] The quote is variously attributed to Mark Twain, Samuel Johnson, and Abraham Lincoln, among others.

verses James returns to an emphasis on actions, moving from exhortation to a negative example of division to a concluding, and positive, list of virtues and a closing blessing.

While there is a consensus that a strong break occurs between 3:12 and 3:13, scholars differ over where to mark the end of the unit that begins at 3:13. Dibelius and Johnson go well into chapter 4 (v. 12 and v. 10, respectively), while Moo sees a break at 4:4. Laws, Martin, Wall, Adamson, and Ropes treat 3:13–18 as a unit, more strongly linked to what precedes than to what follows, but develop the concerns of earlier verses in a rhetorically distinctive way. Their arguments are persuasive.

INNER TEXTURE AND INTERTEXTURE

The shift in tone and theme, from anomalies in nature to a manner of living that shows forth wisdom, is not as abrupt as some interpreters, especially Dibelius, suggest. Instead it is a return to what is arguably the primary theme of the letter – the "good life" (*tēs kalēs anastrophēs*) that demonstrates its underlying wisdom through visible and tangible "works" (*erga*). The passage is carefully, even beautifully, crafted, with attention given to linking the unit with the verses immediately preceding and material found earlier in the letter.

13. This verse is an exemplary *inclusio*, beginning and ending with wise/wisdom (*sophos/sophia*). Those in the community who consider themselves or are considered to be wise and "understanding" (*epistēmōn*, a word not otherwise found in the NT) are exhorted to "show" (*deiksatō*, an emphatic, aorist imperative) or demonstrate this wisdom in their "good life" (*anastrophēs*, a favorite term of 1 Pet – 1:15, 18; 2:12; 3:1, 2, 16 – and 2 Pet – 2:7; 3:11) by their works, echoing a similar exhortation in 2:18, works manifest in gentle wisdom (*en prautēti sophias*). Here James is recalling a contrast between "meekness" (*prautēti*) and various evils (1:21) while anticipating his reiteration of this distinction in the verses to follow.

14–16. Now it gets ugly. The likely source of this ugliness and the intended target of James's words will be considered in the section to follow, but the sharpness of the language matches that found anywhere else in the letter. "But if you have bitter envy [*zēlon pikron*] and selfish ambition [*eritheian*] in your hearts, do not be boastful and false to the truth." The "bitter"-ness recalls the water of v. 11. The "envy" and "selfish ambition" are found here and at v. 16. *Zēlos/zēloō*, as a noun and verb, can mean both jealous and zealous, but when paired with *eritheia* clearly jealousy or envy is intended. A similar pairing is found in Paul, in the well-known "vice lists" (2 Cor 12:20; Gal 5:20), where the similar, but ethnographically distinct term[97] *eris* (strife) is also found. In the present verse (14) the only difficulty in meaning is in the last few words, *mē katakauchasthe*

---

[97] M. Dibelius, *Letter of James* (1975), p. 210.

kai pseudesthe kata tēs alētheia, rendered in the NRSV as "do not be boastful and false to the truth." "Boastful" is the term, unusual in the NT, used by James to describe the "triumph" of mercy over judgment (2:13), and as Johnson remarks, "Some MSS understandably correct to the simple *kauchestai*."[98] How to construe the last phrase is also problematic. "Do not lie against the truth" is most likely, carrying the negative *mē* over to control both verbs in the phrase. The meaning, generally, is clear: those who have jealousy and selfish ambition in their hearts (*kardias*, the seat of the will) have nothing to boast about.

Such so-called wisdom will be contrasted with the true wisdom from above and found to be "earthly, unspiritual, devilish." This trio of terms builds in intensity. The first, *epigeios*, recalls the "cycle of nature," creatures, and the like in vv. 6–7 and stands opposite to the heavenly. The second, *psuchikē*, is found in Paul (e.g., 1 Cor 15:44, 46) and in Jude 19, where the *psuchikē* ("worldly" or physical) is said to be "devoid of the Spirit" (*pneuma mē echontes*), an excellent definition of what James means by the term.[99] The third, *daimoniōdēs*, is likely original to James, calling to mind the *daimonia* who "believed and trembled" (2:19), the opposite of those with true faith, and the various demons and unclean spirits who recognized Jesus but wanted nothing to do with him (Mk 5:1–20).

V. 16 returns to the root of the problem for James. If you find "envy" (*zēlos*) and "selfish ambition" (*eritheia*),[100] then there will also, even automatically, be "disorder" (*akatastasia*, here and 1:8, 3:8) and "wickedness of every kind" (*pan phaulon pragma*, another effective use of alliteration). By this point the reader wants to know why James is so focused on envy and ambition, and where and with whom this envy and ambition led to disorder and wickedness. Is it among the teachers or those who wish to be teachers of 3:1? The juxtaposition of "disorder" and "every" recalls the "person of two minds" in 1:8, who was "unstable" (*akatastatos*) in all (*pas*) ways. Our conclusions must wait until consideration of the sociocultural texture of the passage.

17–18. The pericope does not end on the harsh, condemnatory note of vv. 15–16. Having established the "wisdom" that is "earthly, unspiritual, devilish," James turns, and by making this turn his conclusion emphasizes the wisdom "from above" (*anōthen*). A list of eight features follows (the rhetorical impact lost in translation), as the author begins with a word whose first letter is alpha (*'agnē*/pure), followed by four terms whose first letter is epsilon (*eirēnikē*/peace; *epieikēs*/gentle; *eupeithēs*/yielding; *[mestē] eleous*/[full of] mercy), and concluding with three terms whose first letter is alpha (*agathōn*/good [fruit];

---

[98] L. T. Johnson, *Letter of James* (1995), p. 271.
[99] But see the cautions of M. Dibelius, *Letter of James* (1975) in the excursus "The Term Ψυχικός" on pp. 211–12.
[100] Büchsel, *TDNT* 2.661, states that the term suggests "base self-seeking" and "the nature of those who cannot lift their gaze to higher things."

adiakritos/impartial; *anupokritēs*/sincere). This list of the virtues of the "wisdom from above" compares favorably with the virtue lists of Paul (Gal 5:22–3) and others, but the emphasis is clearly that of James. Most surprising is the first term, "pure," with its ritual connotations otherwise missing in James. The concern for peace, gentleness, yielding, and mercy are set over against the discord of the verses preceding and, as we shall see, those following. Goodness is what comes down from above (1:18) and impartiality a mark of a community acting in faith (2:1 ff.), a community that shows its sincerity by actions and not just words. The concern for good fruit and peace is reiterated in v. 18, an almost gnomic saying that also recalls the concern for righteousness expressed in 1:20, where human anger and divine righteousness are distinguished. The Greek phrasing is ambiguous, and the NRSV does not help matters by choosing to translate *karpos* as "harvest" instead of "fruit," sacrificing the connection with the "good fruit" of v. 17 that seeks to balance the "sow" (*speirō*) of v. 18 and avoiding the fact that fruit is not "sown" like seed. The expression in the dative case at the end of the saying is most likely a dative of advantage (so Dibelius, Martin, contra Johnson) and can be read along with Dibelius, "*by* those who are peaceable – *for* those who are peaceable.... Righteousness is sown and harvested only in peace."[101] In the background may be a better-known Wisdom saying, the seventh beatitude, "Blessed are the peacemakers" (Mt 5:9).

SOCIOCULTURAL AND IDEOLOGICAL TEXTURES

The central question of interest in this section is the identity of those James may have had in mind who exhibited the wisdom that was "earthly, unspiritual, devilish" and what we may be able to determine about the nature of the "disorder" for which they were responsible. As will soon be obvious, this is a discussion that will continue throughout consideration of chapter 4, a thematic continuity that no doubt influenced interpreters who do not see any break between 3:18 and 4:1.

As already noted, the movement in 3:13–18 is from the "wisdom" shown through the "good life" to the "earthly [etc.] wisdom" to "wisdom from above." The first wisdom reiterates the theme of faith and works prominent in chapters 1 and 2. The second seems to develop the objections raised in 3:1–12 about the uncontrollable nature of the tongue and the damage it can cause, while the third recapitulates the first, recalling the "righteousness of God" (1:20) and extending its meaning through an emphasis on peace. Chalk it up to human nature and curiosity, but as hard as James works rhetorically to focus the reader on "the wisdom from above," our sociohistorical interest instead turns to the envy, ambition, disorder, and wickedness. To whom and/or about whom was James

---

[101] M. Dibelius, *Letter of James* (1975), p. 215.

writing? What might we conclude was taking place in the community to evoke such a strongly negative characterization and condemnation?

Martin, continuing his argument about 3:1–12, maintains that James is continuing to speak to and about "teachers" and was concerned with the harm they brought or threatened to bring to the community, both at worship and otherwise.[102] As was the case in considering this argument for 3:1–12, the thesis exceeds the evidence to support it. One use of the word teacher/*didaskalos* and three references to body/*sōma*, though now arguably supported by reference to the "wise person" (*sophos*), are not a sufficient basis on which to re-create a church experiencing conflict and division with its accepted and self-designated teachers. This is not to say that such a scenario is impossible, but to exclude other possibilities, some with wider application, is unnecessary and finally unhelpful. This position is, of course, evidence of this author's interpretive ideology – care should be taken not to exceed the available evidence when examining sociocultural texture. The place for such speculation is the homiletical texture, where the interpreter seeks connections and reconstructions that illumine and make accessible the sacred textures of the text for contemporary readers. Overreading the sociohistorical texture narrows the homiletical texture, and so distorts both.

The culprit, one suspects, is the tendency of interpreters to confuse rhetoric for reality or to overstate the ability to work backward from rhetoric to a reconstruction of historical setting. Indisputably clear in chapter 3 are a word of caution to teachers and those who would be teachers, an extended argument about the danger, real and potential, of the tongue, and a call to embrace the "wisdom from above," a call that suggests familiarity with those who have chosen a different "wisdom" and a growing division between the two groups. This does not exclude teachers, nor does it exclude others within or around the community from and to which James wrote. That James writes in such sharp terms may say as much as or more about his style of argumentation than it does about the danger or threat of some specific group of opponents. A more likely target, textually, for James's strong words are not teachers – a group with which James chose to identify (an identification Martin and others leave out of their arguments) – but the "double-minded" person already met in 1:8, whose instability matches the "disorder" of v. 16, and those showing favoritism (*diakrinō*) to "rich" in 2:1–4, an attitude whose opposite (*adiakritos*) is among the virtues in those who have the wisdom from above.

The biblically and historically intriguing, if ultimately speculative, question is the relationship of those envisioned in this passage and what we know about James from Acts 15 and Gal 2. One must wait for the evidence of James 4 before addressing this question.

---

[102] R. Martin, *James* (1988), pp. 136–7. P. H. Davids, *Epistle of James* (1982), p. 80, and James Adamson, *The Epistle of James* (Grand Rapids, MI: Eerdmans, 1976), p. 149ff., would seem to concur.

SACRED AND HOMILETICAL TEXTURES

"Every good gift, and every perfect giving, is from above, coming down from the Father of lights" (1:17, my trans.).

Just as the historical tendency is to read James as if he were, or should have been, Paul, the inevitable human tendency is to accentuate the negative to an extent that the positive is lost. In reading James this results in an overemphasis on possible divisions, clear condemnations, and an unfortunate lack of appreciation for the letter's own frequent focus on the positive.

In chapter 1 James tells us that the source of every good gift is "from above." Now he tells us what some of those gifts are, first captured in the phrase "the wisdom from above" and then spelled out in a list of eight qualities, or virtues. "But the wisdom from above is first pure, then peaceable, gentle, willing to yield, full of mercy and good fruits, without a trace of partiality or hypocrisy." 3:13–18 begins and ends on this positive note.

We cannot deny that James continues to deal with an element of conflict in these verses. For while the distinction is not as strong as one finds in, for example, the "two ways" document in the Didache,[103] the contrast between "earthly, unspiritual, devilish" wisdom and "the wisdom from above" is pronounced, and it seems most likely that James had some one(s) and some thing(s) in view, if only because generic condemnations rarely reach such level of vituperation. While I am not convinced that James had fellow or rival teachers especially in mind and find the thesis unhelpfully restrictive, there is here a special word for teachers and preachers. More accurately, the words here may have a special resonance for teachers and preachers, as in 3:1 – *we* shall receive the greater judgment.

But upon what will that judgment be based? The content of our teaching? That is the case in the Didache (11–12) and in Paul ("If anyone proclaims to you a gospel contrary to what you have received, let that one be accursed"; Gal 1:8). In James, warnings about the dangers of the tongue notwithstanding, this does not seem to be the case. Instead, and with admirable consistency, James remains focused like a laser beam on conduct, the "manner of life" (*anastrophē*). It is all about the practice.

This suggests two learnings, one sociohistorical and one homiletical. As we saw in chapter 2 and will see most clearly in the passages to follow, the most likely target of James's condemnation were those, within and without the community, who shared in the culture's conventional wisdom favoring the rich and despising the poor. These people's actions, or practice, failed to share in God's special concern for the poor ("Has not God chosen the poor in the world to be rich in faith and to be heirs of the kingdom that he has promised to those who

---

[103] "There are two ways, one to life and one to death, but the difference between the two ways is great" (Did 1:1). See Kurt Niederwimmer, *The Didache*, Hermeneia (Minneapolis, MN: Fortress Press, 1998).

love him?"; 2:5). Attempts to discern teachers or teachings, rivals or wayward partners, with whom James was in dispute, ignore the letter's own emphasis on actions rather than words.

This has homiletical implications for those preaching from or responding to James. It is all about the practice. When considering Jude we will have ample opportunity to speculate on the identity of "certain intruders" who "have stolen in among you" (Jude 4). With James we are consistently (re)turned to simpler, if finally more demanding, questions about one's "manner of life." Whether teacher or initiate, leader or newcomer, what are they "showing forth"? And we who preach? For us as for others, it is not about our doctrine or opinion or even our confession of faith (2:19). The question is this: does our manner of life show "the wisdom from above, [which] is first pure, then peaceable, gentle, willing to yield, full of mercy and good fruits, without a trace of partiality or hypocrisy"? This should be the question central in preaching James. It is all about the practice.

BRIDGING THE HORIZONS – THE PREACHER AS PRACTITIONER

If those who teach will be judged with greater strictness, maybe we had best stick to preaching and leave the teaching to others. It is not, of course, that easy. The line between teaching and preaching is wavy and dotted, and effective sermons are often a combination of both. So let us have no illusions, the "greater strictness" will be applied to preachers as well.

[A]re those who teach and preach also caught in illusions, illusions about their own participation in what they say and in their relationship to those to whom they say it? For instance, some insist that distance both from the message shared and from the listeners is essential to professional competence; to participate personally in the subject matter and in the lives of those who hear tends to reduce the quality of one's work as a communicator. Is this true?

I have been confirmed by SK [Sören Kierkegaard] in my own strong conviction that, whatever may be the talents displayed, the gospel is not communicated by sharing clippings and quotations. This is the work of hirelings, those who scour newspapers, magazines, and books for what can be used.... To this end come those who have lost the passion for their task and who now no longer preach or teach the gospel but who drop the names of famous persons endorsing the product, extol the contributions of Christianity to our civilization, urge attendance to ecclesiastical duties, and occasionally scold the absentees.

[T]he way to understand and to communicate Christian faith is through disciplined participation in that faith. This is not an option for the communicator.[104]

I quote these lines at some length from Dr. Fred Craddock's masterful Beecher Lectures because I find them wise and telling. Conversation with Kierkegaard,

---

[104] Fred B. Craddock, *Overhearing the Gospel* (Nashville, TN: Abingdon Press, 1978), pp. 41–3.

both via biblical interpreters like Craddock and Bauckham, and in my reading of the Danish master himself, has greatly informed my own teaching and preaching, and my Christian practice. This is hardly an accident, because Christian practice and Christian preaching are inextricably linked, and not in the way the maxim about "practicing what you preach" suggests. We do not practice in order to give witness to our preaching; we practice so that we might preach in the first place. Without hearing *and* doing the word we can neither faithfully teach or preach it. Above all and before all, the preacher must be a person of faith and practice.

From the standpoint of the hearers, the qualities of the teller affect the response to the story. The decision that a message is worth listening to is a decision that the teller is worth listening to. If the speaker is not in his speaking, if his absence is evidenced by an overage of clichés, quotations, and secondary sources, the hearers feel deceived and deprived. Anyone could have said it. When we respond, we respond to *someone*.[105]

JAMES 4:1–17 – CONFLICT, FRIENDSHIP, AND WHAT TOMORROW MAY BRING

The fourth chapter of James introduces a level of contentiousness previously unknown in the letter. The first phrase keys the reader to expect as much, speaking of "conflicts and disputes," words that could just as easily be rendered "wars and battles." The audience is referred to as "adulteresses" and accused of being "enemies of God" (v. 4), "sinners" and "double-minded" (v. 8). There are calls to "Lament, mourn, and weep" (v. 9) and a charge that some have set themselves up as judges, not doers, of the law (v. 11).

It is no accident that the subject James addresses so contentiously is contentiousness. The rhetoric of the chapter, especially the first verses, is polished and powerful. The themes, while not new (4:1–3, cf. 1:14–15, 16; 4:4–6, cf. 3:13–17, 1:9–10a, 17; 4:7–10, cf. 1:21; 4:11–12, cf. 2:12–13, 3:1–12, 4:13–16, 1:10b–11; 4:17, cf. 2:14–17), are developed in new ways and extended to include more of those within (and beyond) the community. James draws particularly sharp distinctions and insists that the reader choose – whose friend will you be?

The division of James 4 is more contested than any chapter in the letter. While the unity of 4:1–10 is broadly acknowledged, the relationship of these verses with those preceding and following is broadly disputed. Dibelius links 4:1–10 with 3:13–18 and 4:11–12 under the heading "A Group of Sayings Against Contentiousness." Wall sees a break after 3:18 but links 4:1–10 with 4:11–5:6 under the title "The Wisdom of 'Slow to Anger.'" Adamsom treats 4:1–10 and 4:11–17 separately, each pericope considered as one of the eight major sections into which

---

[105] Ibid., p. 43.

he divides the letter. Johnson reads 3:13–4:10 together as "Call to Conversion" and 4:11–5:6 as "Examples of Arrogance." Martin examines 4:1–5:20 in a single chapter, "Witnessing to Divine Providence," which has six divisions, including 4:1–10 and 4:11–17. Laws treats 4:1–10 and 4:11–17 separately, each constituting one of the fifteen major divisions she reads in the letter.[106] I am convinced by the weight of tradition and by James's signature summary verses at the end of each chapter (1:27, 2:26, 3:18, 4:17, 5:20), to read 4:1–17 as a rhetorical unit with three thematic sections: vv. 1–10, 11–12, 13–17 (so Moo).

JAMES 4:1–10

1 Those conflicts and disputes among you, where do they come from? Do they not come from your cravings that are at war within you?
2 You want something and do not have it; so you commit murder. And you covet something and cannot obtain it; so you engage in disputes and conflicts. You do not have, because you do not ask.
3 You ask and do not receive, because you ask wrongly, in order to spend what you get on your pleasures.
4 Adulterers! Do you not know that friendship with the world is enmity with God? Therefore whoever wishes to be a friend of the world becomes an enemy of God.
5 Or do you suppose that it is for nothing that the scripture says, "God yearns jealously for the spirit that he has made to dwell in us"?
6 But he gives all the more grace; therefore it says, "God opposes the proud, but gives grace to the humble."
7 Submit yourselves therefore to God. Resist the devil, and he will flee from you.
8 Draw near to God, and he will draw near to you. Cleanse your hands, you sinners, and purify your hearts, you double-minded.
9 Lament and mourn and weep. Let your laughter be turned into mourning and your joy into dejection.
10 Humble yourselves before the Lord, and he will exalt you.

INNER TEXTURE AND INTERTEXTURE

1a–2b. James begins his attack in fine diatribal style, with a rhetorical question that works something like the proverbial "Have you stopped beating your spouse?" The author does not ask, "Do you have conflicts and disputes among you?" but "Where do they come from?" That they are present is a given, and the reader is left only to answer to their origin. The first terms, *polemos* and *machē*,

---

[106] M. Dibelius, *Letter of James* (1975), pp. 207–29; R. W. Wall, *Community of the Wise* (1997), pp. 192–247; James B. Adamson, *James: The Man and His Message* (Grand Rapids, MI: Eerdmans, 1989), pp. 165–81; L. T. Johnson, *Letter of James* (1995), pp. 267–310; R. Martin, *James* (1988), pp. 139–71; S. Laws, *Epistle of James* (1980), pp. 166–94; D. J. Moo, *Letter of James* (2000), p. 211.

usually refer to armed conflict, the first a favorite, in noun and verb forms, in the Apocalypse (Rev 2:16; 9:7, 9; 11:17; 12:7, 17; 13:7; 16:14; 17:14; 19:11, 19; 20:8) and the "little Apocalypse" in the Synoptic Gospels (Mk 13 and par.), and the second related to the term for sword (*machaira*, e.g., Mt 26:52 – "all who take the sword will perish by the sword").

Authors answer their own rhetorical questions, and James's answer only sharpens the militaristic language. "Do they not come from your cravings that are at war [*strateuomai*] within you?" The NRSV chooses "cravings" to translate *hēdonē*. In v. 3 it uses "pleasures," thereby obscuring the repetition and diluting the force of the term, which is strong, as is our word group based on it (hedonism, etc.). Luke uses the term in the interpretation of the story of the sower to describe the seed that falls among the thorns as representing those "choked by the cares and riches and pleasures [*hēdonōn*] of life" (Lk 8:14). The NRSV also obscures the use of the word *melos* (bodily part) in the phrase "within you" at end of v. 1. This omission is significant for a more complete discussion (in the next section about the nature of the "war within"): is James talking about armed conflict between members of the community or about the pull and tug of competing desires within the hearts of members of the community?

A CLOSER LOOK – THE LANGUAGE OF DESIRE

The language of desire and conflict continues in the second verse, and while James's intent seems clear there is considerable dispute over his exact meaning. Recalling a word for desire used in 1:15 (*epithumia*), James writes, "You desire and you do not have." The series of second person plural (present active indicative) verbs continues in Greek, *phoneuete kai zēloute kai ou dunasthe epituchein machesthe kai polemeite*, which NRSV translates, "You want something and do not have it; so you commit murder. And you covet something and do not obtain it; so you engage in disputes and conflicts" – twenty-eight words to translate ten, with Greek word order completely ignored. Something must be up. There are two problems, one with punctuation and one, for many interpreters, with the meaning of *phoneuō* (murder). The punctuation problem stems from the fact that in early Greek manuscripts there is none, just as there were no spaces between the words and all the words were in either capitals (uncials) or lowercase (minuscules).[107] The translation problem arises from the apparent anticlimactic and/or hyperbolic use of "murder," and the obvious solution, first proposed by Erasmus, is that there has been a corruption in the text, so that *phthoneite* (jealous) rather than *phoneuete* (murder) was the original reading.[108]

---

[107] See Bruce M. Metzger, *The Text of the New Testament*, 2d ed. (New York and Oxford: Oxford University Press, 1968), pp. 8–23.

[108] M. Dibelius, *Letter of James* (1975), p. 217.

The solution is obvious only so long as the complete absence of any manuscript support is not troubling. Given the "obvious" appeal of this solution to the problem, the wonder is that no copyist has left any evidence of adopting it. Johnson, in his thesis that in chapter 4 James is dependent on a common topos on "envy," points to a solution.[109] Whether or not one agrees with Johnson's thesis in entirety, the solution is rhetorical. As has been the case so often in our reading of James, efforts to identify historical settings for James's community often ignore or dismiss his rhetorical accomplishment. He need not have referred to murder because of a problem with homicide in the community but because he was attempting to demonstrate the seriousness of a problem within the community. Astute readers will be well aware of this, as they will be to the later reference to "adulterers" (v. 4). The problem with punctuation is inevitable, but it does not obscure the meaning when one appreciates the rhetoric.

A   Where comes war and where comes fighting among you?
B   From your desires warring in your bodily members!
C   You long for and have not;
C'   You murder and covet;
B'   But you are unable to obtain.
A'   You fight and make war.

This solution is not perfect, but it retains something of the effect of James's percussive language. The sense of competing desires, at war with one another, is thoroughgoing.

2c–3. These verses build on the impact of the first, continuing the use of second person plural verbs and repeating the verb "to ask" (*aiteō*) three times, twice in the indicative and once in the infinitive. In the first chapter the reader who lacked wisdom was urged to ask but to ask "in faith, never doubting" (1:6). Inadequate and ineffective asking is also the theme here. First comes the failure to ask, "You do not have, because you do not ask," and then asking wrongly, even evilly, "You ask and do not receive, because you ask wrongly [*kakos*]." The reader naturally turns back to 1:5–6, and James illumines both passages in the conclusion to this one, defining what it means to ask wrongly in light of the warring desires of 4:1, "in order to spend what you get on your pleasures [*hēdonai*]." The verb "to spend" (*dapanaō*) can be used neutrally for financial (Acts 21:24; *James's* instructions to Paul) and emotional (2 Cor 12:15) expenditures, but can also suggest a certain sense of squandering, as in the story of the prodigal (Lk 15:14), a sense here reinforced by reference to "pleasures" and forming an *inclusio* with

---

[109] See Luke T. Johnson, "James 3:13–4:10 and the *Topos* ΠΕΡΙ ΦΘΟΝΟΥ" *Novum Testamentum* 25 (1983): 327–47.

the *hēdonē* in v. 1. What is easy to lose in vv. 3c–4 is the topic, prayer. The references to wrong/evil asking, squandering, and pleasures call attention away from where and how the "asking" is taking place – in prayer – to which we will return in considering the sacred and homiletical textures.

4–6. James is hardly finished with harsh language: "Adulteresses!" Some manuscripts add the masculine "adulterer" (*moichoi*) to this unusual, but understandable, use of the feminine plural, and a few others shift to the masculine only, but James knew what he meant. The image comes from the prophetic denunciation of idolatry and the comparison of the covenant between God and Israel with a marriage covenant (Eze 16:1–17; Hos 2; Isa 54:4ff.). God was the husband, and Israel the wife, so the one unfaithful to God, male or female, was an "adulteress." This idea of choosing, over or against, one or the other, a covenant kept or broken, is only furthered in the line following the exclamation. "Do you not know that friendship with the world is enmity with God?" The implication, of course, here as throughout the chapter, is that the readers "know" very well. They are not doing, or they are trying to have it both ways. But James's background in Wisdom and the tradition of the Two Ways make that impossible. The reader must choose, and the choice is all inclusive; as Johnson notes, "It must be remembered above all that 'friendship' involved 'sharing all things' in a unity both spiritual and physical. Thus, friends are *mia psychē*, 'one soul.'"[110] The choice in v. 4 is clear. V. 5 is another matter altogether, for here we are not sure what James means or what he is talking about. The first problem with meaning is in the phrase rendered as a quotation in the NRSV, "God yearns jealously for the spirit that he has made to dwell in us." The second problem is that of source and hence what James intended by "the scripture" (*hē graphē*). This can be addressed in reverse order.

There is nothing in the OT or NT canon similar to this phrase, nor anything very close in Qumran or pseudepigraphic material, and various efforts to find something remain unconvincing. This is unusual, for as Martin reminds us, "In every other case where we read ἡ γραφὴ λέγει (*hē graphē legei*) in the NT this formula introduces a direct scriptural reference or allusion."[111] It is also frustrating, for if one could identify a source one might have some assistance in making sense of the phrase itself. The Greek reads, *Pros phthonon epipothei to pneuma ho katōkisen en hēmin*, and the first thing one notices when comparing this transliteration to the NRSV is the conspicuous absence of the word "God." The Greek does not make clear the subject who yearns/longs (*epipothei*) "with jealousy" (*pros phthonon*) – the latter term always used pejoratively and so never attributed to God in NT and LXX. To add to the confusion is ambiguity about the "spirit" (*to pneuma*) and whether it is "living" or "placed" in us; the aorist form in our text could represent two different verbs, *katoikeō* (live, dwell) or

---

[110] L. T. Johnson, *Letter of James* (1995), p. 279.
[111] R. Martin, *James* (1988), p. 149.

katoikizō (place, put). Whatever this should be taken to mean, it is important, because it is not said "in vain" (*kenōs*).

We will defer discussion of how to understand "scripture" that lacks referent until the next section. (To anticipate, I argue that it is in keeping with James's overall orientation to tradition – biblical, historical, and Jesus material.) The difficult question of the meaning of the phrase remains. The issues may be summarized as follows:

1. The opening phrase, *Pros phthonos*, and main verb, *epipotheō*, are not attributed to God in our literatures, making the NRSV "God yearns jealously" problematic.
2. The noun *to pneuma* could refer to the spirit of God or the human spirit, and could serve as the subject of *epipotheō* or as the object of *katōkisen*.
3. The verb form *katōkisen* is the aorist form of two different verbs, "dwell" and "place."

The solution, following Laws and Johnson, rests in context and rhetoric (again), although multiple possibilities remain. Contextually, James is contrasting worldly and Godly and asking the reader to choose. In the following, thankfully clear, verse, we are told that God gives "more grace" (*meizona de didōsin charin*), which suggests that there is something lacking, or in need of correction, in what preceded. In light of vv. 1–3 it is likely that what needs to be corrected is the jealousy and desires of the human spirit, which Johnson reminds is a part of the topos on jealousy. Rhetorically, along with Laws and Johnson, one notes James's frequent use of rhetorical questions and sarcasm, keeping with the style of diatribe. V. 5 begins with a hint of sarcasm – does scripture speak in vain? – so a rhetorical question following would not be unexpected. Laws reads, "Does the Spirit which he made to dwell in us long enviously?" and Johnson, "Does the Spirit which he made to dwell in us crave enviously."[112] The ambiguity, I think, rests in the absence of a marker (*ou*, *mē*) to determine whether the "question" (there is no punctuation at any point in the tradition to support this reading) expects a positive or negative answer. One's conclusion probably is as much a reflection of one's own anthropology (is the spirit within humans one that craves enviously?) and theology (if it is, should its presence and nature be understood as an act of God?) as it is a construal of James's Greek. In any case the interpreter needs to be careful not to let exegesis grind to a halt, because this is only the midpoint in a larger argument that extends from v. 1 to v. 10.

6–10. As just suggested, it is easy to lose the thread of James's argument when encountering a difficult verse or phrase. Thankfully the text and interpretation of 4:6–10 is comparatively straightforward. Before considering them it would be wise to rehearse the broad outline of James's argument in 4:1–10.

[112] S. Laws, *Epistle of James* (1980), p. 167 and Johnson, *Letter of James* (1995), p. 267.

James 4:1–17 – Conflict, Friendship, and What Tomorrow May Bring

The passage begins with an accusation (there are "conflicts and disputes among you") and an indictment (your desires are the source of the conflicts). These charges are recapitulated, in reverse order, forming a chiasm of accusation, indictment, indictment, accusation (vv. 1–2ab). A supporting indictment is made ("you do not have, because you do not ask," or "because you ask wrongly"; vv. 2c–3). A bit of ad hominem name-calling (Adulterers!) is followed by an implied challenge to choose in what Johnson considers James's "sharpest contrast between two measures of reality and two paths of life": the choice between "friendship with God" and "friendship with the world."[113] It cannot be both (v. 4). In v. 5 a sarcastic taunt, do you think the Scripture speaks vainly? is followed by the confusing noncitation about jealous yearning and the spirit that dwells within us. However one chooses to understand this phrase, it is rhetorically clear that in v. 6 the force of v. 5 is trumped, with a clear affirmation and an actual citation: Prov 3:34, the Greek letter perfect from LXX to James with only a change of names for the deity (LXX, *kyrios*; James, *ho theos*).

"But he gives all the more grace; therefore it says, 'God opposes the proud, but gives grace to the humble'" (v. 6). The relationship of vv. 5–6, in particular the use of citation formulae (one without and one with a citation), is important and revealing, but will be considered in the next section. Here our interest is that *whatever* James meant by v. 5, it is overcome by the greater grace (*charis*) of v. 6, the only time James uses the term, yet in a manner that recalls the "generous act of giving, with every perfect gift" coming from "above" in 1:17. Therefore, the movement of vv. 1–6 is from accusation/indictment, a challenge to choose between God and the world, to a promise of grace to those who choose rightly.

In vv. 7–10 James depicts, with the utmost clarity, what the life of one who chooses rightly will look like. He does so emphatically, using a series of ten verbs in the imperative mood, beginning with "submit" in v. 7 and ending with "humble yourselves" in v. 10. First, and hardly surprising in light of all that has come before, one must "submit" (*hupotassō*) to God. The term is common in NT epistles, generally in reference to the subjection of "all things" to God and Christ (e.g., 1 Cor 15:27-8), of humans to civil authority (e.g., Rom 13:1), and, in various *Haustafeln*, of submission within family structures (e.g., 1 Tim 3:14). James calls for submission only to God, which is further explained in the compelling second half of a memorable, if otherwise unknown, maxim, "Resist the devil, and he will flee from you. Draw near to God, and he will draw near to you" (vv. 7b–8a). The saying is doubly interesting. First, while the verb "to flee" (*pheugō*) is well attested throughout NT and early Christian literature, there is no use comparable to James's idea that the devil will "flee" if resisted. Second, while the verb "draw near" (*engizō*) is even better attested, usually in a geographical sense (e.g., Lk 19:41) but also in the sense of the approaching *kairos* or *parousia* (e.g., Mk 1:15; James 5:8: *hē parousia tou kuriou ēngiken*), and while

---

[113] L. T. Johnson, *Letter of James* (1995), p. 288.

Heb 7:19 speaks of "a better hope" (cf. James's "greater gift") through which "we approach God," nowhere do we find anything similar to the reciprocity of James's "draw near to God and he will draw near to you."

The language of "approaching" calls to mind the psalms of ascent (e.g., Ps 121) and in general the idea of approaching God and approaching God's sanctuary. The cultic and purity overtones of this idea may at first strike the reader as not in keeping with James's focus on ethical concerns, but the tones are unmistakable. And they are clearly reinforced in the next half of v. 8, "Cleanse your hands, you sinners, and purify your hearts, you double-minded," an exhortation that both calls to mind Ps 24:3–4 and maintains James's concern for sin and double-mindedness: "Who shall ascend the hill of the Lord? And who shall stand in his holy place? Those who have clean hands and pure hearts, who do not lift up their souls to what is false, and do not swear deceitfully." LXX (Ps 23:4) does not use the same term (*katharizō*) for the "cleansing" of the hands, using descriptive adjectives instead of verbs, *aōthos* (blameless) for "clean hands" and *katharos* for "pure heart."

James's blending of the moral and cultic as a basis for approaching God is compelling. In the next verse he adds the prophetic. "Lament and mourn and weep. Let your laughter be turned into mourning and your joy into dejection" (v. 9). This is not a call to debasement or masochism but a recollection of the traditional Hebrew prophets' call to repentance (cf. Isa 3:16–24; Joel 2:12–13). But here the "prophet Jacob" calls on the people to choose lamentation and mourning as an act symbolic of the greater reversal promised in v. 10: "Humble yourselves before the Lord, and he will exalt you."

This "prophetic" section also carries many echoes of Jesus material. "Woe to you who are laughing now, for you will mourn and weep" (Lk 6:25) and "For all who exalt themselves will be humbled, and those who humble themselves will be exalted" (Lk 14:11 and par.) come most readily to mind, as well they should. The key terms – laugh (*gelaō*), mourn (*pentheō*), weep (*klauō*), humble (*tapeinoō*), and exalt (*hupsoō*) – are the same in James and the Synoptic Gospels, as are the tone and emphasis on reversal. 1 Peter, which has also included the citation from Prov 3 found in James 4:6, immediately follows the citation with a saying much like v. 10, "Humble yourselves therefore under the mighty hand of God, so that he may exalt you in due time" (1 Pet 5:6). The double use of the maxim, first as citation and then as exhortation, makes vv. 6–10 an *inclusio* and at the same time recalls the opening of the letter (1:9–10).[114]

Vv. 1–10 heighten the language and rhetoric sharply. Repetition, *inclusio*, chiasmus, citations, and allusions to OT and Jesus traditions combine to challenge the reader to look within his or her own life for the source of divisions and

---

[114] Details like these cause one to wonder how so many interpreters, following Dibelius, can conclude that the letter is nothing but a series of unrelated sayings and citations from tradition.

James 4:1–17 – Conflict, Friendship, and What Tomorrow May Bring 113

conflicts within the community of faith. At the center is a compelling call to claim friendship with God over (and against) the "world," to grieve one's sins, and to adopt a manner of life in keeping with one's faith.

SOCIOCULTURAL AND IDEOLOGICAL TEXTURES

Johnson and others have argued that these verses and the argument advanced are pivotal for our understanding of the letter. This is certainly true in terms of the ideological texture, but insights into the social-cultural texture are fewer and farther between, unless one follows the reading of vv. 1–3 advocated by Martin, who maintains that

> in the final analysis a metaphorical understanding of "wars" and "fightings" does not adequately explain the strong language in the text, especially v. 2. Since James and his community were situated in a Zealot-infested society and since it is quite conceivable that (at least) some of the Jewish-Christians were former Zealots (cf. Luke 6:15; Acts 1:13), the taking of another's life is not out of the realm of possibility for church members as a response to disagreement.... While James' community may have not yet experienced and engaged in literal murder on a mass scale, the contingency is a very real one and must be warned against.[115]

After considerable reflection I have concluded that Martin is serious. Incorrect, but serious. Never mind that Martin holds the epithet that opens v. 4 ("Adulterers!") to be no indication of a problem with marital infidelity. "There is nothing in the context to suggest that the literal sin of adultery was a problem in James' church" (p. 148). Apparently murder was common enough that *mass* murder was a possibility to be warned against. Suffice it to say that there is no evidence beyond the anticlimactic placement of murder (*phoneō*) before jealous (*zēloō*) and the connection of "Zealot" with *zēloō* that Martin sees in v. 2 to support his theory. In the desire to understand more about James's setting, rhetoric is mistaken for evidence of historical context.

What we do have support for is the developing evidence of conflict within James's community that was grounded in socioeconomic distinctions (1:9–11; 2:1–7) between the haves and the have-nots. While the focus of 1:9–11, 2:1–7, 4:13–16, and 5:1–6 is on the haves, attention in 4:1–10 is on the have-nots. James contrasts their desires, and the conflicts and disputes that result, with the life of faith of one who is a friend of God and finds the source of the problem.

Interestingly, in light of the passages just mentioned, James does not place the onus on the haves and their misconduct and inadequate practice. Instead the onus is on the have-nots for what is in their own control – their inordinate desires, desires that have even overwhelmed the efficacy of their prayer lives by turning their prayer away from what *God wills* (v. 15) to what *they want*. James operates

---

[115] R. Martin, *James* (1988), p. 144.

from a fundamental ideological conviction that is ultimately empowering of those who do not have. Yes, there is ample blame and condemnation for those who have and do not share faithfully or treat equitably those who have not. But there is no sense of "It's all *their* fault." Rather, those who do not have are also held accountable for the quality of their lives and the faithfulness of their practice, and are reminded that their call is not to be friends "of the world" but friends of God.

By "world" James is not positing a gnostic or dualistic ideology that disparages and disdains the physical and material. Rather he thinks of the world as "a measure of reality, or a system of meaning, which can be contrasted to that of God. Indeed, these passages (3:6, 2:5, 1:27) virtually suggest that 'the world' is a measure that does not take God's existence, and therefore (God's) claims, into account."[116] There is conflict, then, and it is both within the community and between those who have and those who do not. Haves and have-nots, or to use the more traditional language, "rich" and "poor," are both a part of the community of faith to and for which James writes. Moreover, the source of the conflict is not just the disparity, nor the faithless use of wealth by the rich, but the focus on material by all concerned and the negative impact this has on the faith and practice of poor and rich alike. This is not, by any means, a justification for the faithless actions of those who have, both within and without the community – James will focus attention on them in 4:13–16 and 5:1–6. It is a call to those who "have not" to resist being consumed by their desire for what they do not have.

There is a final ideological issue in the passage that must be noticed: James's use of "scripture" (*hē graphē*) and a citation formula, *hē graphē legei* (the scripture says), without a recognizable quote from OT, Qumran, pseudepigrapha, or any other source. James uses similar citation formulae in 2:8 and 2:23, and the quotations that follow are easily recognized, as is the less formal citation formula and quotation in 4:6. Interpreters have sought far and wide, and worked long over the difficult sentence in v. 5b that follows the citation formula to solve the usage puzzle James presents. I suspect the solution is to be found not in some unknown source but in James's own notion of "scripture," a notion in keeping with his understanding and use of "law" and of material that we have come to deem as "Jesus sayings" or "Jesus material." As argued in the Introduction and in examining the intertexture of passages already considered, James has no fixed, precise, and limiting notion. Scripture, law, and Jesus traditions are used in a light and fluid fashion, sometimes with precision and obvious referent, and sometimes not. Forcing upon James our models and interpretive methods distorts his more open use of the spiritual inheritance, written and unwritten, behind the letter.

---

[116] Luke T. Johnson, "Friendship with the World/Friendship with God: A Study of Discipleship in James" in *Discipleship in the New Testament*, ed. Fernando F. Segovia (Philadelphia: Fortress Press, 1985), p. 173.

SACRED AND HOMILETICAL TEXTURES

"Do you not know that friendship with the world is enmity with God? Therefore whoever wishes to be a friend of the world becomes an enemy of God" (v. 4). Of course we *know* this, which is the point of James's rhetoric. The problem is we do not always do it, which in a way is the point of the entire letter.

> **BRIDGING THE HORIZONS – FRIENDSHIP WITH GOD IN THE WORLD**
>
> As mentioned, the "world" is not so much a negative designation of that which is to be avoided as it is an alternative system of meaning constantly seeking to influence the believer and turn him or her away from God. "Friendship" with the world, then, means to affirm the values, choices, and priorities of a meaning system that grounds meaning in material possessions, status, and regard. "Friendship" with God is to affirm the values, choices, and priorities of a meaning system that grounds meaning in the promise of the one who gives every good gift and is both "lawgiver" and "judge," as we will see in vv. 11–12. James means this to be as sharp and either/or as possible, which is very much grounded in Two Ways traditions (e.g. Did 1–6) and in Jesus' distinction between the wise and foolish builders (Mt 7:24–7).
>
> James uses "friendship" as a metaphor, and it is a rich one indeed. Johnson's chapter "Friendship with the World/Friendship with God" is subtitled "A Study of Discipleship in James" and was published in the volume edited by Fernando Segovia entitled *Discipleship in the New Testament*, suggesting that "friendship" is in some sense a synonym for "discipleship." In antiquity friendship was not viewed "in contemporary terms, as a sort of affection, benevolence, or positive attitude toward another. . . . On the contrary, it was regarded as a particularly intense and inclusive kind of intimacy, not only at the physical level but, above all, at the spiritual."[117] The analogy with discipleship, a word not used in James, is appropriate.
>
> Another way to think of "friendship" is as a person's fundamental orientation to life. What is the source of meaning for our lives? If it is the "world," and this may be a usage first and foremost for James, then it is fixed and finite. You may know where you stand, because the "standings" – whether fame, fortune, status, or position – are clear. But you also know that you will never stand anywhere else. *This*, for the one who chooses friendship with the world, is *it*. Most of us realize, some sooner, some later, that *this* is not enough. There is something in us that wants more, a truth that is perhaps what the awkward phrase in v. 5 about yearning and the spirit placed in us is trying to get at.
>
> Nothing less than a complete repudiation of the "world" will do. There is no halfway, no place for a "double-minded" mixing of fundamental

---

[117] Ibid., p. 173.

orientations in life. James is surely right about this. We must choose, and we know it.

Friendship with God looks and feels very different. It is humility, not pride, before the mystery of life and death, and a gracious submitting to God, drawing near to the source of life and meaning, which yields the power to resist the very devil we most fear, who fears and flees in response. James's call is all-encompassing, moral ("resist the devil"), cultic/ritual ("draw near to God," "cleanse your hands/purify your heart"), and prophetic ("lament and mourn and weep"), worth noting given the tendency to read James as if his only concern was for the ethical.

A word about prayer is also needed here. James speaks about prayer explicitly in chapter 5 and has done so implicitly in chapter 1 in much the same way as here in chapter 4. In 1:5 the one who lacks wisdom is to ask for it, knowing that God, "who gives to all generously and ungrudgingly," will give it. "But" (*de*), continues v. 6, "ask in faith, never doubting" (*aiteitō de en pistei mēden diakrinomenos*). In chapter 4 we read, "You do not have because you do not ask. You ask and you do not receive, because you ask wrongly, in order to spend what you get on your pleasures" (vv. 2c–3). Some would say, "There is always a catch." Ask, but don't doubt. Ask, but don't "ask wrongly." Did not Jesus simply say, "Ask, and you will receive"? Yes (Mt 7:7–8 and par.), but also goes on to qualify the saying with a story about the parent who gives bread and fish, not stones and snakes, when the child asks (Mt 7:9–10). But what if the child asks for a snake? "No," as any parent can tell you, is an answer. God "gives good things to those who ask" (Mt 7:11; James 1:17). We do not always ask for good things, nor do we always ask for things for good reasons, which amounts to the same thing and is likely the meaning of "because you ask wrongly" (4:4).

Yes, but sometimes we ask for a good thing, and we ask for it in the right spirit, for the right reason, and we ask without doubting. And that good thing (the healing of a loved one, the end of a war or famine, coming to faith of a friend) is not given. The answer seems to be "No." Here, as unsatisfying as it may be, we are forced to turn back upon the wisdom of James, in this case 4:10: "Humble yourselves before the Lord, and he will exalt you."

JAMES 4:11–12

11 Do not speak evil against one another, brothers and sisters. Whoever speaks evil against another or judges another, speaks evil against the law and judges the law; but if you judge the law, you are not a doer of the law but a judge.
12 There is one lawgiver and judge who is able to save and to destroy. So who, then, are you to judge your neighbor?

These two verses relate clearly to what follows, for vv. 11–12 and vv. 13–16 are about setting oneself apart, in the former apart from others in the community, in the latter apart from God. Both are also about a kind of boasting, vv. 13–16 a boasting that asserts an autonomy that ignores mortality and human dependence on divine protection, vv. 11–12 a boasting that is rooted in condemnation of a brother or sister.

These verses relate clearly to what precedes. "Speaking against" or slander certainly constitutes an example of the wrong use of the tongue condemned in chapter 3, and James's connection of this attitude with judging, the law, and the "one lawgiver" explicitly recalls the condemnation of showing partiality and thereby becoming judges in chapter 2. Moreover, the one who judges another member of the community can hardly be said to have humbled him- or herself or to have drawn near to God, the "one" who is able to save. In this sense vv. 11–12 develop the implications of vv. 6–10 in light of the community concerns of chapters 2 and 3.

At the same time these two verses stand apart. The particular logic of vv. 11–12 is unique to itself, and it forms its own rhetorical unit, beginning with an emphatic imperative and concluding with a typically Jacobean sarcastic rhetorical question. The importance of the issue, presumably for James's community and certainly for many that have followed, also suggests a brief, independent treatment.

INNER TEXTURE AND INTERTEXTURE

All commentators have noted the change in the term of address, from "adulterers," "sinners," and "double-tongued" in 4:1–10 to "brothers and sisters" in v. 11. But it seems an overstatement to call the shift "dramatic" (Johnson). Instead the shift seems more tactical, a change, as Laws writes, "from the pejorative to the personal, from the rhetorical stigmatizing of 'adulteresses' to a reasoned argument with *brothers*."[118] A disputatious tone is retained, however.

There are a number of key terms, including an interesting *hapax*, "lawgiver" (*nomothetēs*), and a second unique designation for God, the one "who is able to save and to destroy." The section begins with a prohibition (*mē* plus the present active imperative):[119] "Do not speak evil against one another" (*mē katalaleite allēlōn* – note the marvelous alliteration in Gk.). The term *katalaleō* is relatively infrequent; it is found here, in Paul (Rom 1:30; 2 Cor 12:20, both vice lists of a sort) and Peter (1 Pet 2:1, 12; 3:16) and occasionally in the LXX (Pss 49:20; 100:5). There is some disagreement about whether "slander" as a technical, legal term is an appropriate translation, but it seems preferable to the NRSV's insertion

---

[118] S. Laws, *Epistle of James* (1980), p. 186.
[119] See the note in D. J. Moo, *Letter of James* (2000), p. 198.

of the word "evil" into the text when it is not present in the Greek. To "speak against" remains the best, and literal, rendering of *katalaleō*, which may develop a more technical sense later in the tradition.[120]

James goes on to say that the one who speaks against a brother or sister judges (*krinō*) them and in doing so speaks against the law (*ho nomos*) and judges the law. The logic here is not obvious, but it is important. We have seen in chapter 2 that James has a characteristically fluid understanding of the law. It includes but is not limited to Torah and the teaching of Jesus. It can be expansive, or specific, and in this instance it seems to be both at once. Central to our understanding is the progression in James's reference to the one who is spoken against/judged.

He begins by referring to "one another" (*allēlos*) then specifies "brothers and sisters" (*adelphos*), but concludes with "neighbor" (*plēsios*) in the rhetorical "who, then, are you to judge your neighbor?" By linking neighbor with law, judgment, and speaking against, James is likely signaling his focal understanding of "law" as that which is found in Lev 19:18 and in half of the summary of the law given by Jesus (Mk 12:28ff. and par.). The logic of the argument is in following, to its natural conclusion, what comes from setting oneself over against others in order to speak critically of them. To do so requires assuming a superior position, which goes against the call to "humble oneself" and against the claim of "the law" to "love the neighbor as oneself" with its implicit equality. James then follows the logic to its extreme. By presuming to be in position to speak against and judge, one adopts a posture that precludes "doing" or practicing the law of "love your neighbor as yourself," and has thereby assumed a role that is already taken: "There is one lawgiver and judge."

The first term, *nomothetēs*, while well attested (the verb form, *nomothetein*, occurs frequently in the LXX in reference to God; e.g., LXX Psa 24:8 and 26:11, but the force is "teacher," as in NRSV), does not carry the force that James intends and is otherwise unknown in this form. James emphasizes the unity and uniqueness of God by placing the word "one" (*heis*) at the beginning of the sentence. As mentioned, referring to God as the "one lawgiver" is not the only unusual reference in the verse, for this one is also termed the "judge" "who is able to save and to destroy." Of course, God is frequently referred to as judge (*kritēs* [5:9]; also, e.g., Heb 12:23; LXX Pss 7:12; 49:6) and as one who saves (*sōsai* [1:21]; also, e.g., LXX Pss 30:3; 69:2; Isa 59:1; Dan 6:28) and destroys (*apolesai*; e.g., Mt 10:28; Job 2:3; Isa 14:25; 34:2; LXX Jer 29:4). What is unique to James

---

[120] *Mandate* 2:2–3 reads, "First of all, do not slander anyone, nor listen willingly to one who does. Otherwise, you the listener will be guilty of the sin of the slanderer, if you believe the slander that you hear, for by believing it, you too will hold something against your brother or sister. Slander is an evil thing; it is an unstable demon, never at peace, but always at home in dissension. So distance yourself from it and you will always have harmony with everyone." Carolyn Osiek, *Shepherd of Hermas: A Commentary*, Hermeneia (Minneapolis, MN: Fortress Press, 1999), p. 105ff. See also G. Kittel, "κατα λαλέω" *TDNT* 4 (1967): 3–5.

James 4:1–17 – Conflict, Friendship, and What Tomorrow May Bring 119

is the combination of save and destroy as descriptive of the activity of the one judge.

The logic leads to an untenable conclusion for anyone who would speak against someone else – to do so is to set oneself as superior to the one spoken against, is to deny the claim of the law to love the neighbor, and is to presume a role that can be held only by God. It is no wonder James concludes the argument with a sarcastic "who do you think you are?" or as the NRSV has it, "So who, then, are you to judge your neighbor?"

SOCIOCULTURAL AND IDEOLOGICAL TEXTURES

In a wonderful book on his first parish, *Open Secrets*, Richard Lischer includes a chapter titled "Gossiping the Gospel."[121] The faithful have ways of keeping one another informed about the life of the community and about the interface of that life with the divine will that to outsiders look and sound a whole lot like gossip. It is a lovely conceit, and Lischer is aware that the line between sharing prayer concerns and spreading rumors is thin indeed. So was James.

"Do not speak evil against one another" reads the NRSV, trying, as we have seen, to render *katalaleō* with appropriate force. James is bringing to bear on the life of the community the dangers of speech that were considered abstractly in 3:1–12. There is no reason to think James's community had a particular problem with critical speech or slander, because the problem itself is universal. The evidence of the Wisdom tradition, the rabbis, and the history of the Church gives ample evidence.[122] In this sense we cannot discern anything revealing in the sociocultural texture.

The logic of James's argument, however, does reveal something of the ideological texture. We have already noted the relatively unusual argument of vv. 11–12. No commandment is cited, although one is surely alluded to: love your neighbor. Nor are the metaphors and analogies about the power and dangers of speech (chapter 3) to be found. Instead James makes two parallel "moves," one in argument and the other in terminology.

---

[121] Richard Lischer, *Open Secrets: A Spiritual Journey through a Country Church* (New York: Doubleday, 2001), pp. 95–102.

[122] The desert fathers and mothers spoke often about slander, comparing it, e.g., (unfavorably!) with fornication and gluttony. See Benedicta Ward, SLG, *The Sayings of the Desert Fathers*, rev. ed. (Kalamazoo, MI: Cistercian Publications, 1984). "He [Abba Matoes] also said 'Satan does not know by what passion the soul can be overcome. He sows, but without knowing what he will reap, sometimes thoughts of fornication, sometimes thoughts of slander, and similarly for the other passions. He supplies nourishment to the passion which he sees the soul is slipping towards'" (p. 143). "He [Abba Hyperechius] also said, 'He who does not control his tongue when he is angry, will not control his passions either.' He also said, 'It is better to eat meat and drink wine and not to eat the flesh of one's brethren through slander'" (p. 238).

The argument unfolds as follows:

Prohibition	Do not speak against one another, brothers/sisters.
Reason	1. The one speaking against a brother/sister
	2. *or* judging their brother/sister
	3. speaks against *and* judges the law.
Result	If you judge the law, you are not a doer of law but a judge.
Affirmation	There is one lawgiver and judge,
	The one who is able to save and destroy.
Indictment	Who are you to judge your neighbor?

Within the argument is a significant shift in terminology. In the prohibition, the one spoken against is slightly distanced, referred to as "one another," while the ones addressed are called brothers/sisters. In the reason for the prohibition the one spoken against or judged becomes the brother/sister, and the one doing the speaking/judging becomes a judge, a title that may only be given to God. In the concluding, sarcastic, indictment comes the major shift. Reference to brother/sister is dropped, as is the opening concern for speaking against. Instead of the expected "Who are you to *speak against* your *brother or sister*?" we find "Who are you to *judge* your *neighbor* [*plēsios*]?" – the latter term found only here and at 2:8, where Lev 19:18 is quoted.

This suggests, I think, a blurring of distinction between brother/sister and neighbor, which itself suggests a blurring of distinction between inside and outside the community, at least insofar as it concerns community practice. And it also suggests the centrality of Lev 19:18, if not the entirety of Lev 19 (Johnson),[123] for James's understanding of community. By making God and God's exclusive role as judge the center of the argument, James places commandment and community in a secondary position. The reason not to speak against another is because to do so is to usurp the role of the only judge, not because it would violate a commandment or harm the community, nor because it might harm a fellow member of the community. Placing God in the center of the argument also, it seems, allows God to serve as a bridge, or at least as a point of contact, between the community and the neighbor.[124]

SACRED AND HOMILETICAL TEXTURES

"There is one lawgiver and judge who is able to save and to destroy." The rhetorical emphasis on "one" in the structure of the sentence has been noted but should be reiterated. James places the word first in the sentence, so that it

---

[123] Luke T. Johnson, "The Use of Leviticus 19 in the Letter of James" *Journal of Biblical Literature* 101 (1982): 391–401.

[124] I am here assuming that James intends some distinction between brother/sister and neighbor by his shift in terminology. The extent to which this depends on Lev 19 is open to debate.

might be literally rendered, "One is the lawgiver and judge, the one able to save and to destroy." James affirms that "God is One" (Deut 6:4; James 2:19) and also claims for God the prerogatives that are God's alone. This affirmation, coupled with the central importance of Lev 19:18, guides the argument of these two verses. We should not speak against others because to do so presumes a standing that is reserved for God and only God. This claim is part of the ideological texture of the letter, but because the claim is theological, the ideological blends into the sacred.

What does it mean to call God "lawgiver" and "judge"? First, it serves to place God at the beginning and end of salvation history, with Moses on Sinai and upon the "mercy seat" at the last day. Second, by reminding the reader that God has power "to save and to destroy," judgment and mercy are lifted up as possibilities (though "mercy triumphs over judgment"; 2:13). Taken together, the reader is chastised for presuming to take God's place, instructed that one should look for judgment to the one who is also the giver of the law, and challenged to rely on the one who is able to destroy or save them.

The homiletical texture of these two verses is treacherous and causes one to raise two questions: (1) How does one preach about/against slander, gossip, and judgmentalism without sounding accusatory and judgmental and perhaps engaging in a little slander? (2) Was James, who earlier in the chapter referred to the readers as "adulterers . . . sinners . . . double-minded," guilty of transgressing his own edict?

The second, first. The answer would seem to be yes, and not just in chapter 4. But this fact, perhaps as much as any other, informs our understanding of what James meant by *katalaleō*, particularizing or distinguishing his usage from the other instances in the biblical tradition and Greek literature. There is a tendency to understand *katalaleō*, as used in Christian teaching, in two ways. The strong form is as "slander" and the mild form as "speak against." In contemporary usage slander is legally actionable defamation and speaking against is criticism or opposition. NRSV, by rendering *katalaleō* as "speaks evil against," holds the possibility of slander and opposition together, despite the absence of any of the Greek words for "evil" (*ponēros, kakos*) in the text.

What tempers all of this is a third question: what if the accusation is true? Then it is neither legally actionable nor unwarranted criticism or opposition. James, whether in these verses, or, for example, those to follow (especially 4:13–16 and 5:1–6), is sharply critical at times. He can be sarcastic, belittling, and belligerent. But if what he says is true, it is not slander; it is shining the light of the Gospel into a dark corner of the life of the community. It is not unwarranted criticism; it is needed reproof and correction.

Here is where the homiletical texture may lead one into temptation and brings us around to the first question. On the one hand, it is possible to hold up 4:11–12 as reason never to offer a critical word to the community and to avoid the need for courageous, prophetic speech when the community or national life cries out for it. On the other hand, it is possible to look at James's own rhetoric as justification for doing precisely what James's command prohibits. But this is much like those who point to Jesus' action in the Temple (Mk 11:12–25 and par.) as justification for their own lack of discipline every time they lose their temper – after all, Jesus got mad, so how can you expect better of me?[125] Such reading and application of vv. 11–12 is indefensible. The preacher must examine the situation, explore his or her own motives, and prayerfully determine what is called for in a given moment. We must neither embrace criticism nor flee from it. Nor should we ever use the pulpit as a place to settle a score or to put someone straight.

JAMES 4:13–17

13 Come now, you who say, "Today or tomorrow we will go to such and such a town and spend a year there, doing business and making money."
14 Yet you do not even know what tomorrow will bring. What is your life? For you are a mist that appears for a little while and then vanishes.
15 Instead you ought to say, "If the Lord wishes, we will live and do this or that."
16 As it is, you boast in your arrogance; all such boasting is evil.
17 Anyone, then, who knows the right thing to do and fails to do it, commits sin.

*A*s discussed in the introductory remarks to chapter 4, the question of the relationship of 4:13–16 to 4:1–12 and 5:1–6 is unresolved. Without doubt the opening expression in 4:13, "Come now" (*age nun*) both signals a shift from 4:12 and links vv. 13–16 with 5:1 ff., which begins the same way. Moreover, the focus on the attitudes and behaviors of merchants and traders in these verses is linked with those of "the rich" (*ho plousioi*) in 5:1 ff. But as we will see, the harshness of James's condemnation in chapter 5 is so much stronger than the warning given in 4:13–16 that it belies easy comparison. And as was argued earlier, the summary exhortation in 4:17 functions to separate 4:13–16 from 5:1, as 1:26–7, 2:26, and 3:18 have in the preceding chapters. Perhaps more than anything the difficulty in determining the contours of the pericopes in chapter 4 gives testimony to the overall unity of the letter. 4:13–17, then, will be treated as the concluding warning of the chapter and the summary reminder recapitulating the link between chapter 4 and chapters 1–3.

INNER TEXTURE AND INTERTEXTURE

13–16. The opening "Come now" (*age nun*), here and at 5:1, rhetorically marks the beginning of the section but does not itself carry any presumption of

---

[125] It is always worth remembering that all four gospels, but especially Mark and John, depict the Temple action as premeditated and nowhere use any of the available words to describe Jesus as "angry" or as "filled with righteous indignation."

condemnation.[126] The use of the singular imperative *age* with the plural *hoi legontes* (you who say) is well attested in Greek literature and is also known in the LXX (e.g., Isa 43:6).[127]

As often before (1:13; 2:3, 16, 18) James expertly captures the speech, and in it the attitude, of those he will oppose in a way that speaks both for and to his audience. In current parlance James examines their "business plan" and finds it wanting. "Today or tomorrow we will go to such and such a town and spend a year there, doing business and making money." The series, all in the first person plural future indicative, has something of the force of the hortatory subjunctive ("let us ..."), and there is some manuscript evidence of a tendency to "correct" the text in this way. In either case, the series is daunting in its self-assurance:

We will go...	*poreuomai*
We will work there one year...	*poieō*
We will trade...	*emporeuomai*
We will make profit	*kerdainō*

It sounds a bit like someone in the late 1990s planning to launch a new technology company – a sure thing! It also sounds a lot like the "rich fool" in Lk 12:17–19.

> 17 "And he thought to himself, 'What should I do, for I have no place to store my crops?' 18 Then he said, 'I will do this: I will pull down my barns and build larger ones, and there I will store all my grain and my goods. 19 And I will say to my soul, 'Soul, you have ample goods laid up for many years; relax, eat, drink, be merry.'"

The difference in the responses of James and Jesus is interesting. Jesus' story continues, "But God said to him, 'You fool! This very night your life is being demanded of you'" (Lk 12:20). James does not have the epithet, but he turns to the same theme, human mortality. "Yet you do not even know what tomorrow will bring. What is your life? For you are a mist that appears for a little while and then vanishes" (v. 14). This response also hearkens back to James's earlier depiction of "the rich" (*ho plouisoi*), who "will disappear like a flower in the field" (1:10) and who "in the midst of a busy life ... will wither away" (1:11). The connections with Lk 12 and James 1 inevitably influence how interpreters view James's attitudes toward the merchants in vv. 13–16, perhaps more than they should.[128] For while James certainly chides those for making such plans when they "do not even know what tomorrow will bring" it is done in a matter-of-fact way, without the harshness of 5:1–6.

---

[126] Contra J. Adamson, *Epistle of James* (1976), p. 178, and P. U. Maynard-Reid, *Poverty and Wealth* (1987), p. 69ff., who is, however, correct about the fatuous nature of the New English Bible (NEB) translation.

[127] See L. T. Johnson, *Letter of James* (1995), pp. 294–5, who cites Homer, Aristophanes, Xenophon, and Epictetus, among others.

[128] The possible identity and activity of the merchant traders James is addressing will be considered in the following section on sociocultural texture.

A CLOSER LOOK — TEXT-CRITICAL ISSUES

V. 14 presents a number of textual problems. First, some manuscripts have, and some lack, a substantivizing definite article before "the morrow," so that it could read "you do not know the things of the morrow" or "you do not know the morrow." Second, some manuscripts include, while others omit, the particle "for" (*gar*) after the interrogative "what?" (*poia*) in the phrase "What is your life?"; other manuscripts have the pronoun in the first person, leading some interpreters to translate the phrase as "What is our life?" — a translation with a very different rhetorical force.[129] Third, the verb "are" in "you are a mist" is found in second person plural and third person singular, "it [life] is a mist," and even in the future tense.

None of these alternatives are particularly significant, and the general thrust of the verse is understood and familiar ("Do not boast about tomorrow, for you do not know what a day may bring"; Prov 27:1). But cumulatively the variants suggest a tension in the verse, despite the familiarity with its central claim, a tension that works on a spectrum from the personal to the more generalized. Is James saying, once again, "all flesh is grass," or is he saying emphatically to *these* merchants that they will disappear like a mist, "that appears for a little while and then vanishes"? The tone and so the choices among variants incline toward the emphatic and thus could be read as, "You are ones who know not what the morrow brings. For what is your life? For you are a mist that appears for a moment and then disappears."

V. 15 suggests a proper attitude and speech in light of mortality, the countercultural (to anticipate the sacred and homiletical textures) "anti"-speech (*anti tou legein humas*): "Instead you ought to say, 'If the Lord wishes, we will live and do this or that.'" Again a hypothetical speech is placed on the tongue of James's readers, and it is not without its own problems, despite having the author's approval. The pattern of the second half of the speech follows that of the speech in v. 13: indefinite designations ("this or that"), future active indicative verbs ("will live and do") with similar "corrections" to hortatory subjunctives in some manuscripts ("let us live and do"). More interesting is the relatively mild affirmation of divine sovereignty over human affairs represented by "If the Lord wishes," the so-called *conditio Jacobaea*, which Dibelius points out is "named after him but is in reality much older."[130] That the saying, in addition to the similar "If God wills" or "if the gods will," predates James and is found in affirmations outside Judeo-Christian sources is indisputable. That James meant the phrase to have some talismanic effect is unimaginable. Nor should the significance of the phrase be dismissed because it has been used to such ends by

---

[129] L. T. Johnson, *Letter of James* (1995), p. 296.
[130] M. Dibelius, *Letter of James* (1975), p. 233.

others. Affirming the centrality of God's will in the life of the believer is as fundamental to Christian faith as the third petition of the Lord's Prayer, "Your will be done" (*genēthetō to thelēma sou*).

"As it is," James finishes – returning the argument to its beginning and again recalling 1:9–10, recasting the speech and attitude of the (hypothetical?) merchants in a significantly less benign way in v. 16 – "you boast in your arrogance; all such boasting is evil." The NRSV "as it is" fails to capture the recapitulation James intends by using *nun de* to parallel the opening *age nun*. The phrase should be rendered, "But now you are boasting" (*kauchaomai* in the present middle indicative, the NRSV losing the sense of continuing action in the present). The following phrase, *en tais alazoneiais humōn*, is difficult to translate. The noun, *alazoneia*, is in the plural, but "arrogances" is confusing in English. The preposition *en* following *kauchaomai* generally renders the object, as in James 1:9 ("Let the believer who is lowly boast in being raised up"; cf. Rom 2:17; 1 Cor 1:31). But who would boast in their own arrogance or pride? Laws is correct to treat the phrase adverbially, as describing the manner of boasting, not that about which one boasts. Moo points out that, "[t]he point of importance here is that 'boasting' is not itself a negative activity or attitude: the question is what it is that one is boasting in (see also 1:9). And so James must qualify the verb to indicate that he uses it to depict a boasting that arises from misplaced pride in one's own ability to chart the future."[131] In any case it is not a pretty picture, nor does James mean it to be, for "all such boasting is evil," only the second use of *ponēros* in the letter; the first was used in describing those who show partiality as "judges with evil thoughts" (2:4).

17. V. 17 is a typical Jacobean summary, reminding the reader that it is the practice that matters and that simply avoiding doing the wrong thing is not enough. Knowing the right thing to do (*poiein*) but failing to do it (*mē poiounti*) is a sin (*hamartia*).

SOCIOCULTURAL AND IDEOLOGICAL TEXTURES

These verses reveal a good deal about the community for and to which James writes, about the values at work, prominent or dominant, in that community, and James's attitude toward both. In this sense it reveals both a greater diversity than is often admitted for the early Church and competing ideologies that are, finally, mutually exclusive. This assumes that "you who say" are members of James's community. Certainly they are members of his intended audience, or at the very least the attitude expressed is present among members of the audience, otherwise the inclusion of the verses makes no sense. To propose that the verses target hypothetical persons who have a hypothetical attitude about a

---

[131] S. Laws, *Epistle of James* (1980), p. 192. D. J. Moo, *Letter of James* (2000), p. 206. Moo goes on to link this attitude with the Greek understanding of *hubris*.

hypothetical trip to engage in hypothetical trade is an inadequate hypothesis. Moreover, there is scant example of NT documents addressing anyone other than real or desired readers, who must have *some* relationship to the addressed community, whether as members, believing visitors, or seekers. "You who say," then, are a part of the community being addressed in the letter (which is not to deny that others might benefit from what James says to them, then and now).

What they say:

Time frame	Today or tomorrow
Travel plan	we will go to
Destination	such and such a city
Duration	spend a year there
Activity	doing business
Goal	making money

As suggested, it looks very much like a model business plan.

Who might be expected to have such a plan? The travel plan and duration indicate that these are not local traders. "The traders envisaged here are not the small-scale business dealers of the local markets . . . but men who make ambitious plans involving movement between cities and looking some way ahead into the future."[132] Such trade requires capital, transportation, and multinational partners, which "those who say" presumably have. The long-held assumption has been that persons of such means were not members of early Christian communities, an assumption I think is mistaken. The first reason has already been stated: it is hard to imagine why James would address someone who would not hear what he had to say. The second reason is offered by Moo. After summarizing James's argument in vv. 13–16 and noting that "James chastises these merchants for failing to look at life from a Christian perspective," Moo concludes, "James would hardly address non-Christians in this way."[133] I concur. The third reason is provided by the overall witness of the NT; there are women with the means to provide for Jesus and the disciples (Lk 8:2–3); another woman, Lydia, is specifically identified as a trader in fine cloth (Acts 16:14); and Paul, by indicating that "not many" (*ou polloi*) of the Corinthians were wise, powerful, or of noble birth, suggests that some in fact were (1 Cor 1:26). I conclude that "you who say" refers to merchants of some means *and* sufficiently connected with James's community as to require some singling out as well as to be expected to respond positively to such admonition.

What, then, about their plans? On paper, the plans look good. But so did the plans of the farmer in Lk 12:18: "'I will do this: I will pull down my barns and build larger ones, and there I will store all my grains and my goods.'" The problem, with merchants and farmer, is ideological and economic. They make their plans as if there is nothing and no one else in the world – the farmer as if

---

[132] S. Laws, *Epistle of James* (1980), pp. 189–90.
[133] D. J. Moo, *Letter of James* (2000), p. 201.

there were no poor who might benefit from his excess; the merchants as if winds never blow ill, or not at all, the roads are always safe, markets are always stable, and so on. Above all, farmer and merchants plan as if there was no possibility that "this very night your life is being demanded of you" (Lk 12:20).

James challenges this ideology with his own: "you are a mist that appears for a little while and then disappears." They make plans for a year in advance, when they "do not even know what tomorrow will bring." In contemporary terms James confronts a thoroughly secular ideology with wisdom from his own tradition and by asking "What is your life?" confronts the plans of worldly merchants with the reality of their own mortality.

SACRED AND HOMILETICAL TEXTURES

Wall describes the orientation of "those who say" as "functional atheism."[134] It is more prevalent today than ever. By bringing something as entangled with the ways of the world as the business plans of a group of merchants under the penetrating question, "What is your life?" James challenges and overturns the very notion of a division between "sacred" and "secular." This is in spite of the distinction earlier in the chapter between "God" and "world." While James's ideology may be dualistic (good/evil) it is not an otherworldly dualism. No understanding of Christian faith that is as focused on practice as James's can afford to compartmentalize existence.

Such compartmentalization is the rule, not the exception, in most corners of the Church today. It is justified in the name of "separation of church and state," evicting faith from the public square and from influence on the decision-making process in many nations. It is justified in the name of "common sense" and "good planning," so that the ethical impulse of faith is excluded from the boardroom and the shop floor.

For the most part, this compartmentalization is found in the pulpit as well. The moral imperatives of the Christian faith are permitted to speak to most aspects of daily life – marriage and family, friendship and neighborliness, human sexuality, compulsions and addictions, and so on – but almost never does the preacher confront the business models and practices of the community or nation. The result? Churchgoing, Sunday-school-teaching corporate executives who systematically defraud, mismanage, and destroy major, multinational businesses. It is impossible to imagine James having no word for Enron's Kenneth Lay or WorldCom's Bernard Ebbers. But it is almost as hard to imagine a preacher who would.

If the Church cannot confront those who "know the right thing to do and fail to do it," what will it say to those we meet in chapter 5?

---

[134] R. W. Wall, *Community of the Wise* (1997), pp. 217–22.

BRIDGING THE HORIZONS — WHEN THE TEXT IS TOUGH

It is one thing to encourage preachers to respond to the challenge of James 4 by challenging their listeners to live as if "the Lord wishes." It is another to offer such a sermon. How does the faithful preacher overcome the resistance of the hearer? Very carefully. More precisely, one should do so intentionally, gradually, and indirectly.

From its opening salvo ("Those conflicts and disputes among you, where do they come from?") to its concluding summary ("Anyone, then, who knows the right thing to do and fails to do it, commits sin"), the fourth chapter of James provides the eager preacher with abundant ammunition. So, what – shoot to kill? Unfortunately it happens; worse, many of us are guilty of firing off a few rounds. The pulpit provides a marvelous vantage point for such blasts; members of the congregation, after all, are sitting all in a row, waiting for a word from the Lord. Why not, "Woe to you!" It is biblical. But is it helpful? Does it build up or does it simply give permission for the preacher to vent frustration at systemic injustices in society, inequitable power dynamics in the community, corporate and individual sin in the congregation, or the less noble things that foster less-than-righteous anger in religious leaders?

Such temptation is to be avoided, for most sermons that attempt a "thus saith the Lord" approach to identifying, reproving, and correcting sin do much harm and little good. To the congregation they sound like pulpit tantrums rather than the intentional, thoughtful, prayerful reflections on the word of God that those in the pew have every right to expect from the one in the pulpit. First, then, calm down, and consider an intentional strategy, over time, for addressing the issues in one's setting that betray "friendship with the world," the tendency to usurp God's responsibility to judge sisters and brothers, or an approach to life and work that denies the limits of mortality and our dependence on God's providence and grace.

Second, after identifying the issue or issues most crying out for homiletical attention, plan to address them gradually. In her book on transformational preaching, Barbara Lundblad suggests strategies that take time, for example, "*moving from the familiar to the strange*" and "*moving from points of lesser to greater resistance.*"[135] A head-on confrontation tends to increase, not lessen, resistance, closing ears and hardening hearts. A gradual approach may seem less "prophetic," but it is likely to be more effective in facilitating openness to change.

Third, following the examples of Jesus and James, consider a strategy of *indirection*, the strategy implied in Lundblad's suggestion and most closely identified with the teaching and preaching of Fred B. Craddock. In his classic 1978 Beecher Lectures published as *Overhearing the Gospel*, Dr. Craddock sharpened the method introduced in his earlier *As One without Authority* "by way of SK" (Sören

---

[135] Barbara Lundblad, *Transforming the Stone: Preaching through Resistance to Change* (Nashville, TN: Abingdon Press, 2001), pp. 53, 55 (emphasis in original).

Kierkegaard).[136] Borrowing from his reading of the parables of Jesus and the writings of Kierkegaard, he suggests the metaphor of "overhearing," understood multivalently, as key to effective communication in our age. Confronted directly, the listener resists. Given time and occasion to ponder, consider, and move with the preacher from situation to conclusion, the listener may well have a Nathan-to-David-like "Thou art the man!" epiphany.

An example of what is suggested in these three moves – intentionally, gradually, and indirectly – will be helpful. Because it is much in the news and little in the pulpit, consider the ethical implications of James 4:13–15, which in its own way models the approach under consideration.

¹³ Come now, you who say, "Today or tomorrow we will go to such and such a town and spend a year there, doing business and making money." ¹⁴ Yet you do not even know what tomorrow will bring. What is your life? For you are a mist that appears for a little while and then vanishes. ¹⁵ Instead you ought to say, "If the Lord wishes, we will live and do this or that."

A direct approach would start with the latest corporate scandal, perhaps one recently viewed on a television "tabloid" or in a news magazine, quote James, and condemn the congregation for failing to do much better. In addition to being ineffective, this fails to heed James's warning in 4:11–12 about being judgmental.

A more intentional, gradual, and indirect approach would be to decide prayerfully, and perhaps in consultation with church staff and leaders, that the question of the implications of Christian faith and practice for work and business was deserving of greater attention. Appropriate adult education offerings might be planned and a sermon series prepared (if one follows the lectionary one will have a different, but not insurmountable, set of planning concerns). The key point is that one does not wake up on Sunday morning and decide that it is time – once and for all is usually the idea – to take a stand against corporate malfeasance. The approach will be gradual in that a foundation is laid, one that invites congregational assent, highlighting the more general ethical implications of the faith and suggesting that our practice is not limited to church and home but touches all parts of our lives. When moving to the more specific issues of faith and work, business ethics, and the like, the strategy of indirection becomes all the more important, allowing the audience to grasp and claim the implications for themselves, as stories unfold, comparisons suggested, and biblical parallels brought into view. Here the likely key will be to invite identification, helping the listeners see the signs and marks of the kind of ethically questionable decisions and practices that are often taken for granted as "the way the world works."

---

[136] F. B. Craddock, *Overhearing the Gospel* (1978) and *As One without Authority*, rev. ed. (Enid, OK: Phillips University Press, 1974).

All this can be done in a single sermon, of course, but will probably be more effective if done collaboratively and over a period of weeks, not minutes.

JAMES 5:1–20 – CRIES, PATIENCE, AND PRAYER: THE LORD IS NEAR

James 5, despite the opinion of those who hold that the work is in no way to be understood as a letter, brings the composition to a coherent, powerful, and in many respects typical epistolary close. There are no farewell greetings, doxology, or benediction, endings customary in many NT epistles (Rom 16; 2 Tim 4:19ff.; 1 Pet 5:12ff.; Jude 24–5), though by no means in all (cf. 1 Jn 5). However, the chapter is replete with warnings, admonitions, and instructions, as is common in the closing chapters of other letters (Phi 4; Tit 3), and the chapter as a whole is interested in eschatological concerns, bringing to focus issues only touched upon earlier in the letter, something we also see in other epistles (e.g., 2 Pet 3).

James 5 is above all a fitting conclusion to chapters 1–4. Much as chapter 1 states in concise, introductory fashion the predominant concerns of the letter – patient endurance in trial (vv. 1–4, 12–15), prayer (vv. 5–6), rich and poor (vv. 9–11), right and wrong use of the tongue (vv. 19–20, 26), and the practice of faith (vv. 22–5), so chapter 5 reprises and summarizes most of those same concerns – rich and poor (vv. 1–6), patient endurance in trial (vv. 7–8, 10–11), right and wrong use of the tongue (vv. 9a, 12), prayer and forgiveness (vv. 13–18), right judgment (v. 9b), and the efficacious practice of faith (vv. 19–20).

From this summary it is easy to see that as was the case in chapter 1, determining the boundary for each pericope in chapter 5 is difficult. The case for making a division between 4:13–16, 17 and 5:1–6 was made in the last chapter and will only be reinforced by what is found in our reading of the latter passage in this chapter. And while there is a clear break between vv. 1–6 and 7–11, there is also a clear and important connection, as James moves from denouncing the rich to encouraging the brothers and sisters, a group that likely included those oppressed by the rich, to be patient. How to treat the remaining verses (12–20) is the problem. V. 12 can easily be treated by itself, yet the treatment of what not to say (oaths) is followed by what to say (prayers, praise, and confession), providing an obvious connection between v. 12 and vv. 13–18. This leaves the final two verses, closing instructions on a faith practice not previously mentioned ("returning" a wandering brother/sister), which can "cover a multitude of sins." Not the most satisfying epistolary ending, to be sure, but certainly in keeping with the tone of the letter as a whole.

It is no surprise then that commentators, and most likely their editors, are divided on how to group these verses. I will follow the pattern of Laws, Johnson, and others and treat vv. 7–11 and vv. 12–20 as rhetorical units. But first we will

James 5:1–20 – Cries, Patience, and Prayer: The Lord Is Near

examine in considerable detail James's final and dramatic words for rich and poor.

JAMES 5:1–6

The concluding and summarizing nature of 4:17, as well as the way in which it followed the pattern of summarizing verses in the first three chapters of James, is a significant reason to see a break between 4:13–16 and 5:1–6. In what follows we will see the other compelling reasons: a dramatic change in tone, a likely change in audience, and a probable shift in the anticipated outcome from repentance (4:13–16) to punishment (5:1–6).

1 Come now, you rich people, weep and wail for the miseries that are coming to you.
2 Your riches have rotted, and your clothes are moth-eaten.
3 Your gold and silver have rusted, and their rust will be evidence against you, and it will eat your flesh like fire. You have laid up treasure for the last days.
4 Listen! The wages of the laborers who mowed your fields, which you kept back by fraud, cry out, and the cries of the harvesters have reached the ears of the Lord of hosts.
5 You have lived on the earth in luxury and in pleasure; you have fattened your hearts in a day of slaughter.
6 You have condemned and murdered the righteous one, who does not resist you.

This is without doubt the strongest, harshest passage in the letter, surpassing even the warnings about the dangers of the tongue in chapter 3. It is also the passage with perhaps the thickest intertexture, virtually every noun and verb resonating throughout the biblical tradition. Throughout these verses also rings a series of sociocultural and ideological questions. Who were these "rich," and where did they get their money? Were they members of James's community? Does James intend any hope for them? And there are finally, for the honest and open reader, an equally significant series of questions about sacred and homiletical textures. Where do I fit in this picture? Where does my community of faith fit, and how should this text be shared with the members of that community? To each in turn.

INNER TEXTURE AND INTERTEXTURE

1. "Come now" James begins, echoing his own summons in 4:13 and the cry of the prophets, for example, Isa 1:18, although Isaiah uses *deute* (LXX) instead of *age*. Such a prophetic summons to judgment (cf. Hos 5:1, Amos 4:1; 5:1) warns James's audiences – and as we will see they are definitely plural – to prepare for strong words.

The use of the vocative, "you rich" (*hoi plousioi*), introduces the direct address found in the entire passage and also the accusatory tone that courses through the verses, immediately seeming to carry a sharper edge than the "you who say" in 4:13. The identity and character of "the rich" will be explored in the following section, but we will learn much about them in the following verses. Their wealth is in the form of clothing (v. 3), gold and silver (v. 4), and land (v. 5). They live in luxury (v. 6) and have stored up wealth (v. 3). In this verse we learn what James believes the future has in store for them.

"Weep and wail for the miseries that are coming to you." The aorist imperative *klausate* (weep) is followed by an absolute participle with marvelous onomatopoeia, *ololuzontes* (wailing), with the force of the imperative. They are to weep and wail because of the miseries (*talaipōriais*) that await them. The commands echo 4:9, where the readers were challenged to "Lament" (*talaipōrēsate*), "mourn" (*penthesate*), and "weep" (*klausate*) as symbol of repentance. Here the sense is "weep and wail" now because you will soon suffer misery. "Wail" (LXX *ololuzete*), says Isaiah, "for the day of the Lord is near" (Isa 13:6). As Moo and Johnson point out, the LXX "uses the verb exclusively in the context of laments in response to the disasters visited on the people by Yahweh for apostasy," both scholars citing Isaiah (10:10; 13:6; 14:31; 15:2–3; 16:7; 23:1, 6, 14; 24:11; 52:5; 65:14), Jeremiah (2:23; 31:20, 31), Ezekiel (21:17), Hosea (7:14), Amos (8:3), and Zechariah (11:2).[137] This is, interestingly, the only use in the NT (although Mk 5:38 uses the synonym *alalazō*).

2–3. In these verses we learn why the rich should weep, if not now, then soon. The tenses of the verbs are significant. The first three, which describe the fate of the materials, are in the perfect, implying that rot, moth, and rust "have done" their work, and the emphasis is on the impact of the destruction. This, of course, would only be for those with eyes to see, for on the surface the materials may look fine. James could be signaling in his choice of tense his awareness that the riches will not last.[138]

A CLOSER LOOK — JAMES'S USE OF THE GREEK TENSE

The sequence of verbs in vv. 2–3 shows a sophisticated use of the various Greek verb tenses to add rhetorical emphasis:

1. your wealth (*ploutos*) has rotted	perfect
2. your garments have become moth-eaten	perfect
3. your gold and your silver have rusted	perfect
4. their rust will witness against you	future
5. and will eat your flesh like fire	future
6. you treasured up in the last days	aorist

---

[137] D. J. Moo, *Letter of James* (2000), p. 211, and L. T. Johnson, *Letter of James* (1995), pp. 298–9 (quote).

[138] P. H. Davids, *Epistle of James* (1982), p. 115.

The first three describe what has (as good as) happened to that upon which the status of the rich is based – rot and moth and rust have already begun, if not completed, their work – but the emphasis in the perfect is on the present effects of the past action. The rhetorical effect is to claim that the goods of the rich are as good as ruined, and by the turn to the future tense the rich are warned that as bad as the loss of their riches might be, something worse is coming, all summed up in the aorist.

James knew perfectly well that gold and silver do not rust, just as he knew that gold and silver were no defense against the ravages of time and the inevitability of death. He was all-encompassing in his assay of the property of the rich, using the generic term for wealth (*ploutos*), specifying apparel (*to himatios*), gold (*chrusos*), and silver (*arguros*) in vv. 2–3 and land in vv. 4–5. The depiction of judgment could hardly be more dramatic, colorful, or compelling.

James seemed to have had the tradition in mind when talking about the fate of these possessions. Jesus speaks of "laying up treasures" (*thēsaurizō*) where "moth and rust" (*sēs* and *brōsis*, not *ios*) do not destroy. In Deut 29:5 the people of Israel are reminded that their clothes (*LXX ta himatia*) did not wear out. Most interestingly, Sirach writes of "losing" (*apollumi*) one's silver on account of a "brother/sister" (*adelphos*) or "friend" (*philos*) rather than letting it rust (*iōthētō*) under a stone and continues, "Lay up your treasure according to the commandments of the Most High, and it will profit you more than gold. Store up almsgiving in your treasury, and it will rescue you from every disaster" (Sir 29:10–12).

The rich have not done so. They have hoarded their wealth, and now (a prophetic "now") the rust and rot of that wealth testifies to their greed. Intertextuality may explain "their rust will be evidence against you." Would that we had such help in understanding the second half of the sentence, "eat your flesh like fire." The individual pieces are clear enough: "eat" is another way to say "corrode" (thus *brōsis* in Mt 6:19–20 means "rust" but in Lk 24:41 and elsewhere in the NT, it means "food"), and the "fire" is surely the fire of eternal judgment (Jude 7, 23). The sense seems to be "as rust 'eats' their gold and silver so will the fire of judgment eat their flesh." But the Greek says that it is the "rust" that will eat their flesh, like or in the manner of fire, not that the fire will eat their flesh. Efforts to emend or repunctuate the sentence are unavailing, nor are the idea of fire as purifying (Sir 2:5 and 1 Pet 1:7) and the fact that *ios* means "poison" in 3:8 helpful.[139]

The confusion carries over into the end of v. 3, "You have laid up treasure for the last days" (NRSV). Wall understands this to be the beginning of a new

---

[139] So L. T. Johnson, *Letter of James* (1995), p. 300. The most elaborate attempt at solving the puzzle by emending the text was offered by J. H. Ropes, *Critical and Exegetical Commentary* (1916), p. 287.

thought in four phrases, from v. 3c to v. 5a ("you have lived on the earth in luxury and in pleasure"), a suggestion undermined by the shift to the specific indictment against the rich in v. 4, signaled by the hortatory "Listen!" (*Idou*). Laying up treasure is clear enough (Mt 6:19–20), and the NRSV tries to help matters by translating the Greek *en* as "for," which it rarely means and probably does not mean here. James meant "in the last days" in the fullest eschatological sense, the sense that pervades the entire chapter, if not the whole letter, and the sense James had of the time he was living in: the last days, when "the coming of the Lord is near" (v. 8) and the judge is "standing at the doors" (v. 9). Here he condemns the rich for living in "the last days" (*en eschatais hēmerais*; cf. Acts 2:17; Jn 6:39–40; 12:48; 2 Tim 3:1) but nevertheless living as if they had all the time in the world and their judgment was not near.

4–6. Listen! (*Idou*), a favorite word for James, especially in this chapter (3:4, 5; 5:4, 7, 9, 11) and many other NT writers (especially Matthew and Luke), the expression serves to "enliven a narrative" and to "introduce something new."[140] Here it introduces a shift away from describing what awaits the rich to the specific actions for which they are being judged. Intended or not, there is also a shift of presumption, from a sense that the crime or sin of the rich is their wealth to indictment for particular acts of oppression and abuse. There are four charges against the rich in these verses:

1. Holding back (or defrauding) wages from workers.
2. Living in luxury and pleasure.
3. Fattening their own hearts for slaughter.
4. Condemning and murdering "the righteous one."

The first and fourth charge pertain to wrong done to others, the third wrong done to themselves, and the second a more general and relative wrong. Attention naturally tends to focus on the first and fourth, but each deserves examination.

"Wages," says James, "cry out." Stones "cry out" against those who "get evil gain for their houses" (Hab 2:11), and Jesus tells the Pharisees the stones will "shout" if his disciples were silent (Lk 19:40). Using a different Greek word (*boaō*), the blood of Abel is "crying out" from the ground (Gen 4:10). In important times and unjust situations even inanimate objects call to God.

More important for James is whose wages these were. He names two groups, workers (*ergatos*) and harvesters (*therisavtos*), the latter group redolent with eschatological significance but both to be understood as farm laborers. The manuscript tradition is not uniform in its choice of verb to describe what the rich have done to these workers. Two similar verbs, with fairly similar meanings, are found in the tradition. *Apostereō* (perfect participle *apesterēmenos*) means

---

[140] *A Greek-English Lexicon of the New Testament and Other Early Christian Literature*, 2d ed., W. Arndt, F. W. Gingrich, and F. Danker, from Walter Bauer's 5th ed. (Chicago: University of Chicago Press, 1979), pp. 370–1.

"defraud," while *aphustereō* (perfect participle *aphusterēmenos*) is found less frequently and means "withhold." Johnson follows Metzger in reading "defraud," or with the NRSV "kept back by fraud," while Laws opts for the less pointed "held back."[141] Given the tone of James's indictment the stronger verb probably makes more sense, which renders the other possibility the more difficult, and thus preferred, reading.

The charge of "holding back" wages specifically recalls another verse from Lev 19: "you shall not keep for yourself the wages of a laborer until morning" (Lev 19:13). On the face of it this is a markedly specific command, one that comes on the heels of commands not to "defraud the neighbor" or "steal," which places "holding back" in the same category. The seriousness of the charge and the desperate situation of day laborers in first-century Palestine, will be considered in the next section. For now this should be kept in mind when we look at v. 6. That the sin is a serious one is underscored by the final phrase in v. 4, "the cries of the harvesters have reached the ears of the Lord of hosts" (*kyrios sabaōth*), the only independent use of this common OT expression in the NT (Rom 9:29 quotes Isa 1:9), which "emphasizes God's power to act."[142]

The middle charges, v. 5, are less compelling (lived in luxury and pleasure) and slightly confusing (fattened your hearts for the day of slaughter). This luxurious living is *epi tēs gēs* (on the earth), an expression perhaps intended to emphasize again the temporal nature of life. That this living is understood to be indolent and heedless of others seems underscored by the phrase, "you have fattened [*trephō*] your hearts [*kardia*] in a day of slaughter [*en hēmera sphagēs*]." The day in question is surely the same as that at the end of v. 3, and James is claiming that the "day" is nigh, if not present. The image of fattening one's own heart to be slaughtered highlights a double-heedlessness. At a time when James has called for voluntary misery as a sign of repentance (4:9), the rich have chosen the opposite, a self-indulging luxury that renders them like fatted calves ready for slaughter.

The last charge is the most serious and the most elusive. "You have condemned [*katadikazō*] and murdered [*phoneuō*] the righteous one." Who was this righteous one (*ho dikaios*), who "does not resist you" (*ouk antitassetai humin*)? Tradition (Oecumenius, Bede) and one reading of "does not resist you" suggests that it was Jesus. Those who hold that this letter was written by disciples of James suggest that it was James himself.[143] Such specificity, however, is not required by the verse.

---

[141] L. T. Johnson, *Letter of James* (1995), p. 302; B. Metzger, *Textual Commentary on the Greek NT* (1994), p. 614; S. Laws, *Epistle of James* (1980), p. 201.
[142] L. T. Johnson, *Letter of James* (1995), p. 303.
[143] "It cannot be coincidental that ὁ δίκαιος became the standard designation by which James was known to posterity; and we may offer the submission that 5:6 is a tribute paid to the historical James whose martyrdom is recalled by his followers who in turn look on themselves as part of the afflicted and righteous remnant. R. Martin, *James* (1988), p. 182.

First, there is ample evidence in the tradition indicting some, including the rich, for killing "the righteous." "The wicked watch for the righteous [*ton dikaion*] and seek to kill them" (Psa 37:32; LXX 36:32). "It was for the sins of her prophets and the iniquities of her priests, who shed the blood of the righteous [*diakion*] in the midst of her" (Lam 4:13). "[T]hey sell the righteous [*dikaion*] for silver, and the needy for a pair of sandals" (Amos 2:6). Second, as we will see in the section to follow, the consequences of defrauding workers of their wages were dramatic enough to warrant this additional charge. Third, understood from the perspective of the workers, the exploitation necessary to acquire sufficient property to become "rich" may be described as "murder."

The indictment is a serious one. Unlike other passages, filled with the rhetorical questions and hypothetical responses of the diatribe, no response is allowed or given, perhaps because, as far as James was concerned, there was no more to be said. The "rich" were condemned by their actions. We turn now to consideration of who the rich might have been for James and then to consideration of who the rich are today.

SOCIOCULTURAL AND IDEOLOGICAL TEXTURES

The prophet Isaiah wrote, 800 years or so before James was written, "Ah, you who join house to house, who add field to field, until there is room for no one but you, and you are left to live alone in the midst of the land" (Isa 5:8). Elsa Tamez wrote, 1,900 or so years after James was written, "In our day the oppression has intensified. Salaries are very low and often withheld. Racial and sexual discrimination is common. Who can deny that the *ptōchos*, the poor, are many in Latin America?"[144] The more things change, the more they stay the same. Jesus said, "You always have the poor with you, and you can show kindness to them whenever you wish" (Mk 14:7). What about the rich? Are they always with us, and what can we do with or to them? In looking at 1:9–11 and 2:1–8, we sketched an understanding of rich and poor in ancient Mediterranean cultures. It is time to complete that picture.

In chapter 2 we began this sketch by pointing to three realities of ancient Mediterranean cultures generally: (1) there was extreme socioeconomic stratification; (2) a relatively fixed, and limited, amount of goods were available for consumption; (3) the vast majority (eighty to ninety percent) of people living in such cultures were by any standard poor, and for many subsistence was a daily struggle. In this section we will develop the significance of these realities with additional insights from cultural anthropology and social-scientific critics that will help us better appreciate the social-scientific texture of 5:1–6.

Surprising as it may be to many in our social location, not all people in all times and places have shared the priorities widely held in North America and Western

---

[144] E. Tamez, *Scandalous Message of James* (1990), p. 78.

Europe today. Without wishing to sound judgmental, it is impossible not to mention the emphasis on personal physical comfort and an ever-increasing consumption of material goods prevalent in society. That serious debate could even take place over the contemporary maxim "greed is good" would stun most everyone in the ancient Mediterranean world, not just the members of James's community. Without belaboring points better discussed in material devoted to the topic,[145] our understanding of 5:1–6 will be aided by further consideration of the dynamic of an honor/shame culture, patron/client relationships, the impact of limited goods on daily life in antiquity, all enabling us to offer clearer identification of "rich" and "poor" in James.

Two of the primary social values in antiquity were honor and its correlate, shame. Both honor and shame were positive values. Honor

stands for a person's rightful place in society, a person's social standing. This honor position is marked off by boundaries consisting of power, gender status, and location on the social ladder. From a functionalist point of view, honor is the value of a person in his or her own eyes plus the value of that person in the eyes of his or her social group. Honor is a claim to worth along with the social acknowledgment of worth. The purpose of honor is to serve as a sort of social rating which entitles a person to interact in specific ways with his or her equals, superiors, and subordinates, according to the prescribed cultural cues of the society.

Shame in this context refers to a person's sensitivity to what others think, say, and do with regard to his or her honor.[146]

Honor was ascribed to individuals on all levels of the socioeconomic pyramid described in chapter 2, not just to those at the top. The preservation of honor and sensitivity to dishonoring, an appropriate sense of shame, were important to all, from peasant to emperor. Furthermore, honorable relationships were possible not only between members of the same social class but across and between all classes.

One of the primary ways by which such honorable relationships could be maintained across social classes was recognition (and manipulation) of the patron/client relationship. In its simplest form this relationship described the boundaries of dealings between persons of unequal social class in a way that recognized the difference without shaming – the client does not ask for more than the patron can provide (e.g., a day's work), and the patron provides what it is expected by society (a day's wage). Theologically, in the letter of James, God is the patron "who gives to all generously and ungrudgingly" (1:5), the reader is the client who is to "ask in faith, never doubting" (1:6) and having received "every perfect gift" (1:17) is to be "quick to listen, slow to speak, slow to anger" (1:19). The patron/client relationship is reciprocal, each having responsibilities. Practically,

---

[145] See the references in the Suggested Reading list under "Sociocultural Texture."
[146] B. J. Malina, *New Testament World* (1993), pp. 54–5.

when one member of the community sees a brother or sister in need and responds only with a blessing, "Go in peace; keep warm and eat your fill" (2:16), that person has failed in his or her obligations, and the shame is on him or her.

Maintaining one's honor was perhaps of heightened import because materially most of the people in antiquity had so little. We might glibly say, "All I have is my good name," while that could be close to literally true for others. The primary way in which one maintained one's honor was not by getting ahead but by retaining the honor one inherited from one's ancestors. Ancient Mediterranean society was a society of limited goods, which was referred to in chapter 2 as a "zero-sum society." That is, the amount of wealth available was fixed, not ever-expanding (due to gains in productivity, e.g.) as we understand it today. This meant two things. First, it was somewhere between extremely difficult and impossible to in fact get ahead in any economically meaningful sense. There was little or no excess capacity (e.g., unused arable land) available, discoveries to be made, or increases in productivity to be achieved. And if there were, the economic system was designed to ensure that only the elites (at most, the top five percent, more likely the top one or two) benefited. Second, those who did get ahead did so at the expense of others and at the cost of their own honor. "By and large, only the dishonorable rich, the dishonorable non-elites, and those beyond the pale of public opinion (such as city elites, governors, and regional kings) could accumulate wealth with impunity."[147] Taxation consumed more than fifty percent of production, perhaps more than two-thirds if various Temple taxes were paid.[148] With land also unevenly distributed (a handful of elite families controlled the majority of arable land), those who farmed were condemned to small plots and meager incomes. The only way to get ahead was not to work hard but to work the system. "In preindustrial societies, profit and gain normally refer to something that accrues to a person by fraud or extortion, that is, something other than wages, customary rent, reciprocal lending, or direct sale from producer to consumer."[149]

Zaccheus (Lk 19) is a well-known example. There were also, apparently, examples among those known to, if not members of, the community to and for which James wrote. This is shown, I think, on two levels. When some in the community show favoritism to the well attired and shunt those in ragged clothing to a spot on the floor, they have "dishonored the poor" (*ētimasate ton ptōchon*, 2:6). As noted, if they fail to provide for the physical needs of another, they have shamed themselves by not fulfilling their obligations. The merchants in 4:13–16 bring dishonor on themselves by failing to acknowledge their dependency on the benevolence (patronage) of God. All of this, I think, is imaginable within community, and James's rebukes are meant to call the community back to a sense of its own place (honor) and responsibility.

---

[147] Ibid., p. 104.
[148] K. C. Hanson and D. E. Oakman, *Palestine* (1998), p. 113ff.
[149] B. J. Malina, *New Testament World* (1993), p. 105.

The same cannot be said for the verbal assault on "the rich" in 5:1–6. These rich either always have been or have at some point placed themselves outside the life and practice of the community. But they are known to the community. How well known it is not possible to say, but they either never have been or are not now members of the community. This condemnation of the rich, particularly as offered in full eschatological significance in 5:1–6 and entirely in the tradition of Isaiah, Amos, Hosea, and Jesus, is offered here for the "benefit" of the victims. The immediate turn to words of consolation in v. 7 ("Be patient, therefore, beloved, until the coming of the Lord") underscores the point. Whereas "the rich" in chapters 1, 2, and 4 most likely heard and understood the words of James as addressed to them from within community, the rich oppressors of chapter 5 did not. The poor oppressed, however, did hear and were intended to be encouraged and comforted by the promised judgment and the coming reversal at the coming of the Lord.

That is not all they were expected to hear, however. There was a warning for the poor as well, a warning that likely traces back to those of 4:1–3. In chapter 4 the community was chastised for conflicts that grew from unfulfilled desires, desires for what would be "spent on our passions" (4:3). In chapter 5 James depicts those whose desires were "fulfilled," who now live "in luxury and in pleasure." Condemnation of them is stronger than that of the "adulterers" in chapter 4. Perhaps James is also saying "be careful what you ask for, because you might get it!"

The condemnation highlights the loss of honor, particularly if one appreciates the metaphorical significance of the gold, silver, and wealth of the rich, now spoiled, as the fading of hopes, dreams, and desires, of life itself. We tend to read everything in crassly economic terms, as if individual prosperity was all that matters (Lk 12:15). It was not this way in James's day. Kinship, village, and community – the group – were valued as much as or more than the individual, and maintaining one's honor was critically important. There was no shame in being materially destitute. If anything, the dishonorable status was to be rich.

SACRED AND HOMILETICAL TEXTURES

The famous line in the movie *Taxi Driver* could well be adapted for the contemporary reader of James 5:1–6: "Are you talkin' to me?" We hope not, but James is. The very act of holding this book in your hand, whether purchased (via your access to the Internet?) or borrowed from a library (to which you also have access), coupled with your ability to read it, marks you, on most any international standard, as among the rich. There is no need to rehearse the statistics of national and individual per capita gross domestic product (GDP) and gross national income (GNI) by nation (go to the World Bank's website for all the information you could ever want). We are rich. What are we going to do about it?

Of course, we will try to avoid cheating our employees (or stockholders, like Enron, WorldCom, etc.). And we would never "condemn and murder the righteous one." But we may be fooling ourselves by concentrating on the obvious felonies while hoping no one will notice the everyday misdemeanors. Sondra Wheeler, author of *Wealth as Peril and Obligation*, has noticed:

> In view of the seriousness of the charges of judicial murder (5:6) and fraudulent labor practices that amount to stealing bread from the poor (5:4), perhaps the severity of the promised judgment upon them comes as no surprise. But we are not accustomed to think of the other two charges as properly crimes at all; while most people regard charitable giving as praiseworthy, few regard its absence as culpable, much less actually punishable. Similarly, although some might find fault with the judgment or even the taste of those who live in luxury, few would treat their self-gratification as a serious offense. In general, even those within the church regard the disposal of income beyond what is needed to meet basic financial obligations as a matter of individual choice, and any material "lifestyle" that can be supported as morally acceptable.[150]

Damnation by bad taste or conspicuous consumption? Probably not. But a free ride from the pulpit? All too often.

NT scholar Craig Blomberg has also noticed, and presses us to consider, the wider implications of these verses for both our own choices and public policy:

> In light of the numerous Two-Thirds World countries today, not least in Latin America, in which vast tracts of land are owned by a handful of wealthy people or, in many instances, large multi-national corporations that fail to pay decent wages to their labourers, would-be Christians need to reflect long and hard on this passage in James. To what extent do we tacitly endorse such injustice by our purchases from such companies, often without even being aware of their practices, or by supporting politicians who promise tax cuts for the upper and middle classes, when programmes helping the needy at home and abroad are slashed in the process and not likely to be replaced by private-sector equivalents.[151]

Throughout this commentary we have argued that what matters is the practice. For James talk is cheap. On one level this includes the talk of homily and sermon. On another, more fundamental level, however, the proclamation of the Gospel is very much a central practice. For that practice to be fulfilled it must faithfully and consistently confront the inconsistencies and hypocrisies that undermine the witness of the Church.

The sacred and homiletical textures of James are very much of a piece. What James reveals to us about God, about faith in God, and about proclamation of that faith is demanding and should yield demanding sermons. Unless those sermons are matched by the personal and corporate practice of the proclaimer and the community of faith, however, the message of James has been lost. The

---

[150] Sondra Wheeler, *Wealth as Peril and Obligation: The New Testament on Possessions* (Grand Rapids, MI: Eerdmans, 1995), p. 105.

[151] Craig L. Blomberg, *Neither Poverty nor Riches: A Biblical Theology of Material Possessions* (Grand Rapids, MI: Eerdmans, 1999), p. 158.

implications of this for our material consumption, charitable giving, volunteer commitments, and political choices is every bit as real as it is for our sermon topics. Or we had best keep silent.

JAMES 5:7–11

7 Be patient, therefore, beloved, until the coming of the Lord. The farmer waits for the precious crop from the earth, being patient with it until it receives the early and the late rains.
8 You also must be patient. Strengthen your hearts, for the coming of the Lord is near.
9 Beloved, do not grumble against one another, so that you may not be judged. See, the Judge is standing at the doors!
10 As an example of suffering and patience, beloved, take the prophets who spoke in the name of the Lord.
11 Indeed we call blessed those who showed endurance. You have heard of the endurance of Job, and you have seen the purpose of the Lord, how the Lord is compassionate and merciful.

James follows his sharp denunciation of the rich with words of consolation to the wider community. This pattern, often referred to as "afflicting the comfortable and comforting the afflicted" is very much in keeping with the classical prophets, from Amos to Zechariah, and was certainly a part of the teaching of Jesus. The verses are clearly a unit, although the place of v. 9 within the pericope is often questioned. Johnson considered 5:7–11 sufficiently important to merit designation as one of the eight sections making up the letter as a whole.

Most interpreters note the thematic connection between these verses and 1:9–12 and have, at least since Francis in 1970,[152] understood the passage as part of a rhetorical framing device (with 1:2–12), introducing and closing the main body of the letter, with 1:1 and 5:12–20 opening and closing the letter proper.[153] Certainly 5:7–11 revisits the theme of patient endurance, so important to the opening verses of the letter, and both use pastoral images to illustrate points, but beyond that the connections are slight, and as we will see our verses relate more clearly to 5:1–6, standing on their own as a call to endurance, while vv. (12) 13–20 serve as the true closing verses of the letter. Hypotheses of a double-framing, one to the letter and one to the main body of the letter are not finally persuasive.

---

[152] Fred O. Francis, "Form and Function of the Opening and Closing Paragraphs of James and 1 John" *Zeitschrift für die neutestamentliche Wissenschaft* 70 (1970): 110–26.
[153] So, e.g., R. W. Wall, *Community of the Wise* (1997), pp. 248–73.

INNER TEXTURE AND INTERTEXTURE

7–8. After the harshness of vv. 1–6 and the challenges of 4:13–16, James again addresses the reader as "beloved" (*adelphoi*). The section begins with an exhortation to patience, "Be patient, therefore" (*makrothumēsate, oun*), and both words are important. The particle *oun* signifies a shift in topic or place in the argument. Those who read v. 7 as the beginning of the conclusion of the letter (or the main body of the letter) see the *oun* as relating to the whole of the letter, "I take it that the author does not intend to draw a conclusion from 5:1–6 alone, but for his entire composition."[154] This seems an overreading of a simple word and an underreading of the link between 5:1–6 and 7–11. As we will see later in this chapter, the opening of v. 12 offers a more decisive turn toward the letter's conclusion.

James's vocabulary in vv. 7–11, beginning with the choice of *makrothumeō*, has occasioned much comment. As Johnson notes, "James' choice of words is puzzling."[155] The choice also undermines Wall's thesis of an *inclusio* on the topos "patience" between 1:2–12 and 5:7–11, because James does not use the same terms in chapters 1 and 5. In 1:2–4 the reader is encouraged to "consider it nothing but joy" when facing trials because these will produce "endurance" (*hupomonē*). In 5:11 we will encounter the same term. But in 5:7, 8, and 11 James will call for "patience" using the verb *makrothumeō* and the noun *makrothumia*. Laws notes, "the verb *makrothumeō* denotes a patient waiting rather than an active endurance of suffering, for which (although the verbs are to some extent synonymous) *hupmoneō* would be the usual expression."[156] More precisely, while the terms cluster around the same family of meaning, they do not mean the same thing. NT usage suggests *makrothumeō* is used to describe the attitude we are to have in our dealings with persons (1 Th 5:14; 1 Cor 13:4), while *hupomoneō* is used for the attitude required when confronting difficult situations (Rom 5:3–4 cf. James 1:3–4; Rev 2:2–3). As Moo phrases it, "Or, to put it simply, we are *patient* with other people and *endure* difficulties."[157] This does not mean the terms are mutually exclusive, for they can and do occur side by side, for example, Col 1:11, "may you be prepared to endure everything with patience" (*pasan hupomonēn kai makrothumian*). It does suggest that the emphasis in vv. 7–8, in relation to vv. 1–6, is in response to the people whose actions and eventual fate is described in the earlier verses, and to waiting for their imminent judgment.[158] This reading is supported by two features in the passage: the pastoral image used to illustrate

---

[154] Ibid., p. 251.
[155] L. T. Johnson, *Letter of James* (1995), p. 312.
[156] S. Laws, *Epistle of James* (1980), p. 208.
[157] D. J. Moo, *Letter of James* (2000), p. 222.
[158] Martin's suggestion that the verses may be meant to discourage those who may be thinking of taking the law into their own hands and murdering the rich is fanciful (*James* [1988], p. 191).

patience (v. 7b) and the emphasis on the imminence of the coming judgment (vv. 8, 9). Just as the condemnation of v. 4 echoed the parable of the Laborers in the Vineyard (Mt 20:1 ff.), the agricultural image in v. 7 recalls the parable usually referred to as the Seed Growing Secretly in Mk 4:26–9, a story with vocabulary (earth, fruit, harvest) and rhythms ("sleep and rise night and day"), as well as a basic attitude that the growth and fruit are provided, not earned, much like v. 7.

The textual problem in v. 7 is fairly straightforward: the best Greek manuscripts do not include the word "rain" (*huetos*) after "the early and the late" (*proïmon kai opsimon*). Later traditions, East and West, provide the word, and a few insert "fruit" (*karpon*) instead, but because the addition of one or the other noun is easier to explain than its omission, the word "rain" is only to be inferred. The extent to which this provides evidence of a Palestinian provenance will be considered in the next section.

As the farmer is patient so also should be the reader. Moreover, the readers should "strengthen" (*stēriksate*) their hearts (*kardia*) because "the coming of the Lord is near" (*hē parousia tou kuriou ēngiken*). However one decides to understand the fattened hearts of v. 5, the strengthened hearts of v. 8 are surely opposite (Wall). Laws points out that the call to patience and for strengthened hearts suggests crisis, while the metaphor of the patient farmer and use of *makrothumeō* suggest the ordinary waitings of daily life.[159] While Laws did not offer this, and the supposition may well be a "reading into" the text, it seems to me that the tension present here in terminology, metaphor, and situation are part and parcel of James's eschatology. This brings us to "the coming of the Lord."

That *parousia* can mean the ordinary arrival or presence of any person is well documented (see 1 Cor 16:17; 2 Cor 7:6–7). That the term is also generally used as a technical term in the NT for the second coming of Christ (Mt 24:37, 39; 1 Th 2:19; 3:13; 4:15; 5:23; 2 Th 2:1, 8; 2 Pet 1:16; 3:4; 1 Jn 2:28), and is so used here, is generally agreed upon (Laws, Johnson, Martin, Moo, Wall). The eschatological stakes are raised by James in the claim that the parousia "is near" (*ēngiken*), a claim recalling Jesus' proclamation of the coming of the kingdom of God (Mk 1:15 and par.) and James's own call to "draw near" (*engisate*) to God in 4:8.

9. Dibelius objects that the warning in v. 9 "disrupts the continuity" and that attempts to relate the groaning/grumbling implied in the admonition to the oppression of vv. 1–6 are "only psychological possibilities which do not explain the juxtaposition of these imperatives."[160] He has a point, up to a point. I will leave it to others to defend the worthiness of the "psychological" relation of

---

[159] S. Laws, *Epistle of James* (1980), p. 210.
[160] M. Dibelius, *Letter of James* (1975), p. 242 and note 2 on 242–3.

oppression and grumbling.¹⁶¹ I note the following in support of the relation of v. 9 to vv. 7–8 and 10–11: (1) the assonance of "strengthen" (*stēriksate*) and "grumble" (*stenazete*); (2) the use of *adelphoi* in vv. 7, 9, and 10; (3) the heightened eschatological awareness in vv. 8 ("the coming of the Lord is near") and 9 ("the Judge is standing at the doors").

The verb translated in the NRSV as "grumble," *stenazō*, also (and more frequently) means "groan" or "sigh" in the NT (Rom 8:22, 23; 2 Cor 5:2, 4; Heb 13:17) and LXX (e.g., Lam 1:8, 21; Eze 26:15; Nah 3:7). The context requires an understanding of "grumble," one does not generally groan "against one another," and in some manuscripts this reading is strengthened by placing the latter phrase (*kat' allēlōn*) immediately after the verb.¹⁶² The warning against grumbling is placed in the same context of judging found in the warning against slander in 4:11–12 and fits James's overall concern with right use of the tongue. The logic here more closely reflects that of Mt 7:1 ("Do not judge, so that you may not be judged") than was found in 4:11–12 but seems to share the emphasis in 4:12 on the prerogatives of the one judge, who is now described as "standing at the doors" (*idou ho kritēs pro tōn thurōn hestēken*). In Rev 3:20 Jesus is standing at the door and knocking. In Mk 13:29 and par., when "these things" (the events of Mk 13) take place you will know that "he" (the Son of Man) is "very near" (*engus*), at the "gates" (*thurais*). The combination of "door" and "judge" is eschatologically charged, to say the least.

10–11. In chapter 2 James used two exemplars of the kind of faithful practice he calls for, one expected and appreciated by contemporary readers (Abraham), one not (Rahab, who we saw would have been appreciated by James's own contemporaries). In chapter 5 James will mention two more by name, and one entire "class" – the "prophets who spoke in the name of the Lord."¹⁶³ James refers to these as "examples" (*hupodeigma*), the word Jesus uses to describe his own actions in washing the feet of the disciples ("I have set you an example, that you also should do as I have done to you"; Jn 13:15). This is precisely what James intends in citing the "example of suffering and patience" of the prophets – that we are to do likewise. "Suffering and patience" (*tēs kakopathias kai tēs makrothumias*) should be understood as "patient suffering," that is, endurance (see vv. 7–8), as the beginning of v. 11 confirms, "Indeed we call blessed those who

---

¹⁶¹ D. J. Moo, *Letter of James* (2000), p. 224, writes, "grumbling against those who are close to us is particularly likely to occur when we are under pressure or facing difficult circumstances.... So it would be quite natural if James's readers, under the pressure of poverty and persecution (cf. 5:1–6), would turn their frustrations on one another."
¹⁶² L. T. Johnson, *Letter of James* (1995), p. 316. His suggestion of a link to Lev 19 seems unsubstantiated in either textual tradition.
¹⁶³ Here we see the problematic way in which James uses the word "Lord" (*kurios*). In vv. 7–8 we argued that James clearly meant "Jesus" when he used the term *kurios* because of the use of parousia. Just as clearly, in v. 10 *kurios* should be taken as referring to "God" because of the context – the prophets never spoke in the name of Jesus.

showed endurance." Exactly how James wants us to understand the exemplary behavior of those who spoke in the name of the Lord is not clear, but presumably he was referring to their martyrdom (Lk 13:34). Given James's emphasis on faithful practice and right speech, however, it is not inconceivable that he also intended a reference to the fact that they "spoke in the name of the Lord."

After holding the prophets out as example it is not surprising that James mentions someone by name. What is surprising is that the name he mentions is Job. Yes, we have all heard of the patience of Job. We had not heard that Job "was among the prophets." And those who have heard of Job by reading the Book of Job know that while his life was marked by suffering his behavior seemed anything but patient. Instead there was a lot of grumbling/groaning, both against his "friends" and against God. This has led many commentators to seek a source for the idea of Job's patience in extra-testamental literature, specifically the *Testament of Job*.

The dating of this document is far from clear, however. Nor need one necessarily find a source for James's idea. Dibelius writes, "the conception of Job as the righteous sufferer, the model of "steadfastness" (ὑπομονή), is older than the Book of Job and goes back to the ancient popular legend of Job, who did not sin in spite of all his misfortune (cf. Job 1; 2:1–10; 42:10–16)." Johnson concludes, "It would seem that James has considerable responsibility for shaping the perception of 'endurance/patience' as the most memorable feature of Job."[164] There is another possibility, which will have to wait until we explore the sacred and homiletical textures of vv. 7–11: perhaps James wanted to hold out the example of Job in all his complexity and not just as a legendary caricature.

SOCIOCULTURAL AND IDEOLOGICAL TEXTURES

From the prophets whom he mentions in v. 10 James received an active expectation of ongoing and decisive participation in human affairs by God. From the traditions of Wisdom James inherited a firm conviction that the judgment(s) of God would overturn and reverse the injustices of the present age. From the teaching of Jesus James learned that such decisive intervention and judgment was imminent. Throughout the letter this set of expectations pervades the ideological character of the text. Unless James was writing against the ethos of his community, which does not seem likely, it seems fair to characterize that ethos as one of thoroughgoing eschatological expectation.

Dibelius, however, would disagree, finding in James what we might call a reluctant eschatology. "[T]he Christian who wrote this (1:10) was thinking of the parousia and the cosmic transformation connected with it, and yet there

---

[164] M. Dibelius, *Letter of James* (1975), p. 246; L. T. Johnson, *Letter of James* (1995), p. 319. Johnson goes on to acknowledge that this conception is "emphatically shared" by *T. Job*.

is no eschatological passion glowing in his words."[165] I frankly find this reading of James inexplicable, except as evidence of a reading too grounded in its own preconceptions that James is a derivative work, that its "author" a rather bumbling editor who clumsily reworked traditional Jewish material. Moo, for one, finds that "future eschatology is clearly the dominant perspective in James. He frequently warns believers about the coming judgment. . . . And he reminds them of the reward they can look forward to. . . ."[166] Johnson is more outspoken in his reading of James's eschatology, finding that "James' expectation of the judgment appears to be imminent rather than distant" and concluding:

> In short, James gives every indication of sharing in an eschatological expectation that is intense and focused on the return of Jesus as the judging Lord. It is not possible to move directly from this conclusion to one concerning James' historical placement. It is conceivable, after all, that a document written well into the second century could imaginatively construct an eschatological scenario with this degree of internal coherence. But it must be said that nothing in James' language itself would lead to such a conclusion. Far from appearing as an archaizing expression of "primitive eschatology" in the face of diminishing expectations, his language seems a direct and fresh expression of genuine convictions concerning an imminent intervention.[167]

I concur with both of Johnson's conclusions, the one he makes explicitly (James gives us a powerful expression of imminent eschatological expectation) and the one he makes implicitly (this expression is best understood in the context of earliest Christianity).

A CLOSER LOOK – JAMES'S THOROUGHGOING ESCHATOLOGY

Surprisingly, few have commented on the thoroughgoing way in which James expresses his eschatological expectations. Virtually every pericope touches in some way or another on a theme with some eschatological overtone, which is revealed by even a short account of such themes.

1. trials and endurance	1:2–4, 12; 5:7, 8, 10–11
2. reversal	1:9–11; 2:5; 4:6, 9–10; 5:1–3
3. salvation	1:21; 2:5; 5:11, 15, 19–20
4. judgment	2:12–13; 3:1; 4:12; 5:4, 9
5. hell	3:6 (set on fire by Gehenna/ *tēs geennēs*)
6. life is fleeting	1:10–11; 4:14
7. coming of the Lord	5:7, 8, 9

The pervasive appearance of these themes and the prominent role they play in the passages in which they are found argue persuasively for reading the letter as steeped in its author's expectation of the imminent return of Jesus.

---

[165] M. Dibelius, *Letter of James* (1975), p. 87.
[166] D. J. Moo, *Letter of James* (2000), pp. 29–30.
[167] L. T. Johnson, *Letter of James* (1995), p. 322.

> Is this also true of James's audience, and if it is, what may we conclude about their social setting? The answer first depends on how one reads the nature of the various warnings James offers as part of the expectation he shares. If life is fleeting, and life is hard, what is the ground for hope? If judgment is coming soon, should one wait with hope or dread? Certainly there is an element of dread in a statement like "The judge is standing at the doors" (5:9), and in 1:10–11 and 5:1–6 one group, the rich, receives ample reason to fear the coming of the Lord, "for judgment will be without mercy to anyone who has shown no mercy" (2:13). But if they are in any way a part of the community, they are not the primary audience. And for the primary audience the coming of the Lord will be the occasion for both judgment and reversal, the judgment itself promised to be tinged with mercy, "for mercy triumphs over judgment" (2:13), a statement that can be read as promising an eschatological victory for those who have themselves shown mercy. Moreover, there is a "crown of life" that "the Lord has promised to those who love him" and have endured "temptation" (1:12). God gives "every perfect gift" (1:17), including the gift of "the implanted word that has the power to save your souls" (1:21).

The vast majority of James's readers would be encouraged by his words, sharing his expectations. We can conclude, then, that James was writing for and to a community that awaited the coming of the Lord in the immediate future, an expectation generally agreed to be found in the earliest Christian communities (cf. 1 and 2 Th). The thoroughgoing nature of the eschatological expectations in the letter of James argues for similar expectations in the community for and to which he wrote.

SACRED AND HOMILETICAL TEXTURES

How does the old saying go? "Everybody wants to go to heaven, but nobody wants to die." When we encounter someone who says with seriousness that they look forward with joy to the end of the age, we are more likely to ask if they are still taking their medication than we are to ask about their eschatology. And while no book of the Christian Bible is more popular for study series and lectures than Revelation, the popularity is based not on how John teaches the reader to live as one awaiting an imminent parousia but on whether or not "this is it!" Do the stars and storms, the latest Middle East crisis, and the most recent candidate to star as "the Beast" add up to 666?

In this sense, despite its thoroughgoing eschatology, James does not figure in discussions of apocalyptic literature. While a non-eschatological apocalyptic is hard to envision, a non-apocalyptic eschatology is common, and James is an example. The absence of apocalyptic features may have been what Dibelius had in mind when commenting on the routine way James discusses human mortality, divine judgment, and the promise of status reversal. In any case, the force of the absence of apocalyptic serves to encourage emphasis on the ethical, which is more or less exactly what one finds in James.

Eschatological and apocalyptic speculation is a spectator sport – asking when "these things" will take place and what "the end" will look like has not stopped since Peter, James (the other James, the brother of), John, and Andrew asked, "Tell us, when will this be?" (Mk 13:4). Such speculation encourages questions that have no answers and endless debate about how various apocalyptic pieces fit into the eschatological puzzle. The real fun is that since all the answers are wrong,[168] every answer is just as credible as any another.

Every preacher must choose what she will emphasize, and every teacher what she will stress. Certainly to move from James to a consideration of end times as revealed in the Apocalypse of John is unwarranted, but once the term parousia is spoken the temptation of speculation is great. But the stress in the letter of James is different. Two will be noted. First, because James is a realist, the beginning point of his eschatology is personal. He starts with the reality of human mortality, a truth no one can avoid or forever deny. There is an eschatological exclamation point to every life, poor and rich. The first underlying eschatological question for James, then, is: because we are all going to die, how should we live? Second, because James is a person of faith, he awaits the *parousia tou kyriou* (the coming of the Lord), anticipating the judgment and status reversal promised by the prophets and by Jesus. Therefore, the second underlying eschatological question for James is: because the Lord is coming soon, how should we live?

The answer to both questions is the same – we live in faith, and faith is lived in practice, in word and deed, controlling our tongue, loving our neighbor, drawing near to God.

JAMES 5:12–20

We come now to the conclusion of the letter of James. As noted in the introduction to chapter 5, perhaps the greatest point of controversy in the division of the letter is v. 12 of this chapter, and it has been a pivotal verse for many commentators. Those like Dibelius who view the letter as a compendium of disparate and often unrelated exhortations understand the verse as independent from the prior and following verses.[169] Others, especially Johnson, who argue for the letter's compositional and rhetorical integrity, emphasize the relation of the verse to the rest of chapter 5. Wall's comment clarifies the issues well.

The difficulty of the text for scholars is determining its "fit" within the present compositional surrounding.... What makes this contextual ambiguity more maddening to the interpreter is the importance the author seems to attach to it. The initial phrase, "above

---

[168] "But about that day or hour no one knows, neither the angels in heaven, nor the Son, but only the Father" (Mk 13:32).

[169] M. Dibelius, *Letter of James* (1975), p. 241.

James 5:1–20 – Cries, Patience, and Prayer: The Lord Is Near   149

all," typically introduces statements that climax preceding arguments or claims. Even more remarkable is the final purpose clause (*hina*) that this action is taken "so that you may not fall under judgment (*krisis*). Evidently the proverb found in between carries significant meaning for the readers.[170]

That "proverb" is an admonition not to swear any oath, a final example of prohibited speech. The "judgment" is the same one warned about in 5:9, 4:11–12, and 2:12–13. Continuity in theme and term is apparent. The verse also begins the most sustained set of instructions to the community in the letter, something typical of letter closings within and without the NT. We will treat vv. 12–20 as a unit, and as the conclusion of the letter, reminding the reader of many important themes and bringing most of them to a rhetorically satisfying, if ethically demanding, close.

12 Above all, my beloved, do not swear, either by heaven or by earth or by any other oath, but let your "Yes" be yes and your "No" be no, so that you may not fall under condemnation.
13 Are any among you suffering? They should pray. Are any cheerful? They should sing songs of praise.
14 Are any among you sick? They should call for the elders of the church and have them pray over them, anointing them with oil in the name of the Lord.
15 The prayer of faith will save the sick, and the Lord will raise them up; and anyone who has committed sins will be forgiven.
16 Therefore confess your sins to one another, and pray for one another, so that you may be healed. The prayer of the righteous is powerful and effective.
17 Elijah was a human being like us, and he prayed fervently that it might not rain, and for three years and six months it did not rain on the earth.
18 Then he prayed again, and the heaven gave rain and the earth yielded its harvest.
19 My brothers and sisters, if anyone among you wanders from the truth and is brought back by another,
20 you should know that whoever brings back a sinner from wandering will save the sinner's soul from death and will cover a multitude of sins.

INNER TEXTURE AND INTERTEXTURE

12. As we will see, the primary interest of most commentators is the intertexture of this verse. Consequently its tight structure and the emphatic quality of its insistence on a prohibition of the use of oaths is little noted. The opening *pro pantōn* likely serves three purposes: (1) signaling the turn toward the conclusion of the letter, and so serving as a kind of epistolary "marker," (2) preparing the reader for the importance of what is to follow, thus bringing the emphasis of

---

[170] R. W. Wall, *Community of the Wise* (1997), p. 259.

"above all" to vv. 12–20 in its entirety, and (3) calling special attention to the immediate issue of oath-taking.[171]

For the fourth time in six verses James addresses the community with his favored *adelphoi* before admonishing them with a prohibition in the present imperative second person plural, "do not swear" (*mē omnuete*). There follows a tripartite, all-inclusive series detailing that by which oath-taking was forbidden, "neither by heaven or by earth or by any other oath" (*mēte ton ouranon mēte tēn gēn mētē allon tina orkon*). The strict prohibition then occasions positive instruction, "but let your 'Yes' be yes and your 'No' be no" (*ētō de humōn to Nai nai kai to Ou ou*), which is followed by the rationale, also in the form of a negative, "so that you may not fall under condemnation" (*hina mē hupo krisin pesēte*). The structure of the verse – opening summons, prohibition, instruction, rationale – has something of a prophetic quality to its tone and arrangement. Intertextually the verse includes the closest parallel to a saying of Jesus in the entire letter. A comparison of the two will be helpful.

A CLOSER LOOK – JAMES AND JESUS ON SWEARING AN OATH

"Again, you have heard that it was said to those of ancient times, 'You shall not swear falsely, but carry out the vows you have made to the Lord.' But I say to you, Do not swear at all, either by heaven, for it is the throne of God, or by the earth, for it is his footstool, or by Jerusalem, for it is the city of the great King. And do not swear by your head, for you cannot make one hair white or black. Let your word be 'Yes, Yes' or 'No, No'; anything more than this comes from the evil one." (Mt 5:33–7)	Above all, my beloved, do not swear, either by heaven or by earth or by any other oath, but let your "Yes" be yes and your "No" be no, so that you may not fall under condemnation. (James 5:12)

Lev 19:12 – "And you shall not swear falsely by my name, profaning the name of your God: I am the Lord" – lies behind the antithesis in the Sermon on the Mount, and that Jesus' teaching is cast in the form of an antithesis while James's is in the form of an admonition accounts for much of the difference. But the precise relationship of Mt 5:33–7 and James 5:12 is hardly clear. Johnson notes that "the agreement of Matthew and James on the asyndetic *nai, nai, ou, ou* is especially striking."[172] Martin offers the rather sweeping, "James is usually thought to

---

[171] "The phrase *pro pantōn* indeed may give special significance to oath-taking, but it also functions as a thematic transition to acts of speech within the community" (L. T. Johnson, *Letter of James* [1995], p. 327).

[172] Ibid., p. 238.

embody a more primitive form of the prohibition than those in Matthew and Justin" but makes no conclusion about literary dependence, while Johnson in his later *New Interpreter's Bible* commentary writes that James "represents a stage of the saying prior to its incorporation in the synoptic tradition."[173] Dibelius holds that James was not a paraphrase of Matthew, and Bauckham maintains that "since James is not in the habit of reproducing sayings of Jesus as such, it is very doubtful whether James 5:12 can be used ... to reconstruct an alternative traditional form or a more original form of the saying of Jesus in Matthew 5:33–37."[174]

Intertexture, even "oral-scribal inter-texture" (Robbins), is not limited to seeking textual parallels and answering questions of literary dependence or priority, which Robbins calls "recitation."[175] The recontextualization and re-configuration of texts and traditions are also important. While we can conclude with some confidence that James 5:12, like other passages already considered, reflects James's awareness and use of Jesus material, we cannot with equal certainty determine which version of this or other sayings is more "authentic." We can say that James and in this case Matthew have each contextualized and configured a traditional saying that reflects and responds to the prohibition against false oaths in Lev 19:12. Both Matthew and James follow a similar order: an absolute prohibition against swearing an oath, followed by three examples of the manner of oath forbidden, concluding with a model of the kind of speech that is welcome and a warning against speech that exceeds this model. But different contextualizations of the prohibition result in different emphases. In Matthew the prohibition is found on the lips of Jesus in the middle of a series of six antitheses contrasting traditional teaching ("you have heard it said") with the teaching of Jesus ("but I say to you"). In James the saying is offered without attribution, and the Lev 19:12 reference is only implied. Though earlier discussions in the letter about the dangers of the tongue would be in the background, the force of the prohibition would be more absolute than that in Matthew where the impact of the prohibition is mitigated by attention to the contrast between Torah and the teaching of Jesus.

There is scant attested tradition against swearing an oath in the Hebrew Bible, Judaism, or elsewhere in antiquity.[176] The traditions are against swearing an oath

---

[173] R. Martin, *James* (1988), p. 199; Luke Timothy Johnson, "James" in *New Interpreter's Bible*, vol. 12 (Nashville, TN: Abingdon Press, 1998), p. 222.
[174] M. Dibelius, *Letter of James* (1975), p. 250; Richard Bauckham, *James: The Wisdom of James, Disciple of Jesus the Sage* (London: Routledge, 1999), p. 92.
[175] Vernon Robbins, *Exploring the Texture of Texts* (Valley Forge, PA: Trinity Press International, 1996), pp. 40–8.
[176] The closest to an exception is Philo, *Decal.* 84–5: "To swear not at all is the best course and most profitable to life, well suited to a rational nature which has been taught to speak the

falsely or perjury (Gk. *epiorkia*). In fact the tradition Jesus inherited generally held oaths in positive regard.

On the whole, the Old Testament evidence shows that oaths as such were viewed positively and that misuse was to be avoided as contrary to Torah.... In what must have been an inner-Jewish debate at the time, the Sermon on the Mount not only formulates an ethical response to perjury but also develops theoretical ideas about the roots of perjury and the nature of oaths as such.[177]

5:12 reflects the same development. Johnson understands the admonition against swearing oaths in James as integral and introductory to the section on the positive uses of speech for building up the community. "James' prohibition of oaths is, in reality, the encouragement of plain speech in the community of faith.... It is a call to simplicity and truthfulness."[178] This may be true for the second half of the verse, but it fails to account for the striking, absolute prohibition against oaths. The prohibition is if anything the conclusion of James's warnings and admonitions on negative speech, not the beginning of a section on the positive uses of speech. An oath, far from being viewed as the positive vow it apparently was in much of the biblical tradition, was seen by James (and Jesus) as a negative to be avoided "above all," the final example of the dangers of the tongue.

"Rhetorically, the phrase, 'Yes, yes, no, no' is *epanadiplosis*, the repetition of important words for emphasis. This rhetorical feature, however, is an indication of a weakness of the human language itself. Through manipulation of the words or through deception, a 'yes' can become a 'no' and vice versa."[179] Paul, defending himself against charges of having planned disingenuously a double visit to Corinth, used the same phrase in 2 Cor 1:16–19:

16 I wanted to visit you on my way to Macedonia, and to come back to you from Macedonia and have you send me on to Judea. 17 Was I vacillating when I wanted to do this? Do I make my plans according to ordinary human standards, ready to say "Yes, yes" and "No, no" at the same time? 18 As surely as God is faithful, our word to you has not been "Yes and No." 19 For the Son of God, Jesus Christ, whom we proclaimed among you, Silvanus and Timothy and I, was not "Yes and No"; but in him it is always "Yes."

truth so well on each occasion that its words are regarded as oaths; to swear truly is only, as people say, a 'second best voyage,' for the mere fact of his swearing casts suspicion on the trustworthiness of the man." This is not, of course, a prohibition against swearing, and Philo goes on to give advice on taking care in making an oath and avoiding perjury (86–95). *Philo*, LCL, vol. 7, trans. F. H. Colson (Cambridge, MA: Harvard University Press, 1950), pp. 48–9. Epictetus, *Enchiridion* 33.5, also advises one to "refuse, if you can, to take an oath at all, but if that is impossible refuse as far as circumstances allow." Again, this is hardly a prohibition. *Epictetus*, LCL, vol. 2, trans. W. A. Oldfather (New York: G. P. Putnam, 1928), pp. 516–17.

[177] Hans Dieter Betz, *The Sermon on the Mount*, Hermeneia (Minneapolis, MN: Fortress Press, 1995), p. 262.
[178] L. T. Johnson, *Letter of James* (1995), p. 341.
[179] H. D. Betz, *Sermon on the Mount* (1995), p. 272.

Thus the saying "Yes, yes, no, no" was current in the Jesus tradition circulating in the mid-first century CE and/or was a rhetorical commonplace known to Matthew, James, and Paul.[180]

13–16a. V. 13 begins without transition, implying a natural continuity with v. 12 that, if in fact it is to be found, centers around James's ongoing emphasis on the uses of speech. It is clear that in vv. 13–14 we find a series of three, nicely balanced hypothetical conditions (if not grammatical conditionals), alternating between the statement of the situation (suffering/cheerful/sick, *kakopathei/euthumei/asthenei*) in the present active indicative and commanded response (pray/sing/summon-pray, *proseuchesthō/psalletō/proskalesasthō-proseuksasthōsan*) in the present active imperative. The first two situations are given comparatively short shrift. The verb "suffering" first mentioned serves to recall the noun form of the same term, *kakopathia*, in v. 10 and to connect these concluding verses with their emphasis on prayer with the preceding verses and the emphasis on patience. It also recalls the opening verses of the letter, which also move between a kind of suffering and a call for prayer (1:2–6). The second situation uses a verb, *euthumeō*, without comparable attestation; it is found four times in Acts, three of those in Acts 27, where the sense has to do with courage more than good cheer. The contrast with the first and third conditions makes the meaning clear enough, however, as does the response: to sing. The verb *psallō* is common in the LXX (e.g., the aorist imperative *psalate* occurs eighteen times in the Psalms) but fairly rare in the NT (five times). Our term "Psalm" comes from the same root, but it is probably an overtranslation to render *psalletō* as "sing to God" or "sing praises."

The real interest in this section of the passage is with v. 14. The situation imagined is illness, the term *astheneō* meaning "sick" or "weak," usually in a physical sense, although not in Rom 4:19 and 1 Cor 8:7. The present meaning is surely physical. It is a sickness of such gravity that some are unable to be moved. Instead others are to be summoned. These are referred to as "the elders of the church" (*tous presbyterous tēs ekklēsias*), and they are to "pray over them, anointing them with oil in the name of the Lord." We will defer discussion of the sociocultural significance of the verse to the next section. Here we need only be clear on the sequence and significance of the actions described.

The first action is to summon. The sick person is to reach beyond him- or herself, and beyond the household, to a specific group, the elders of the church. These come (the action is implied) and offer three (or two, depending on how one interprets "in the name of the Lord") actions: prayer, anointment with oil, and invocation of the name of the Lord. We are given no hint about the content of the prayer, the oil was almost certainly common olive oil, and calling on the name of the Lord recalls the role of the prophets in v. 10, as well as the variety

---

[180] L. T. Johnson, *Letter of James* (1995), p. 329.

of activities in the life of an early Christian community done in the "name" of Jesus,[181] from baptism (Acts 2:38) to exorcism (Acts 16:18; humorously in Acts 19:13 ff.) to forgiveness (1 Jn 2:12) to healing (Acts 3:6, 16). In other words, what James instructs those in the community to do is routine, not extraordinary, something we will consider in the next section, along with the implications of "elders of the church," "anointing with oil," and James's apparent understanding of the relationship of sin, sickness, healing, and forgiveness. Innertextually it is the emphasis on prayer that impresses.

"The prayer of faith will save the sick" (*kai hē euchē tēs pisteōs sōsei ton kamnonta*). At the beginning of the letter we found a pattern similar to what we find in vv. 14–15. In 1:5 those who lack wisdom are called on to "ask God," which is then qualified in v. 6 with an admonition to "ask in faith" (*aiteitō en pistei*). Similarly, in 4:3 the reader is told, "You ask and do not receive, because you ask wrongly." Clearly, in the letter of James not every prayer and asking receives the desired response, only the prayer of faith does, which 1:6 defines as "never doubting" (*mēden diakrinomenos*). It is interesting that James uses other terms for "sick" and "pray" (*kamnō* and *euchomai*) in 5:15, much less common terms in the NT but nonetheless terms with the same range of meaning as *astheneō* and *proseuchomai*. The term "save" (*sōzō*) is used almost interchangeably in the NT for healing (e.g., Mk 6:56), physical deliverance (e.g., Acts 27:20), spiritual salvation (e.g., Jn 3:17), and the occasional fascinating mix of all three (e.g., Mk 5:34).

This ambivalence is continued in the phrases to follow: "the Lord will raise them up" (*eyerei auton ho kyrios*) and "anyone who has committed sins will be forgiven" (*kan hamartias ēi pepoiēkōs aphethēsetai autō*). The uses of *egeirō* extend from "waking up" (Mk 4:27) to the resurrection of the dead (1 Cor 15:15); it is also used in connection with healing (Jn 5:8). The overtones, however, of combining *sōzō* and *egeirō* are decidedly soteriological. The ambiguity in the final phrase of v. 15 is not lexical but contextual. Does James intend this saying to apply to the same persons who have been saved/healed and raised up in the earlier part of the verse, or is it a general maxim, one with dominical overtones (cf. Lk 17:4–5; also 1 Jn 1:9)? The construction, as Johnson points out, is periphrastic and may be translated literally as "and if (he) should be (one) who has done a sin it will be forgiven to him."[182]

Further complicating the picture is that confession of sin is not mentioned until v. 16a, and there as an apparent conclusion and application of vv. 14–15: "Therefore [*oun*] confess your sins to one another, and pray for one another, so that you may be healed [*iathēte*]." This is not what the reader expects. First, we

---

[181] I understand the various "names" – Lord, Lord Jesus, Jesus, Jesus Christ, Lord Jesus Christ – to function similarly in early Christianity and am reading James's usage as another example of his fluid appropriation and adaptation of the tradition. The textual variants (see B. M. Metzger, *Textual Commentary on the Greek NT* [1994], p. 614) indicate the tendency of the tradition to maximize the appellations.

[182] L. T. Johnson, *Letter of James* (1995), p. 333.

expect confession to be mentioned prior to forgiveness, not after. Second, we expect that after confessing to one another and praying, one would be forgiven, not healed (the word, frankly, one would have expected in v. 15 instead of *sōzō*). What we find is an almost complete, and seemingly indiscriminate, mixing of sin, sickness, confession, healing, and forgiveness, with a little salvation and resurrection thrown in for good measure. The question of whether this mixing represents a theological conviction or compositional carelessness must wait for the next section.

16b–18. These verses are a little more straightforward, though not without their own surprises. They begin with what appears to be another maxim, "The prayer of the righteous is powerful and effective," although there is nothing comparable in the tradition. James introduces yet a third term for "prayer," *deēsis*, as if he wanted to include in these few verses all the important vocabulary of prayer and petition. The participial form of *energeō*, translated in the NRSV as "effective," has elicited much comment. There is doubt as to its voice (middle or passive) and the implications that such difference might make (presumably taking it to be passive places greater emphasis on the activity of God), but it is likely a (rare) example of middle voice and should be understood attributively.[183] What is unremarked upon is the tendency of the verb to be joined with nouns of "power" (*dunamis*; Mk 6:14 and par.; Eph 3:20; Col 1:29) and strength. As for "the righteous" (*dikaios*), whose prayers are so efficacious, this certainly points back to v. 6, the righteous one condemned and killed by the rich. And in this way it points ahead and also clarifies what or whom James has in mind.

Following the maxim is the example, in this case, Elijah. This would at first seem to confirm that James meant in v. 6 one of the prophets, whose suffering was mentioned in v. 10 and whose martyrdoms were on the way to becoming part of the tradition. But then we read that Elijah, "was a human being like us" (*anthrōpos ēn homoiopathēs hēmin*). *Homoiopathēs* literally means "of like passions/feelings" but is taken to mean "of like nature" (Paul and Barnabas in Lystra, Acts 14:15).[184] Rather than emphasizing Elijah's extraordinary nature and charisma, James compares us to him favorably. Then he uses as an example an incident in Elijah's career that would not make most "top ten deeds of Elijah" lists, although it does have the virtue of being the first time his name is mentioned in the Bible (1 Kgs 17:1). As most commentators point out, no mention is made of prayer on Elijah's part; only the instruction of the Lord is given. "After many days the word of the LORD came to Elijah, in the third year of the drought, saying, 'Go, present yourself to Ahab; I will send rain on the earth'" (1 Kgs 18:1). Clearly it is God whose power and effectiveness is on display in the Elijah narrative,

---

[183] Following D. J. Moo, *Letter of James* (2000), p. 246, and L. T. Johnson, *Letter of James* (1995), p. 335.
[184] See L. T. Johnson, *Letter of James* (1995), p. 336, for classical usage.

which may well be part of the point James is trying to make in saying that Elijah was like us. It is God who "sends rain on the righteous and the unrighteous" (Mt 5:45) and who shuts up the heavens (2 Chron 6:26).

Of course the most striking thing about this example is that Jesus also used it (Lk 4:25–6), and James's way of telling the tale suggests some level of acquaintance. "But the truth is, there were many widows in Israel in the time of Elijah, when the heaven was shut up three years and six months, and there was a severe famine over all the land; yet Elijah was sent to none of them except to a widow at Zarephath in Sidon." The time span and the mention of "heaven" are not from 1 Kings but are found in Lk 4. The very choice of Elijah and of this incident in his narrative also suggest the possible influence of Jesus' saying. In addition, there is considerable elaboration, on James's part (that Elijah was praying for it not to rain, then for it to rain and that the earth brought forth fruit), but the possible awareness and influence of Jesus' saying is significant.

19–20. The problem most interpreters have with these verses is that, while they may make a good ending to chapter 5, they seem to make a very poor ending to a letter. Francis has shown that both the beginning and ending of James find parallels in biblical and classical epistolary literature,[185] The NT is no stranger to unsatisfying endings, as any reader of Mark and Luke–Acts is likely to agree.[186] There is no denying the absence of closing greetings, doxology, benediction, or any of the accoutrements of an epistolary ending in the Pauline tradition, but this finally only serves to remind us that this is not a letter in the Pauline tradition.

The ending is finally satisfying in its own way, on its own terms. James has encouraged and chastised for five chapters, and there may be some who hear and are discouraged by the demanding standard James admittedly sets. There may also be those hearing the letter who have friends and family members who have "wandered from the truth." The opening phrase, following James's final use of "brothers and sisters," posits a hypothetical, conditional situation, which could be literally translated as "if someone from among you might wander from the truth and another might return him." James seems so tentative in postulating the situation that one wonders whose feelings he is trying to spare. He concludes, "you should know that whoever brings back a sinner from wandering will save the sinner's soul from death and will cover a multitude of sins." The NRSV seeks to clarify the ambiguity in the Greek by mentioning "sinner" twice, but the Greek leaves it unclear whose soul is saved – the wanderer or the one who returns the wanderer. In all likelihood the NRSV has it right. In like manner, it is not clear whose sins are covered and what exactly the covering of sin means.

---

[185] F. O. Francis, "Form and Function" *ZNW* (1970).
[186] See my "Means of Absent Ends" in *History, Literature, and Society in the Book of Acts*, ed. Ben Witherington III (Cambridge: Cambridge University Press, 1996), pp. 348–62.

Presumably it is the one who returns the wanderer whose sins are covered, and "covering" means forgotten, if not exactly forgiven. It is clear that James and, in all likelihood, 1 Pet 4:8 ("love covers a multitude of sins") are dependent on Prov 10:12, "Hatred stirs up strife, but love covers all offenses." *Kaluptō* is the verb in all three passages, and while 1 Peter and James have the verb in different form, they use the same expression, *plēthos hamartiōn*, for what is "covered."

SOCIOCULTURAL AND IDEOLOGICAL TEXTURES

Given the breadth of topics covered in vv. 12–20, and the importance of these topics for the life of Christian faith throughout its history, one should not be surprised at how dense the sociocultural and ideological textures of the passage are. We will focus on the following: (1) oaths and oral culture; (2) elders in the church; (3) healing and anointing with oil; (4) sickness, sin, forgiveness and health; and (5) saving souls.

Oaths and Oral Culture

"Above all . . . do not swear." We have seen that the opening "above all" (*pro pantōn*) functions rhetorically to mark the turn toward the conclusion of the letter, adding emphasis to what follows in vv. 12–20 and also to v. 12 alone. But in what sense might one understand the importance of not swearing an oath? The tradition prior to this saying did not prohibit any oath but oaths sworn falsely, and God is found to offer an oath in the divine name on occasion (Gen 22:16; Jer 44:22).

There is, of course, something inherently problematic about any taking of oaths, for to offer or require an oath is to presume that a person's word cannot be trusted without one. The one who volunteers an oath is essentially asking not to be personally trusted, only for the oath to be trusted as a guarantor. This is especially true within family, clan, or community, where trust is such cornerstone of every relationship that it is assumed. Remove the assumption of trust, and you shake the foundation of the primary relationships around which one constructs one's life.

In our own day and our own experiences (about which more will be said in the next section), actions that have brought about loss of trust undermine marriages, weaken kinship ties, and threaten churches to an extraordinary degree. How much more would this be the case in a culture that relied almost exclusively on the trustworthiness of the spoken word? Paul Minear has reminded us just how true this was in ancient Mediterranean cultures. The primacy of orality in communication, the virtual absence of written contracts, and the relative inaccessibility of the legal system (which is perhaps presupposed in 2:1ff.) all underscore just how important it would be for people to know that "my word is my bond." In such cultures the trustworthiness of speech is a cornerstone of community. At stake is not just individual honor or assurance and confidence in personal and commercial transactions but the fabric of society. Hence the seriousness of the Corinthians' charge against Paul, and hence the seriousness of James's condemnation of those whose yes is not yes. Minear offers an apt summary: "In a culture which depends on oral speech, therefore, the intrusion of the intent to deceive pollutes reality at its very source and invokes the ultimate penalties on speakers."[187]

Elders in the Church

"Are any among you sick? They should call for the elders of the church." Laws has written that "This is one phrase which gives a specifically Christian colouring to the epistle."[188] How so? Who were these elders (*presbyteroi*)? What did James intend by referring to "the church" (*hē ekklēsia*)? The critical question about both terms, which were common throughout LXX and NT and the secular literatures of antiquity, is whether James meant them as technical terms designating a distinctive standing (elder) and gathering (church). In both cases the answer appears to be yes.

Elders and Offices in the Early Church

"Elder," which can designate both an age distinction (Lk 15:25) and a person of advanced years (1 Tim 5:1, 2), was a common designation for a leader or local ruler in the Judaism of James's day and is so used throughout the Gospels and Acts. In Acts the word is also used for leaders of the early Christian community, paired with "apostles" in Acts 15, and on one occasion, Acts 20:17, is in the exact phrase we have here, *tous presbyterous tēs ekklēsias*. The self-designation of the author of 2 and 3 John is "the elder" (*ho presbyteros*), and the term is found in Peter and the Pastorals. Moo writes:

> The prominent role of the elders in Acts and the description of the office in the Pastoral Epistles suggest that the elders were spiritually mature men who guided the spiritual development of local congregations. Since the Ephesian elders were to "shepherd," or "pastor," their flocks (Acts 20:28), and "pastors" are never mentioned along with elders in the NT, it is probable that the function of what we know as the pastor or minister was carried out by the elders.[189]

Moo also writes that "Both Peter (1 Pet 5:1) and James assume the ministry of elders in the church, showing that the office was well established in the early church." But how early and what is meant by "office"? If the early dating for

---

[187] Minear, "Yes or No: The Demand for Honesty in the Early Church" *Novum Testamentum* 13 (1971): 13.
[188] S. Laws, *Epistle of James* (1980), p. 225.
[189] D. J. Moo, *Letter of James* (2000), p. 237.

James (c. fifties CE) is accepted, it seems more likely that the functions or tasks being carried out are better described relative to the elders of a synagogue than to contemporary pastors or ministers, and that the idea of "office," understood as a role with stated duties, obligations, and responsibilities, may be premature. Instead of an office, what we have in James is an emerging role, and as Dibelius argued, "It is not known just when this development was completed within those churches who called their leaders 'elders' after the Jewish model."[190]

The singular use of the term "church" is complicated by James's use of *sunagōgē* in 2:2. NRSV appropriately translates *eis sunagōgēn humōn* as "into your assembly" because, as we saw in chapter 2, it is not entirely clear what James meant to designate by the term. Does it refer to a location or to a manner of gathering, and in any case, what sort of gathering (in chapter 2 the issue was whether a legal proceeding was intended)? Because *ekklēsia* and *sunagōgē* are used to designate an "assembly" or "gathering" without any spiritual or ritual overtones, but are also used to designate specifically Jewish and Christian assemblies, how should 5:14 be read, and how does it relate to 2:2? The problem is really about what James meant by *sunagōgē* in 2:2, for throughout the NT *ekklēsia* is used for a gathering of believers. Laws writes, "*ekklēsia* became at a very early stage the chosen self-designation of the Christian community, whether considered as an individual local unit . . . or as the whole body of believers."[191] The "elders of the church" then, while not the same as "the pastoral staff of the local Christian congregation," were certainly more akin to that than "some old people gathered in the town square."

Healing and Anointing with Oil

"Are any among you sick?" Then for heaven's sake call a doctor. That is what we would say. That is not what James said, and while this verse has been used to justify the refusal of medical treatment on religious grounds, that would be a reading of the ideological, not sociocultural, texture.[192] From a sociohistorical perspective the reader must accept that there was no doctor to call, no emergency room to visit, and no insurance forms to file (it was not all bad).

---

[190] M. Dibelius, *Letter of James* (1975), p. 253.
[191] S. Laws, *Epistle of James* (1980), p. 225. See also the article "ἐκκλησία," by K. L. Schmidt in *TDNT*, vol. 3 (Grand Rapids, MI: Eerdmans, 1965), pp. 501–36 for general background on the term.
[192] Luther, of course, took great exception to the use of these verses to defend what had become by his day the "sacrament of extreme unction," arguing in "The Babylonian Captivity of the Church" that those who "believe the apostle's words" (and Luther is not sure that the author of the letter *was* an apostle) "change and contradict them" and asking "Why do they make an extreme and a special kind of unction out of that which the apostle wished to be general?" Martin Luther, *Three Treatises*, trans. A. W. Steinhäuser, rev. ed. (Philadelphia: Fortress Press, 1970), p. 251. Luther is here (in 1520) really rather kind to James, saving his venom for the 1522 "Preface to the New Testament."

This does not mean, however, that there was no system, only that it was quite different from ours. The distinctions and alignments differed, as did the expectations. John Pilch reminds us of our tendency to read ancient healing narratives as if we were reading the *New England Journal of Medicine*.[193] We bring all of our contemporary assumptions to bear on material that may share almost none of them. Central is the medical anthropological distinction between the meaning clusters "illness/cure" and "disease/healing." While it may involve oversimplification to some extent, anthropologists contrast contemporary medical care, which involves the diagnosis of symptoms leading to the cure of an illness, to ancient and traditional medicine, which sought to bring healing to one who was diseased.

This healing primarily involved bringing understanding and meaning to a situation – making sense of the world, or better, (re)creating a world that comprehended the disease – and restoration of the diseased person to full participation and acceptance in the life of the community. One of the things Pilch's insights teach us is that questions about the possible medicinal quality of olive oil and how those qualities might have been understood by James and his community probably miss the point.

The distinction between summoning the elders and summoning a physician is one that we would make, just as we would between antibiotics and olive oil. Asking if the anointing with oil was intended medicinally, pastorally, symbolically, or sacramentally[194] is to begin in the wrong place, assuming distinctions simply not present in the ancient Mediterranean world. Instead, as we will see, the meanings cluster in ways unfamiliar to us.

Sickness, Sin, Forgiveness, and Health

Are you sick? Call for the church leaders. They will pray and anoint you with oil. You will be saved, raised, and forgiven. So confess your sins and pray, and you will be healed.

That makes absolutely no sense. To us. If we are sick we go to a doctor (we can "summon" all we want, it won't help). If we have sinned, we confess our sins and are forgiven. The physical and the spiritual are two entirely different things, and we intend to keep them that way – unless, of course, the medicine is not working, or the diagnosis is dire. Then the spiritual, driven by a confrontation with our own mortality, is suddenly welcome, and we pray like crazy. So who is crazy, we who wait until the doctor says, "There is nothing more we can do. All we can do is pray" before attempting to deal with our own mortality, or James, who recognizes it in 1:10–11 and begins to pray at the first sign of illness?

---

[193] John J. Pilch, *Healing in the New Testament: Insights from Medical and Mediterranean Anthropology* (Minneapolis, MN: Fortress Press, 2000).

[194] See, e.g., D. J. Moo, *Letter of James* (2000), pp. 238–42.

James looks at the world differently than most of us do, but he did not look at it much differently than his contemporaries. He may have had greater confidence in the power of prayer ("the prayer of faith *will* save the sick, and the Lord *will* raise them up") but not in the appropriateness of it. Following in the example of Jesus ("Which is easier, to say to the paralytic, 'Your sins are forgiven', or to say, 'Stand up [*egeire*] and take your mat and walk'?"; Mk 2:9) and in the assumptions of the culture,[195] James addressed sickness, sin, health, and forgiveness together.

Part of this, to be sure, reflects the scientific limitations of 2,000 years ago. Disease, contagion, and the like were not generally understood to have primarily physical causes, and medicinal treatments were limited. But there was and is great wisdom in the fundamental insight about what it meant to be "made well" and to be "saved" and "raised." They were part and parcel of one another. They still are.

Saving Souls

"If anyone among you wanders from the truth and is brought back by another, you should know that whoever brings back a sinner from wandering will save the sinner's soul from death and will cover a multitude of sins" (5:19–20).

Among others, Witherington notes that the concerns of the letter of James are exclusively limited to the needs and practices of the community, and likens the disposition of the letter to a kind of "battening down the hatches" in the face of various trials and possible persecution.[196] Certainly one of James's frequent refrains, especially in chapter 5, is "among you" (*en humin* – 3:13; 4:1; 5:13; 5:14, 19; "of you," 1:5; 2:16). Then again, given the designation of the addressee as "the twelve tribes of the Dispersion" the "you" could be a fairly large group.

Nevertheless, the concern is not for evangelism but for restoration. The provisions are not as formal as those found in Mt 18:15 ff. for reconciliation, but the sense of urgency is greater. The sinner who has wandered from his way (the Greek for this phrase, *ek planēs hodou autou*, includes the technical term "way," used for the "way of salvation" throughout our literature) recalls the "double-minded" (*anēr dipsuchos*) who is "unstable in every way" (*akatastatos en pasais tais hodois autou*) in 1:8. Evidently it is one such as this, so roundly condemned at the beginning of the letter, who is now the subject of great concern.

It would be wonderful for the sacred and homiletical textures of James if the concern was not so parochial, but evangelism was simply not an expressed priority in the letter. It is all about the practice, but that practice apparently

---

[195] The scribes did not disagree with the prevailing cultural attitude, they just did not want Jesus to heal or forgive (cf. Mk. 3:1ff.).
[196] B. Witherington, *Jesus the Sage* (1994), p. 246.

did not include outreach. Could this, in part, have contributed to the eventual collapse of the Jerusalem church? That is unfounded speculation, but it *is* true of many a contemporary congregation. In fact most contemporary congregations do not even follow the practice James commends for restoration, preferring what has been termed a "Little Bo Peep philosophy" as in "Leave them alone and they'll come home." James realizes that they do not come home of their own accord but must be restored. Was this a significant problem for the community to which James wrote? Again we can only speculate, but rhetorically, where one chooses to end is almost as suggestive as where one begins, so it is likely that it was. That such outreach is difficult may be why, in his rationale, James reminded the community that such acts of restoration cover a multitude of sins, the point being that restoration benefits all concerned.

SACRED AND HOMILETICAL TEXTURES

If Paul Minear and others are correct, and the prohibition against oaths with which our section begins must be read against a background not only of Lev 19:12 but of a culture that depended on truthfulness in oral communication as the foundation of commerce, governance, and daily life, how do we read the prohibition in our culture? Our culture seems to be the opposite of James's. If anything, our assumption is to *dis*trust or at least regard with suspicion every communication sent our way, be it oral, written, or electronic, from every source, not only the commercial and political, but the ecclesial and interpersonal as well. We are conditioned to expect everyone to have an "angle." We expect to be exploited or at least for the other to try. We do not trust, we polygraph, DNA test, and take an affidavit.

This is why the prohibition against oaths and a call for "the encouragement of plain speech in the community of faith ... a call to simplicity and truthfulness"[197] are as vital to the Church and Christian today as they ever have been. First it is a responsibility, both a keeping of commandment and a modeling within community, so that our every exchange, interaction, and decision is founded on honesty and respect. Second, it is a prescription for the well-being of Church and family, as the destructive and tragic consequences for beloved institutions and partnerships whose trust is broken by deceit too well attests. Finally, it is an opportunity, in a culture of alienation and distrust, for the Church to be that community of integrity and faith whose witness speaks powerfully of a better way.

As yet unremarked on in our consideration of James's many instructions on appropriate speech is the instruction in v. 13b, "Are any cheerful? They should sing songs of praise." How typical and unfortunate, to skip over the call to praise and the instruction to share with the community and with God our joy

---

[197] L. T. Johnson, *Letter of James* (1995), p. 341.

and gladness (Lk. 15:6, 9, 22–24). What, after all, is the chief end for which God created humanity? To glorify God and enjoy God forever.[198] It is common, but superficial, to chide James for being a somewhat dour letter, when it is anything but – it is earnest, yes, but not without bright spots.

Still it was James who devoted more attention to sickness and sin, forgiveness and healing than to song and cheer, and this cluster does capture our attention. Luke Johnson invites readers to understand James's insights on this cluster within the context of the Church as what might be called a "community of healing." Sickness threatens community in profound ways and can be as divisive as harmful speech. Sickness also alienates persons from themselves, their faith, and their God. When we do not feel like ourselves and when we "wonder what I did to deserve this?" we experience such alienation. When we imagine God visiting such distress on us we forget that God tempts no one (1:13). We also know, however, that guilt is both a powerfully negative motivator and a destructive power within us. "Confession is good for the soul" and, in keeping with James's understanding of the interrelation of body and spirit, doesn't hurt the body either.

The "prayer of faith" should thus be understood not just as a prayer of petition but as a prayer of praise, a prayer of confession, and prayer for wholeness. In this believers may need to raise their expectations. The prayer of faith expects that something *will* happen. Such pray-ers do not doubt (1:6) and are not of two minds in their request (1:6–8; 4:3), but trust in the God "who gives to all generously and ungrudgingly" (1:5).

Such raised expectations are also appropriate when reaching out to a brother or sister who has "wandered." Most churches, frankly, are better at recruitment than retention, the steady stream of those who "come forward" to join the church matched or exceeded by those who slip quietly out the back, rarely to return. The truth is most pastors and church leaders do not necessarily want to know why someone has "wandered." It may not be them, it may be us. But if we reach out, individually and corporately, lives and souls may be saved, and a multitude of our own sins "covered." That we wonder how this can be suggests a failure of imagination with regard to God's desire to forgive us our sins (vv. 15–16 also).

With this encouragement to sing, pray, confess, forgive, and reach out to the wandering our reading of James comes to a close. That James closes with practices vital to the community's life of faith is not accidental. It is all about the practice, personally and corporately. James is both wise guide and faithful witness to this central point, something he shared with his brother, Jesus. Before turning to the very different witness of the other brother of the Lord, Jude, a few general reflections on reading and preaching James seems appropriate.

---

[198] Westminster Shorter Catechism (1674).

BRIDGING THE HORIZONS – PREACHING JAMES

In considering the homiletical texture of the letter of James I have offered suggestions for approaching the challenges individual passages present to anyone who stands in a pulpit. But what of the larger questions about how to interpret and proclaim the message of James for the Church? Our study of James hints at the possible unspoken reason for the difficult reception the letter has received throughout its history, a reason that recalls the response to Jesus' "bread of life discourse" in Jn 6 – "This word is hard. Who is able to hear it" (Jn 6:60, my translation).

Yes, James's word is hard, to hear and to live, which makes it hard to proclaim in many so-called first world contexts. And there is good reason for that. To the extent that the modern reader of the letter of James sits in a position of relative privilege, comfort, convenience, education, prosperity, and power, she or he is always forced to read against the grain of the text, because James was not written with such as us primarily in mind. This does not mean that we do not have much to learn from the letter, for indeed we do. What it means is that we may need to learn new ways of reading, hearing, and preaching to benefit fully from James's message of God's special concern for the poor and how that concern is to be manifest in our faith and practice.

My own most formative learning experience in the reading and preaching of the letter of James occurred in the churches, villages, and schools of Nicaragua as the guest of Dr. Gustavo Parajón, pastor of the First Baptist Church of Managua, and founder of Providenic, a series of health clinics around the country, and CEPAD (Consejo de Iglesias Pro-Alianza Denominaciones), the Protestant ecumenical association created after the 1972 earthquake. In Nicaragua this presumed teacher and preacher became a true student. Thinking that I would have opportunity to share James's message of God's concern for my poor sisters and brothers, I instead learned a powerful lesson about riches that do not rust and about faithful practice that is profoundly mature. The words of James 1:2–5 came alive before my eyes.

2 My brothers and sisters, whenever you face trials of any kind, consider it nothing but joy, 3 because you know that the testing of your faith produces endurance; 4 and let endurance have its full effect, so that you may be mature and complete, lacking in nothing. 5 If any of you is lacking in wisdom, ask God, who gives to all generously and ungrudgingly, and it will be given you.

In prayer, study, and worship with pastors and people whose faith had been tested time and again by war, hurricane, earthquake, famine, and flood I *saw* endurance having its full effect. Amidst people who, materially, lacked just about everything, I realized that in the most profound way they were lacking in nothing, possessing a wisdom that I could only ask God to give to me.

Not everyone has the opportunity to teach and preach among people of faith in a different country, language, culture, and sociopolitical location. But we all have the opportunity to listen to their voices and to reflect on their words and allow their lives and faith to be reflected in our preaching and teaching. In their insightful book *The Liberating Pulpit*, Justo and Catherine González offer "some pointers on biblical interpretation" that are helpful. After showing the inadequacy of "Lone Ranger" biblical interpretation (the presumption of moving from private, individual study and devotion to proclamation for the community), the authors give seven pointers (as opposed to methods) to assist in overcoming the individualism, isolation, and narrowness that characterizes much preaching and that makes preaching James almost impossible. They can be summarized as follows:

1. *Read the political situation.* Be aware that the same text may sound very different to persons in the same congregation, or the same city, but in different social locations.
2. *Include the wider context.* Do more than make note of the presence of difference; allow the differences to inform interpretation and preaching.
3. *Consider the politics of the text.* The politics can be overt (Amaziah and Amos in Amos 7) or covert (James 4:13 – "Come now you who say . . . "), but the dynamics of power are often at work.
4. *Reassign the cast of characters.* We love to give ourselves the starring role when we imagine a biblical narrative. What happens when we place ourselves in a less prominent, or powerful, role?
5. *Imagine a different setting.* You may not be able to go to Nicaragua, or the South Bronx, but you can imagine what it would be like to be there. What would it be like to interpret James from that imaginative place?
6. *Consider the direction of the action.* Attend not only to what is going on but to where the dynamics, especially the power dynamics, of the narrative are heading. While the historical situation behind a text cannot be re-created, in many ways the direction the text points can be.
7. *Avoid avoidance.* We cannot simply skip over the difficult passages (like most of the letter of James!) but must read even more closely those words that we tend to resist.[199]

Effective proclamation must enter into the world of the text and the world of the congregation. No surprise there. Faithful proclamation must take the congregation through the text to the wider world, a world hidden from our

---

[199] Justo L. González and Catherine G. González, *The Liberating Pulpit* (Nashville, TN: Abingdon Press, 1994), esp. chapter 4, "Some Pointers on Biblical Interpretation."

> eyes, or perhaps more accurately, from which we hide our eyes. Our coming to a richer understanding of the wider world to which the letter of James speaks will afford us an opportunity to speak of James more deeply and to invite speaker and hearer to practice the faith to which James so faithfully gave witness.

THE LETTER OF JUDE – HAVE MERCY ON SOME WHO ARE WAVERING

As stated in the Introduction, while I recognize that many scholars find Jude to be of indeterminate authorship, provenance, audience, and date, I believe there is insufficient basis for reading against the tradition. Therefore, I read the letter of Jude as a work of Jude, brother of James and Jesus, and interpret the letter as written from or near Jerusalem, before the destruction of the Temple (70 CE), to an audience struggling with issues of interpretation and authority.

Informed by the rhetorical insights of Watson,[200] the inner texture and intertexture of Jude will be examined according to the following divisions, and the sociocultural, ideological, sacred, and homiletical textures considered as a whole.

Jude 1–2	Salutation
Jude 3–4	Introduction and thesis (intruders, designated for judgment, are among you)
Jude 5–10	Three proofs from the tradition (5–7, out of Egypt, angels/watchers, Sodom)
	First summation (8, these dreamers defile, reject, blaspheme)
	Example of judgment (9, Michael, the devil, and the body of Moses)
	Second summation (10, these people blaspheme, are destroyed)
Jude 11–16	Three proofs from the tradition (11, Cain, Balaam's error, Korah's rebellion)
	Third summation (12–13, blemishes on *agapē*, waterless clouds, etc.)
	Example of judgment (14–15, Enoch's prophecy)
	Fourth summation (16, grumblers, malcontents, flatterers, etc.)
Jude 17–23	Four exhortations to the faithful:
	17–19, remember the words of the apostles
	20, build yourselves up and pray
	21, keep yourselves in the love of God
	22–23, have mercy on some, save others
Jude 24–5	Benediction

---

[200] Duane F. Watson, *Invention, Arrangement, and Style: Rhetorical Criticism of Jude and 2 Peter* (Atlanta: Scholars Press, 1988), pp. 29–79.

The Letter of Jude – Have Mercy on Some Who Are Wavering

INNER TEXTURE AND INTERTEXTURE OF JUDE

JUDE 1–2

1 Jude, a servant of Jesus Christ and brother of James, To those who are called, who are beloved in God the Father and kept safe for Jesus Christ:
2 May mercy, peace, and love be yours in abundance.

1–2. Jude begins in the classic form of a typical Hellenistic letter, first identifying the sender and addressee, and closing the introduction with a blessing or thanksgiving in salutation.[201] That said, however, it is the anomalies from the classic pattern that stand out, in particular the absence of certainty, at least to modern readers, as to the identity of the sender and the general, or "Catholic," designation of the addressees.

> **A CLOSER LOOK – "JUDE" IN THE NT**
>
> The names "Jude" or "Judas" render the same Greek words, *Iouda, Ioudan, Ioudas*, and occur thirty-six times in the NT.
>
> - twenty-three references are to "Judas Iscariot, who betrayed him" (Mk 3:19)
> - three references in Acts to "Judas called Barsabbas" (Acts 15:22) who accompanied Silas
> - two references to "Judas son of James" (Lk 6:16) in Luke's list of the twelve
> - one reference to "Judas (not Iscariot)" in Jn 14:22, presumably the other disciple
> - one reference to "Judas the Galilean" (Acts 5:37), leader of a popular revolt
> - one reference to the "house of Judas" (Acts 9:11) in Damascus
> - two references to the "brother of James and Joses and Judas . . ." (Mk 6:3; Mt 13:55)
> - one reference to "Jude, a servant of Jesus Christ and brother of James" (Jude 1).
>
> This list helps to place the last reference in its NT context, reminding us that in comparison to other "Judes" the author of this letter relates a great deal about himself. The problem, of course, is that "Jude" does not tell us all of the things we would like to know. Or does he?

The opening phrase is more compelling, and revealing, in Greek than the NRSV translation: *Ioudas Iēsou Christou doulos, adelphos de Iakōbou,*

---

[201] Following the canons of rhetoric (see ibid., pp. 8–28, 194), these verses are understood as forming an epistolary prescript, or "*quasi-exordium*," which sets and frames (vv. 24–5 function as an epistolary postscript) the deliberative and epideictic rhetoric of the body of the composition within epistolary convention.

juxtaposing Jude and Jesus at the beginning of the phrase, with James coming at the end, so that a literal translation would read "Jude (of) Jesus Christ a slave, a brother of James." The emphasis is therefore on the relationship with Jesus, which is described in terms of servanthood, a description recalling the one who "did not regard equality with God as something to be exploited, but emptied himself, taking the form of a slave [*doulos*]" (Phi 2:6–7). While the LXX consistently uses *doulos* to describe David's relationship to God (2 Sam 7:25 ff.), Moses (Deut 34:5), Abraham, Isaac, and Jacob (Ex 32:13), and Samuel (1 Sam 3:9) are among those described as or themselves claim to be "servants" (Heb. *ebed*) of God. Paul (Rom 1:1), Epaphrus (Col 4:12), Peter (2 Pet 1:1), and James (1:1) are all described as servant/slave (*doulos*) of Jesus Christ or God.

The designation "slave [*doulos*] of Jesus Christ" is therefore an honorific one, as is the designation "brother of James." What the reader may wonder is why the author did not claim identity as a "brother of the Lord." One approach to answering this question has been offered earlier in this commentary and in the Introduction – what would be true for one brother, James, would be true for the other, Jude: identification as "the brother(s) of the Lord" was not necessary. The identification with James is also significant, supporting the understanding of Jude's brother developed earlier in the commentary. First, it tells us that the "James" in question was of sufficient stature to the audience as to need no qualifications, a status that can only be ascribed to James the Just/of Jerusalem, the "brother of the Lord." Second, it tells us that the author of Jude was confident enough in the identification of James and Jesus that he need not claim it for himself – identification with James accomplished both.

The recipients of the letter are referred to in tripartite fashion: (1) beloved in God the Father, (2) kept for Christ Jesus, and (3) called (the order in Greek). The descriptions are not specific but inclusive. The specificity comes later in the letter, when dealing with opponents. Nevertheless, by emphasizing the relationship of the addressees to God as beloved, claiming that they are guarded or kept for Jesus,[202] and acknowledging their standing as those who are called, the author bestows significant honor on his readers.[203]

The blessing bestowed on the readers, "May mercy, peace, and love be yours in abundance," is also unique. "Mercy" (*eleos*) and "peace" (*eirēnē*) are common in NT salutations, though not as common as the Pauline "grace and peace" (Rom 1:7; 1 Cor 1:2; 2 Cor 1:2; Gal 1:3; Eph 1:2; Phi 1:2; Col 1:2; 1 Th 1:1; 2 Th 1:2; Phm 1:2), as is the hope that they be had "in abundance" (*plēnthuntheiē*, 1 Pet 1:2; 2 Pet 1:2), but the two are more commonly joined by "grace" (1 Tim 1:2, 2 Tim 1:2, 2 Jn 1:3), not Jude's use of "love" (*agapē*).

---

[202] That the readers are guarded or kept for Jesus is a claim with eschatological overtones; see R. Bauckham, *Jude and 2 Peter*, Word Biblical Commentary (Waco, TX: Word Books, 1983), p. 26.

[203] See the following section, on sociocultural and ideological textures of Jude, for a fuller discussion of honor and shame in Jude.

JUDE 3–4

3 Beloved, while eagerly preparing to write to you about the salvation we share, I find it necessary to write and appeal to you to contend for the faith that was once for all entrusted to the saints.
4 For certain intruders have stolen in among you, people who long ago were designated for this condemnation as ungodly, who pervert the grace of our God into licentiousness and deny our only Master and Lord, Jesus Christ.

3. Jude begins the verse with his third use of *agapē* in the first 25 words, here signaling the beginning of the body of the letter, for which these verses are the introduction, and continuing the author's efforts to elicit the good will (*pathos*) of his readers.[204] It is a common epistolary convention to refer to earlier correspondence or communication (see Acts 1:1), but it is not clear to what Jude might be referring. It appears that Jude intended to write (*poioumenos graphein humin*) a general letter to this general audience on their general (common) salvation, but events interceded so that now it is "necessary to write you" (*eschon grapsai humin*) on a more pressing topic. Whether or not there was actually a half-finished composition set aside or only the intention to write on the more comprehensive topic, the reference works effectively to heighten the importance of the composition in hand, the letter of Jude.

The language is "charged" throughout v. 3, preparing the reader for the seriousness of the charge that will be leveled in v. 4. After the affectionate opening, "beloved," Jude writes of his zeal, *pasan spoudēn*, to write to the readers about "our common salvation" (*tēs koinēs hēmōn sōtērias*). Now, however, something even more pressing necessitates (*anagkēn*) writing, an "appeal to you to contend for the faith that was once for all entrusted to the saints." Here the author is using vocabulary in an almost Pauline way – necessity (*anagkē*; 2 Cor 9:7), saints (*hagioi*; Phi 4:2), faith (*pistis*; Gal 1:23), entrust (*paradidōmi*; Rom 6:17) – which argues against those who see in Jude's language here (and elsewhere) evidence of the presence of a fully formed doctrine and ecclesiology, and thus evidence of a late dating for its composition. Instead what we do see is a successful attempt to create a great sense of urgency.

4. "For certain intruders have stolen in among you" (*pareisedusan gar tines anthrōpoi*). The verb is otherwise unattested in the NT, although Paul's use of *pareisaktous* and *pareisēlthon* in Gal 2:4 is strikingly similar: "because of false believers *secretly brought in*, who *slipped in* to spy on the freedom we have in Christ Jesus." The language is shadowy and secretive, "certain people" (*tines*

---

[204] D. Watson, *Invention* (1988) understands v. 3 as the *exordium*, "which aims to make the audience attentive, well-disposed, and receptive to the speech that follows" (p. 21), and v. 4 as the *narratio*, "the persuasive exposition of that which either has been done, or is supposed to have been done . . . a speech instructing the audience as to the nature of the case in dispute" (p. 21, quoting Quintilian, *Institutio Oratoria* 4.2.31).

anthrōpoi; cf. Lk 10:30, *anthrōpos tis*), whose names are never known and whose identity is revealed only through the biblical and extra-biblical examples in the body of the letter, have appeared in the community. That they are unnamed and that their deeds are mentioned only in generalities and analogies suggest that it is only modern readers who struggle to identify the "certain people" in question; Jude's implied readers would have known exactly who they were.

It is significant, and rhetorically effective, that before Jude begins to tell the reader anything about the offenses of these people he biases the reader against them by suggesting that their very presence and manner of entrance are problematic, and then claims that their condemnation (*to krima*) was foretold/written of long ago (*hoi palai progegrammenoi*, using a compound form of the verb, *(pro)graphō*, twice in v. 3). This claim references no verse in the Hebrew Bible or tradition in particular, but a host of references in general, and serves to introduce the six proofs (v. 5, out of Egypt; v. 6, angels/"watchers"; v. 7, Sodom and Gomorrah; v. 11a, way of Cain; v. 11b, Balaam's error; v. 11c, Korah's rebellion) and two examples of judgment (v. 9, Michael, the devil, and the body of Moses; vv. 14–15, Enoch's prophecy) that form the body of the letter (vv. 5–15).

Before moving to the proofs from the tradition Jude makes three central claims, or charges, against the intruders, and as noted, argues that sentence against them has been passed "long ago." The claim of ancient condemnation was a favorite rhetorical strategy and served two purposes. First, in a culture that valued the well known and antique over the unfamiliar and new, older was always better and oldest best, so by placing his interpretation and treatment of a new and present threat, Jude seeks to gain the advantage and weight of the tradition for his position in what was likely a difficult debate.[205] Second, given the apocalyptic undertones of the letter, it is not surprising to see one of the central themes of most all apocalyptic prominent in the letter: despite any and every appearance to the contrary, God is in charge and what we are experiencing today was anticipated long ago (and here is the text to prove it!).

The three charges against the "certain intruders" are serious, vague, and familiar, and function opposite the threefold standing of Jude's readers as "called . . . beloved in God . . . and kept safe for Jesus Christ" (v. 1). First, they are "ungodly" (*asebeis*), a favorite term of Jude (here, v. 15, v. 18). This ungodliness is manifest in two general ways: they "pervert the grace of our God into licentiousness" and "deny our only Master and Lord, Jesus Christ." NRSV "pervert" may be something of an overtranslation, influenced by the noun "licentiousness" (*aselgeia*), which we will see carries an appropriate overtone of

---

[205] On the importance of ancient antecedent in the ideology of antiquity, particularly in Judaism and early Christianity, see Arthur J. Droge, *Homer or Moses* (Tübingen, Germany: J. C. B. Mohr, 1990).

sexual immorality and complements the earlier use of *asebeis*. The verb itself (*metatithēmi*), however, can simply mean "change." The final charge, that they deny (*arnoumenoi*) Jesus, is accentuated by the postpositive placement of the preposition and the heaping up of titles upon the one who is denied — master (*despotēs*, used only here and in 2 Pet 2:1 in reference to Jesus), Lord (*kyrios*), Jesus Christ (*Iēsous Christos*). How is it possible to "deny" (cf. 1 Jn 2:22–3) one such as this? Only through great wickedness, which is what Jude sets out to show in the next twelve verses.

The standing of the "certain intruders" is a matter of some significance. Does Jude take them, despite all the condemnation heaped up against them, to be members of the community to which he writes or as outsiders? The NRSV "among you" in v. 4 is likely an overtranslation, and because *pareisduō* is, as noted, a NT *hapax*, we will have to await consideration of the sociocultural and ideological textures prior to venturing a conclusion.

Before turning to those verses in detail, a few words about Jude's rhetorical strategy may be useful. One of the features of the letter commented on most frequently is Jude's "citation" of noncanonical material, from *1 Enoch* (vv. 14–15) to, apparently, the *Testament of Moses* (see discussion on v. 9), along with a citation attributed to "apostles of our Lord Jesus Christ," which has no known referent. In a pair of helpful articles J. D. Charles and T. Wolthuis examine Jude's use of traditional materials.[206] Both find Jude using materials from the tradition, canonical, noncanonical, and historical, in ways within "Jewish haggadic tradition" (Charles) and "within the Jewish-Christian tradition of the early Church" (Wolthuis), much in the way Bauckham refers to Jude as "midrash" in "the general sense of an exegesis of Scripture which applies it to the contemporary situation."[207]

What is problematic and insightful is the sense in which Bauckham uses the word and idea of "text" upon which Jude "comments." As Charles shows, none of the examples, which I refer to as rhetorical proofs, can be understood simply on the basis of a biblical citation but must be interpreted in light of understandings prevalent in the first century of our era. A familiar example (by now, I hope) of this was seen in James 2, where the treatment of Rahab as an exemplum of faith reflected the appropriation of Rahab as a convert to Judaism and as a model of faith common to James's day, and not simply to Josh 2 and 6. Further, as we argued in the chapters on James, such use of traditional materials can best be described as fluid, the boundaries between canonical text and traditional interpretation and appropriation far from fixed. Much as James references Jesus' sayings without attribution, so Jude uses material we now

---

[206] J. D. Charles, "Jude's Use of Pseudepigraphical Source-Material as Part of a Literary Strategy" *New Testament Studies* 37 (1991): 130–45; T. Wolthuis, "Jude and Jewish Traditions" *Calvin Theological Journal* 22 (1987): 21–41.

[207] R. Bauckham, *Jude and 2 Peter* (1983), p. 4

hold to be canonical (e.g., out of Egypt, Korah's rebellion), apocryphal (e.g., Moses' body, Enoch's prophecy), and a mixture of the two (e.g., Sodom and Gomorrah, the angels/watchers) without discrimination between the sources. If there is any caution here it is that once again the interpreter must take special care not to let her or his interests, questions, and concerns (dating, sources, identity of author, audience, and presumed opponents) overwhelm the interests, questions, and concerns apparent in the text (apostasy, immorality, threat to the community, warning, and encouragement of the faithful).

JUDE 5–10

5 Now I desire to remind you, though you are fully informed that the Lord, who once for all saved a people out of the land of Egypt, afterward destroyed those who did not believe.
6 And the angels who did not keep their own position, but left their proper dwelling, he has kept in eternal chains in deepest darkness for the judgment of the great Day.
7 Likewise, Sodom and Gomorrah and the surrounding cities, which, in the same manner as they, indulged in sexual immorality and pursued unnatural lust, serve as an example by undergoing a punishment of eternal fire.
8 Yet in the same way these dreamers also defile the flesh, reject authority, and slander the glorious ones.
9 But when the archangel Michael contended with the devil and disputed about the body of Moses, he did not dare to bring a condemnation of slander against him, but said, "The Lord rebuke you!"
10 But these people slander whatever they do not understand, and they are destroyed by those things that, like irrational animals, they know by instinct.

5. "Now I desire to remind you" (*hupomnēsai de humas boulomai*). Jude knows that they know ("you are fully informed"/*eidotas humas panta*; cf. James 3:1, "you know [*eidotes*] that we who teach will receive the greater judgment") so presumes only to remind.[208] There is an interesting resonance here to the "appeal" (*parakalōn*) in v. 3, for other than scattered uses in 2 Peter and the Pastorals, the only uses of *hupomimnēskō* are Johannine. Jn 14:26 reads, "But the Advocate [*ho paraklētos*], the Holy Spirit, whom the Father will send in my name, will teach you everything, and remind [*hupomnēsei*] you of all that I have said to you." Jude, in language similar to that of Jesus in Jn 14, is here reminding the readers what the Lord has done,[209] "once for all" (*hapax*). The adverb is

---

[208] D. Watson, *Invention* (1988) holds the body of the letter, vv. 5–16, to be the *probatio*, "the part of the oration which by marshaling arguments lends credit, authority, and support to our case" (p. 21, citing Cicero, *De Inventione* 1.24.34).
[209] *ho kyrios* – here referring to God's saving action, not Jesus' as in v. 4; but see R. Bauckham, *Jude and 2 Peter* (1983), p. 49.

problematic, particularly in light of its use in v. 3 to describe the "faith." In v. 3 the force is different from the sense in v. 5, the earlier use absolute and the present case seemingly sequential: "once for all [*hapax*] saved... afterward [*to deuteron*, literally "the second time"] destroyed." Speculation about the meaning of *to deuteron* stretches from the time of wandering in the wilderness to the parousia, and in a way is appropriate for both, the first as example and the second as warning.

The reference is half commonplace ("saved a people out of the land of Egypt"), half innovative interpretation ("destroyed those who did not believe"). Referring to God's deliverance of the Israelites out of Egypt is familiar (Pss 78:12; 105:23, 38; 136; Hos 2:5; Amos 2:10; Hag 2:5; Heb 11:23–9), and to a certain extent so is mention of the rebellion(s) and disbelief that followed (see Stephen's speech, especially Acts 7:39ff.). "From the time when the Lord brought our ancestors out of the land of Egypt until today, we have been disobedient to the Lord our God, and we have been negligent, in not heeding his voice" (Bar 1:18). In response to this disobedience, perhaps best captured in Ex 32 but also in episodes such as Num 14, "the people," even Moses, did indeed die (*apōlesen*) before Joshua crossed the Jordan (one among many possible "seconds," in parallel to the crossing of the Red Sea).

6. In v. 6 we move quickly from biblical referent to traditional, apocalyptic, and pseudepigraphic material. There is here much more than a hint of Gen 6:1–4, which itself is hardly the best-known passage in the Hebrew Bible.

1 When people began to multiply on the face of the ground, and daughters were born to them, 2 the sons of God saw that they were fair; and they took wives for themselves of all that they chose. 3 Then the LORD said, "My spirit shall not abide in mortals forever, for they are flesh; their days shall be one hundred twenty years." 4 The Nephilim were on the earth in those days – and also afterward – when the sons of God went in to the daughters of humans, who bore children to them. These were the heroes that were of old, warriors of renown.

The tradition, especially that of *1 Enoch* 6–19,[210] expanded this text to describe the rebellion and fall of the angels in order to account for the presence of evil on the earth.[211] The reference to the angels being "kept in eternal chains in deepest darkness for the judgment of the great Day" is perhaps the strongest apocalyptic image in the letter and brings to mind in Rev 20:1-3 the binding of the "dragon, that ancient serpent, who is the Devil and Satan."

---

[210] *1 Enoch* is best understood as a collection of writings "as dependent on the Old Testament as it is influential upon the New Testament and later extracanonical literature." E. Isaac, "1 (Ethiopic Apocalypse of) Enoch" in *The Old Testament Pseudepigrapha*, ed. James H. Charlesworth, vol. 1 (New York: Doubleday, 1983), p. 9. For a full treatment of this intriguing work see the commentary by George W. E. Nickelsburg, *1 Enoch*, Hermeneia (Minneapolis, MN: Fortress Press, 2001).

[211] R. Bauckham, *Jude and 2 Peter* (1983), p. 51.

The sin of the angels (*angeloi*), significantly, is described not as engaging in forbidden relations with humans, but as not keeping "their own position" and leaving "their proper dwelling." As we will see in discussion of the sociocultural texture, issues of boundaries and pollution are strongly at work here. Noteworthy also is Jude's repetition of the verb "keep" (*tēreō*). The readers are those who are being "kept" for Jesus Christ (v. 1) and who are to "keep" themselves in God's love (v. 21). The angels did not "keep" to their proper place or relationships and so now are being "kept" in eternal chains.

7. The third example in this series is the most familiar and perhaps the most problematic, not the least because of Jude's use of "likewise" (*hōs*) and "in the same manner" (*ton homoin tropon*) to connect the two examples (angels/watchers and Sodom and Gomorrah).

Sodom and Gomorrah is a much better-known example than the angels/watchers (Isa 1:9–10; Jer 23:14; Eze 16:46–56; Amos 4:11; Lk 10:12; 17:29 and par.; Rom 9:29), but an example of what? This reference does not afford opportunity to unpack what is meant by "indulged in sexual immorality" (*ekporneusasai*) and "pursued unnatural lust" (*apelthousai opisō sarkos heteras*), and what little can be said about the use of this passage in current discussions on human sexuality is more appropriate in consideration of its homiletical texture. Two things are problematic here. First, the ambivalence in most discussions of the "sin" of Sodom and Gomorrah: was it homosexual practice per se or failure to provide protection and hospitality to the strangers in their midst? Second, because those "strangers" happened to be angelic visitors (Gen. 19:1) and the sin of the angels in Jude 6 was that they "did not keep their own position," is the analogy ("likewise") to the sexual practice or to the violation of angelic/human boundaries? That it may be at least in part the latter is suggested by the return to matters angelic in v. 9. In any case, their punishment is certain – they will be an example (*prokeinai deigma*) by burning in eternal fire (*puros aiōniou*), another apocalyptic image.

In the first round of biblical examples Jude compares his opponents to the ever-grumbling, never-thankful, always-near-rebellion children of Israel, a group of fallen angels, and the infamous residents of Sodom and Gomorrah. In the next verse he tells us what he really thinks of them.

8. "Yet in the same way" (*homoiōs*) Jude continues but now wants to make a different kind of comparison, not between the angels/watchers and the people of Sodom and Gomorrah, but between his opponents and all three examples detailed in vv. 5–7. "These dreamers" (*houtoi enupviazomenoi*) is itself an important phrase. "These . . . are" (*houtoi eisin*) is a favorite introductory phrase in Jude (vv. 8, 10, 12, 16, 19) for unnamed opponents and is always followed by a negative example or phrase. Dreamers, of course, are often positive biblical characters (Jacob, Joseph), and dreams are often sources of visions and instructions

(Jacob, Joseph the husband of Mary, Peter). Here the contrast is negative, and "dreamers" are those who do not keep "awake" (Mk 13:37 and par.; 1 Th 5:6). These dreamers are guilty of three things that reflect and anticipate charges made more specifically elsewhere in the letter. They "defile the flesh" (cf. v. 7, Sodom and Gomorrah), "reject authority" (cf. the disobedience in the wilderness, v. 5 and "Korah's rebellion" in v. 11c), and "slander" (*blasphēmousin*)[212] "the glorious ones (*doxas*)" (cf. the discussion of vv. 9–10). What is meant by "the glorious ones" is not apparent. The consensus, offered with little enthusiasm by most commentators, is that the glorious ones represent "one of the species of angels."[213]

9–10. Jude sets forth two "texts" (Bauckham) containing judgment against those to whom he compares his opponents. The second (vv. 14–15) is taken from the pseudepigraphic *1 Enoch*. The example in vv. 9–10 is taken from traditions around Moses, which are alluded to in extant material but not fully available.[214] Two texts that are available to us provide the biblical background. In Deut 34 we read of Moses' death but 34:6 adds "no one knows his burial place to this day," exactly the sort of opening creative writers love. In Zech 3:1 we see "Joshua standing before the angel of the LORD, and Satan standing at his right hand to accuse him." 3:2 continues, "And the Lord said to Satan, 'The LORD rebuke you, O Satan!'" In the *Testament of Moses* these texts are combined with a tradition about the Lord sending the archangel Michael to bury Moses. Satan, in his original role as accuser (as in Zech 3), resists the granting of such an honor on the grounds that Moses murdered an Egyptian, a biblical datum problematic for the tradition. Jude is not so much interested in the fate of Moses' corpse as in the fact that Michael "did not dare to bring a condemnation [*krisin*] of slander [*blasphēmias*] against him" but looked to the Lord for judgment, quoting Zech 3:2, "The Lord rebuke you."

This response is contrasted with that of "these people" (*houtoi*), who slander (*blasphēmousin*) "what they do not understand" (*hosa men ouk oidasin*) and will in turn be "destroyed by those things... they know by instinct" (*hosa de physikōs... epistantai*), a nice parallelism indeed.

---

[212] The translation of *blasphēmeō* as "slander" rather than "blaspheme" in vv. 8–10 reflects both the usage of the term in Greek and the desire to preserve "blaspheme" for slander against God, something that is not at stake here.

[213] Jerome Neyrey, *2 Peter and Jude*, Anchor Bible 37c (New York: Doubleday, 1993), p. 69, citing Sellin; also R. Bauckham, *Jude and 2 Peter* (1983) and J. N. D. Kelly, *A Commentary on the Epistles of Peter and Jude* (New York: Harper and Row, 1969).

[214] See R. Bauckham's excursus, "The Background and Source of Jude 9" in his commentary, *Jude and 2 Peter* (1983), pp. 65–76. Also G. Nickelsburg, ed., *Studies on the Testament of Moses* (Cambridge, MA: Society of Biblical Literature, 1973) and J. Priest, "Testament of Moses" in *The Old Testament Pseudepigrapha*, ed. James H. Charlesworth, vol. 1 (New York: Doubleday, 1983), pp. 919–34.

JUDE 11–16

11 Woe to them! For they go the way of Cain, and abandon themselves to Balaam's error for the sake of gain, and perish in Korah's rebellion.
12 These are blemishes on your love-feasts, while they feast with you without fear, feeding themselves. They are waterless clouds carried along by the winds; autumn trees without fruit, twice dead, uprooted;
13 wild waves of the sea, casting up the foam of their own shame; wandering stars, for whom the deepest darkness has been reserved forever.
14 It was also about these that Enoch, in the seventh generation from Adam, prophesied, saying, "See, the Lord is coming with ten thousands of his holy ones,
15 to execute judgment on all, and to convict everyone of all the deeds of ungodliness that they have committed in such an ungodly way, and of all the harsh things that ungodly sinners have spoken against him."
16 These are grumblers and malcontents; they indulge their own lusts; they are bombastic in speech, flattering people to their own advantage.

11. After the implied condemnation of the intruders (v. 9) and second summary of the charges against them (v. 10), Jude moves quickly to his second set of three examples, prefacing the very terse references with a prophetic "Woe to them" (*ouai autois*). Aside from one use in Paul (1 Cor 9:16) and fourteen uses in six verses of Revelation, the other twenty-nine uses of *ouai* are on the lips of Jesus in the Synoptic Gospels, very much in the same sense of judgment found here, "Woe to them because . . . " (e.g., Mt 11:21).

The three examples Jude offers are at best only clues to the author's likely meaning, really only a name and a verb: (1) *go* the way of *Cain*; (2) *abandon* themselves to *Balaam*'s error for the sake of gain; (3) *perish* in *Korah*'s rebellion. Each example has a clear biblical referent, if not a clear interpretation, and should be looked at in turn.

1. Go the way of Cain. The name Cain occurs sixteen times in Gen 4 and not again in the Hebrew Bible or NT until 1 Jn 3:12 ("We must not be like Cain who was from the evil one and murdered his brother") and Jude 11, which does not leave the biblical commentator much on which to build.[215] In the biblical account we are told only that the Lord "had regard for Abel and his offering, but for Cain and his offering he had no regard. So Cain was very angry" (Gen 4:4–5). The tradition has always presumed that Cain murdered Abel because of that anger, an anger born of jealousy (cf. James 4:2, "You want something and do not have it, so you commit murder"). But the text itself is silent, and we can only speculate

---

[215] Nor is there much else in extra-biblical material. See T. Wolthuis, "Jude and Jewish Tradition" *CTJ* (1987), pp. 31–2.

about Jude's intent, the sort of speculation reserved for consideration of the ideological texture of Jude.

2. Balaam's error. Balaam is known from Num 22–4; his story is complex and in many ways amusing. He does not appear to be an enemy of God, nor a particularly cunning adversary. He is a little slow to catch on, perhaps, and certainly no favorite of the Society for the Prevention of Cruelty to Animals (Num 22:21–9). But when one considers the text carefully Balaam seems mostly faithful to his calling, the very opposite of those who prophesy "for the sake of gain." Nevertheless, haggadic traditions attempting to explain the "plague" that killed 24,000 Israelites before Phinehas killed an unnamed Israelite and the Midianite woman he had "brought into his family" build on the proximity of the Balaam saga to this strange plague and the mention some chapters later that the Moabite women, "on Balaam's advice, made the Israelites act treacherously against the LORD in the affair of Peor, so that the plague came among the congregation of the LORD" (Num 31:16). Balaam thus is considered responsible for the death of the 24,000, and despite his rather innocuous story in Num 22–4, is in certain parts of the tradition – and obviously a part with which Jude, and presumably Jude's readers, were familiar[216] – considered a prototype of evil. None of this, however, really explains what Jude specifically thinks Balaam's "error" (*planē*) should be taken to be. Room for more speculation.

3. Korah's rebellion. Terra firma at last. In Num 16:1–40 we read of Korah's (plus Dathan's and Abiram's) challenge to the authority of Moses and Aaron. "They assembled against Moses and against Aaron, and said to them, 'You have gone too far! All the congregation are holy, everyone of them, and the LORD is among them. So why then do you exalt yourselves above the assembly of the LORD?'" (Num 16:3). The challenge results in a competition, "dueling censers at dawn" if you will. The upshot? The earth "opens up" and swallows Korah and all his possessions (Dathan and Abiram too), and fire comes from heaven and destroys their 250 supporters. Message received.

In this second round of biblical examples, Jude compares his opponents to a fratricide, a for-profit prophet, and an infamous challenger to the authority of Moses. In the next verses he gives us our first real clue as to their identity.

12–13. "These are blemishes on your love-feasts" (*houtoi eisin hoi en tais agapais humōn spilades*). Two problems must be addressed immediately: the meaning of "love-feasts" and the translation of "blemishes." The word translated as

---

[216] See R. Bauckham, *Jude and 2 Peter* (1983), pp. 81–2, who cites G. Vermes, "The Story of Balaam: The Scriptural Origin of Haggadah" in *Scripture and Tradition in Judaism: Haggadic Studies* (Leiden, Netherlands: Brill, 1961), pp. 127–77.

"blemishes," *spilas*, is more commonly used with the meaning "rock," which some extend to mean "reef," or a rock on which a ship may run aground,[217] which would help if Jude was talking about a boat, but the aquatic imagery comes later in the verse. Here the concern is with a community meal, and the translation "blemish" or "stain," perhaps understood as a misspelling of *spilos* (cf. Eph 5:27; James 3:6), makes more sense. But a stain on what? NRSV has "love-feasts" for *hē agapē*, a form and usage otherwise unattested in the NT. We have here the first technical use of *hē agapē* to describe the central fellowship meal of the early Christian community, equivalent to Paul's one reference to the "Lord's supper" (*kuriakon deipnon*) and Luke's mention of "breaking bread" (Acts 2:46). "The agape or Lord's Supper was a real meal (1 Cor 11:20–34; Acts 2:46), held in the evening (Acts 20:7, 11), and was not, in the NT period, distinct from the Eucharist . . . , for which NT writers have no term which distinguishes it from the agape."[218] Jude confirms that more than bread and wine are involved, chastising his opponents for "feasting without fear" in much the same way that Paul chastises the Corinthians for their indulgence at the Lord's Supper (1 Cor 11:20–3). Jude concludes this section of the verse by denouncing his opponents for "feeding themselves," a deeply resonant phrase, *heatous poimainontes*, that literally means "shepherded themselves," recalling Jesus' command to Peter to "tend my sheep" (Jn 21:16) and Ezekiel's condemnation of the "shepherds" in Eze 34:2–4.

2 [P]rophesy against the shepherds of Israel: prophesy, and say to them – to the shepherds: Thus says the Lord GOD: Ah, you shepherds of Israel who have been feeding yourselves! Should not shepherds feed the sheep? 3 You eat the fat, you clothe yourselves with the wool, you slaughter the fatlings; but you do not feed the sheep. 4 You have not strengthened the weak, you have not healed the sick, you have not bound up the injured, you have not brought back the strayed, you have not sought the lost, but with force and harshness you have ruled them.

The passage is quoted at length because it seems likely to be in the background of Jude's accusation,[219] and if it is, it provides the first real hint of what Jude found lacking in his opponents: those who would be, or should be, leaders and shepherds were taking care only of themselves. And doing so fearlessly (*aphobōs*). There follows a series of compelling images of abject emptiness, each drawn from nature, with biblical and extra-biblical intertextures. (1) "Waterless clouds carried along by the winds" (cf. Prov 25:14: "Like clouds and wind without rain"); (2) "autumn [*phthinopōrina*] trees without fruit, twice dead" (cf. especially Mk 11:12–14, 20–5: the fig tree without fruit "for it was not the season for figs," which Jesus curses – prefiguring the action in the Temple to follow – which the next day is "withered away to its roots"; (3) "wild waves of the sea [*kumata agria thalassēs*],

---

[217] R. Bauckham, *Jude and 2 Peter* (1983), p. 85.
[218] Ibid., pp. 84–5.
[219] Ibid., p. 87.

casting up the foam of their own shame" (cf. James 1:6: "for the one who doubts is like a wave of the sea [*kludōni thalassēs*], driven and tossed by the wind" and Isa 57:20: "the wicked are like the tossing sea" [*kludonithēsontai*]); (4) "wandering stars [*asteres planētai*], for whom the deepest darkness has been reserved forever" (the "wandering" [*planētai*] recalls Balaam's "error" [*planē*]).[220] The emphasis in all four images is emptiness and random motion. A great deal of activity, but nothing positive is happening.

14–15. "This is the only section of his midrash in which Jude provides a formal quotation from a written source as his text."[221] That the "text" in question is noncanonical and pseudepigraphic has been problematic for readers of Jude from the start. In the letter itself the citation works in the same way as the reference to the archangel Michael, the devil, and the body of Moses in v. 9, allowing Jude to pronounce judgment without himself having to be the one to do it. Enoch, "the seventh generation from Adam," does it for him.[222] The judgment itself is noteworthy.

> "See, the Lord is coming with ten thousands of his holy ones,
> to execute judgment on all,
> and to convict everyone of all the deeds of ungodliness
> that they have committed in such an ungodly way,
> and of all the harsh things that ungodly sinners have spoken against him."

Three verbs of divine action (coming/*ēlthen*, execute judgment/*poiēsai krisin*, convict/*elegksai*) are paralleled by a threefold emphasis on the ungodliness (*aseibeia*) of the actions, both deeds (*ergos*) and speech (*laleō*).

16. Jude concludes the extended section of condemnation (vv. 5–16) with a second summation, referring to the opponents as "grumblers" (*goggustai*) and "malcontents" (*mempsimoioroi*) and detailing three areas of sinful behavior: "indulge their own lusts" (*kata tas epithumias heautōn poreuomenoi*, literally "walk according to their own desires"); "bombastic in speech" (*to stoma autōn lalei huperogka*); and flatter to their own gain (*thaumazontes prosōpa ōpheleias charin*). The last is a difficult expression that has to do more with showing partiality or favoritism (cf. James 2:1ff.) than oral flattery. The overall meaning is clear, however – they dissemble for their own benefit. Almost as clear, given the nature of the charges, is that those whom Jude has in mind were asserting themselves as presumed leaders of the community.

---

[220] Ibid., p. 89, argues for a reference in *1 Enoch*.
[221] Ibid., p. 93.
[222] Two factors at work – you cannot find a much greater claim to antiquity than "the seventh generation from Adam," and because the biblical tradition tells us only "Enoch walked with God; then he was no more, because God took him" (Gen 5:24) there is almost no limit to what a creative author could imagine Enoch as having seen and heard.

JUDE 17–23

17 But you, beloved, must remember the predictions of the apostles of our Lord Jesus Christ;
18 for they said to you, "In the last time there will be scoffers, indulging their own ungodly lusts."
19 It is these worldly people, devoid of the Spirit, who are causing divisions.
20 But you, beloved, build yourselves up on your most holy faith; pray in the Holy Spirit;
21 keep yourselves in the love of God; look forward to the mercy of our Lord Jesus Christ that leads to eternal life.
22 And have mercy on some who are wavering;
23 save others by snatching them out of the fire; and have mercy on still others with fear, hating even the tunic defiled by their bodies.

17–19. Jude has cited apocrypha (v. 9) and pseudepigrapha (vv. 14–15) and now cites "the predictions of the apostles of our Lord Jesus Christ," for which we have no reference. A sort of noncanonical hat trick.[223]

The change in tone signaled by "But you, beloved" (*humeis de ayapētoi*) precedes the change in content, which begins with the repeat of the phrase in v. 20. This serves to make the change in tone all the more noteworthy. Even while continuing to speak of "scoffers" and "worldly people . . . causing division" Jude is no longer speaking of their condemnation but reminding the readers that their appearance was predicted. This reminder (*mnēsthēte*) recalls the reminder (*hupomnēsai*) in v. 5, creating an *inclusio* that brackets vv. 5–16, and the double series of biblical examples, judgments, and summaries that form the body of the letter.

The reminder carries its own set of problems. How long ago did the "apostles" (*apostoloi*) issue these "predictions" (*tōn rēmatōn tōn proeirēmenōn*)? Whom did Jude intend in the reference to apostles? And is not Jude among the apostles? One possibility, and it is perhaps a natural possibility, is to see in the idea of an apostolic prediction a reference to a bygone era, particularly because we have no other use or phrase comparable to Jude's sweeping "apostles of our Lord Jesus Christ." But there is nothing in the text itself that requires the words to have been spoken "long ago," only before the appearance of the opponents. In other words, the phrase cannot be used as evidence that Jude wrote long after some distinct period known as "the apostolic age." Such reading is anachronistic (see the Introduction on the dating of Jude).

Whom did Jude intend, then, in using the term *apostoloi*? Of course, an *apostolos* can simply be a messenger, but surely Jude's use is more technical than that. If so, how technical? Limited to "the twelve"? Or the twelve and a

---

[223] D. Watson, *Invention* (1988) takes vv. 17–23 as the rhetorical *peroratio*, "recapitulating the main points of the *probatio* and arousing emotions for our case and against that of the opposition through amplification" (p. 21).

few others, perhaps including "super-apostles" (2 Cor 12:11) like Apollos? We cannot finally know, but the number would seem to be small (cf. 1 Cor 12:29, "Are all apostles?"). That Jude would not appear to be among them suggests at least two possibilities: that as "a brother of the Lord" the office of "apostle" was redundant and the title unneeded, or that the "office" was parochial, and Jude did not hold that position in the eyes of the readers.[224]

As for the warning itself, it echoes warnings found in the Synoptics. "And if anyone says to you at that time, 'Look! Here is the Messiah!' or 'Look! There he is!' – do not believe it. False messiahs and false prophets will appear and produce signs and omens, to lead astray, if possible, the elect. But be alert; I have already told you everything" (Mk 13:21–3). The time designation, "in the last time" (*ep eschatou [tou] chronou*), makes explicit what has been apparent to the reader throughout – this is a work steeped through and through with apocalyptic eschatology. Jude's opinion of the opponents, now connected with an apostolic warning, remains condemnatory until the end of the letter. "It is these worldly people, devoid of the Spirit, who are causing divisions" is our second piece of evidence about the identity of Jude's opponents: those who are dividing the community.

20–3. The contrast between "these," Jude's opponents, and Jude's "beloved," the audience, is made clear in vv. 20–3.

"these"	"beloved"
Jude's opponents cause divisions.	Jude's beloved are to build themselves up.
Jude's opponents are bombastic in speech.	Jude's beloved pray in the Holy Spirit.
Jude's opponents indulge their own lusts.	Jude's beloved keep themselves in God's love.
Jude's opponents are destroyed and will perish.	Jude's beloved look forward to mercy.
Jude's opponents show partiality/flatter for their own gain.	Jude's beloved have mercy.

Much else in the verses is not clear, however, for as we will see, the text of vv. 22–3a is disputed.

A CLOSER LOOK – THE TEXT OF JUDE 22–3

The final exhortation of the letter is intriguingly similar to the final exhortation in the letter of James ("My brothers and sisters, if anyone among you wanders from the truth and is brought back by another, you should know that whoever

---

[224] R. Bauckham, *Jude and 2 Peter* (1983) argues that "the apostles" referred only to those who had founded the community to which Jude now writes, that Jude himself was not one of those founders, and that, "as 'the Lord's brother' he was probably not known as an apostle" (p. 104).

brings back a sinner from wandering will save the sinner's soul from death and will cover a multitude of sins"; James 5:19–20). Nevertheless, it is a formidable text-critical challenge.[225] To summarize, there are two textual clusters, one with a longer version referring to three groups of people to be saved/shown mercy, the other with a shorter version referring to two groups of people and omitting the verb "save."

Longer version (NRSV)	Shorter version (P[72])
And have mercy on some who are wavering; save others by snatching them out of the fire; and have mercy on still others with fear	Snatch some out of (the) fire, have mercy on the waverers in fear

Most recently the Bodmer Papyrus (P[72]), c. third century CE, supports the shorter reading, as does *Stromateis* 6.8.65 of Clement of Alexandria. Other major codices (e.g., ℵ and A) support the longer reading, as does Jude's preference for grouping in threes.[226] The more difficult reading, however, is the shorter version, and this is the position of Bauckham and Neyrey. No final resolution is yet possible, as good arguments are made to support either reading. Fortunately the sense of the passage – save some who might otherwise be lost – is clear.

As was the case in James, it is fascinating to end the correspondence on the theme of outreach, at least among "fallen" members of the community. This is especially so in the case of Jude, where the language of condemnation is consistently harsh. In that light it seems likely that the encouragement to "have mercy" is limited in scope. The "some who are wavering" (*diakrinomenous*) includes not the opponents but those who are perhaps being influenced negatively by the opponents. This view is supported by the warning that accompanies the encouragement: have mercy "with fear," and don't get too close, "hating even the tunic defiled by their bodies." The apocalyptic backdrop ("snatching them out of the fire") is pronounced.

JUDE 24–5

24 Now to him who is able to keep you from falling, and to make you stand without blemish in the presence of his glory with rejoicing,

25 to the only God our Savior, through Jesus Christ our Lord, be glory, majesty, power, and authority, before all time and now and forever. Amen.

---

[225] R. Bauckham writes, "It is probably impossible to reach an assured conclusion as to the original text of vv. 22–23a" (ibid., p. 108).

[226] B. M. Metzger, *Textual Commentary on the Greek NT* (1994), pp. 658–61, and D. Watson, *Invention* (1988), note 346, p. 74.

Letters close in a number of different ways. Jude closes with a benediction and doxology.[227] For most it is the best known part of the letter; for many it is the favorite part of the letter.

While vv. 24–5 share formal similarities with other NT doxologies (Rom 16:25–7 and Eph 3:20–1, e.g.), it remains distinctive in style and content, and pushes at the widely held distinction between doxology and benediction. In traditional form, the opening is in the dative case ("to him who is able to keep you") and maintains the letter's concern with "keeping" or "guarding" already noted. *How* one is kept also echoes an important theme, that of blemished versus spotless. A new note is sounded at the end of v. 24 – "rejoicing" (*en agalliasei*). In v. 25 the focus shifts back to the deity, and while there is no mention of the Holy Spirit (v. 20) the doxology is offered "to" the only God, our savior (*sōtēri hēmōn*), "through" (*dia*) Jesus Christ our Lord. What is asked for is all-encompassing: glory (*doxa*), majesty (*megalōsunē*), power (*kratos*), and authority (*exsousia*). It is an unprecedented doxology.

SOCIOCULTURAL AND IDEOLOGICAL TEXTURES

The sociocultural and ideological textures of the letter of Jude are rich, complex, and, in comparison to those of James, difficult to discern. In his Anchor Bible commentary on *2 Peter and Jude* Jerome Neyrey, a pioneer and leader among scholars who apply the canons of social-scientific criticism to NT texts, makes mention of five "pivotal values" important for any reading of Jude concerned with its social-scientific texture: (1) honor/shame; (2) patron/client relationships; (3) purity and pollution; (4) the physical body; and (5) group/individual orientation.[228] The present reading will focus on the first and third, while touching on the others. Before considering specific values and how they operate in and underneath the text of Jude we should first note how a form of "contest" central to the first value, honor/shame, provides the dynamic that undergirds and energizes the letter as a whole.

Jude as Riposte: Defending the Honor of the Lord

Watson has noted that the letter does not fit neatly into one or another of the three main species of Greek rhetoric but is an amalgam of deliberative (giving advice and encouraging or discouraging a specific course of action) and epideictic (praise and blame seeking assent to some value). One might also argue that the accusations, condemnations, and reference to divine judgment

---

[227] D. Watson, *Invention* (1988) refers to these verses as the "Quasi-*peroratio*" and distinguishes them from an epistolary postscript (p. 76), a distinction that is not necessary. As throughout the letter, there is a mixing of rhetorical and epistolary convention.

[228] J. Neyrey, *2 Peter and Jude* (1993), pp. 3–20.

add some sense of the third species, the judicial, although there is no actual or imagined legal setting. In view of this rhetorical miscellany it is significant that the letter throughout evidences a single dynamic important from a social-scientific perspective: Jude is arguably best understood as a riposte to an honor challenge. Neyrey notes,

> The document may profitably be examined as the author's riposte to an honor challenge. The world of Jude and indeed the first-century Mediterranean is rightly described as highly agonistic. On the level of peasants and artisans there was an ongoing social game of push and shove, of honor claimed and honor challenged. Jude claims a certain honor by virtue of blood relations with James (and Jesus); his official status is that of "servant" of Jesus. But "certain men" are obviously challenging this status. This letter constitutes the author's riposte, a defense both of the honor of Jesus which is slighted (vv. 4, 8) and of the honor ascribed to Jude which is challenged.[229]

The essential elements of an honor/shame value system are best presented by Malina, Pilch, Hanson and Oakman, and others whose work is found in the Suggested Reading list under "Sociocultural Texture" and will be summarized.[230] The dynamics of an honor challenge and riposte is best illustrated from the Synoptic Gospels.

A CLOSER LOOK – A CHALLENGE TO JESUS' HONOR

Honor, a favorable opinion and status in one's own eyes and that of one's community, is either inherited, garnered, or granted, then confirmed by family and community. If one's honor is challenged, be the challenge great or small, it must be defended. If it is not honor is lost. The measure depends on the significance of the challenge. Some challenges, for example, Nathanael's "Can anything good come out of Nazareth?" require little more than Philip's, "Come and see" (Jn 1:46), a riposte in defense of Jesus' honor echoing Jesus' own words to "two disciples" of John the Baptist (Andrew, and one unnamed) a few verses earlier (Jn 1:39). Other challenges, for example, the Jerusalem scribes' accusation, "He has Beelzebul, and by the ruler of demons he casts out demons" (Mk 3:22 and par.), demand a more complete response.

Jesus has garnered great honor by his successful exorcisms ("He commands even the unclean spirits and they obey him"; Mk 1:27), healings, and compelling teaching ("They were astounded at his teaching, for he taught as one having authority, and not as the scribes"; Mk 1:22). As a result, "At once his fame began to spread throughout the surrounding region of Galilee" (Mk 1:28). In Mk 2 we read of scribes and Pharisees who challenge this honor and of Jesus' response in

---

[229] Ibid., p. 52.
[230] See, e.g., B. J. Malina, *New Testament World* (1993), pp. 28–62 (includes an excellent bibliography).

deed (Mk 2:1–12) and word (Mk 2:16–28). The sparring continues into chapter 3, and while the dispute over "Beelzebul" is better known, the challenge/riposte that begins chapter 3 serves as a more economic example.

> 1 Again he entered the synagogue, and a man was there who had a withered hand. 2 They watched him to see whether he would cure him on the sabbath, so that they might accuse him. 3 And he said to the man who had the withered hand, "Come forward." 4 Then he said to them, "Is it lawful to do good or to do harm on the sabbath, to save life or to kill?" But they were silent. 5 He looked around at them with anger; he was grieved at their hardness of heart and said to the man, "Stretch out your hand." He stretched it out, and his hand was restored. 6 The Pharisees went out and immediately conspired with the Herodians against him, how to destroy him. 7 Jesus departed with his disciples to the sea, and a great multitude from Galilee followed him; 8 hearing all that he was doing, they came to him in great numbers from Judea, Jerusalem, Idumea, beyond the Jordan, and the region around Tyre and Sidon.

Jesus' honor has been well established in Mk 1 and 2. The challenge, in the form of a man with a "withered hand," is offered in response to the dispute about the sabbath that ended chapter 2 and appears to be a setup or trap – Jesus' opponents "watched him." Jesus' response is both verbal and physical riposte, rebuking his opponents ("Is it lawful to do good...?") and then healing the one presented in challenge ("his hand was restored"). Honor challenges always have winners and losers, and those bested by Jesus in this contest do not take it well (they "conspired... against him, how to destroy him"). The judgment of the narrator, however, emphasizes the breadth of Jesus' victory in the contest, as "great numbers" from Jerusalem to Sidon come to him.

In the letter of Jude honor is established in the first verse. Jude's honor is inherited ("brother of James") and earned ("servant of Jesus"). Moreover, Jude is generous in bestowing honor, referring to his audience as "called... beloved in God... kept for Jesus." The reader is further honored three times by being addressed as "beloved" (vv. 3, 17, 20). As Neyrey puts it, there is "honor all around."[231] But the honor is not for everyone, nor is the honor of Jude universally acknowledged. Here we lack details and may only infer from what we do have in the letter. Two things seem clear, based on the level of vituperation in Jude's characterization of his opponents: (1) Jude's honor and authority have been seriously challenged; and (2) Jude uses the occasion of this writing (v. 3) to offer a withering, scathing denunciation of those who have challenged him.[232] Apart from the opening and closing (vv. 1–2, 24–5), and to a certain, albeit mixed extent in the final exhortation to "have mercy on some who have wavered" (vv. 22–3),

---

[231] J. Neyrey, *2 Peter and Jude* (1993), p. 46.
[232] See S. Joubert, "Persuasion in the Letter of Jude" *Journal for the Study of the New Testament* 58 (1995): 75–87.

the letter of Jude is one long response to the challenge presented by the "certain intruders."

If we list the charges Jude levels against his opponents it looks something like this:

1. intruders who have "stolen in among you"
2. long ago designated for "this condemnation"
3. ungodly
4. pervert the grace of God
5. licentious
6. deny "our only Master and Lord, Jesus Christ"
7. dreamers
8. defile the flesh
9. reject authority
10. slander "the glorious ones"
11. slander "whatever they do not understand"
12. like animals
13. destroyed by "those things . . . they know by instinct"
14. blemishes on love-feasts
15. without fear
16. feed themselves (only)
17. waterless clouds, fruitless trees, wild waves, wandering stars
18. grumblers
19. malcontents
20. indulge their own lusts
21. bombastic in speech
22. flatterers to their own advantage
23. worldly people
23. devoid of the Spirit
24. causers of division

As if these are not enough, Jude's opponents are compared to

unfaithful Israelites in the desert	Cain
fallen angels	Balaam
people of Sodom and Gomorrah	Korah

And finally they are condemned, directly or indirectly, by the rebuke of the archangel Michael (v. 9), the prophecy of Enoch on "ungodly sinners" (vv. 14–15), and the prediction of the apostles of our Lord Jesus Christ that "In the last time there will be scoffers, indulging in their own ungodly lusts" (v. 18).

That is an impressive amount of condemnation to squeeze into 25 verses! But it is characteristic of a riposte to an honor challenge. Recall Jesus' response to the scribes and Pharisees in Mt 23. Just a partial list of the shorter phrases includes the following:

"do not do as they do, for they do not practice what they teach," v. 3
"they do all their deeds to be seen by others," v. 5
"they love to have the place of honor," v. 6
"hypocrites!" vv. 13, 15, 23, 25, 27, 29
"blind guides," vv. 16, 24
"blind fools," v. 17
"you strain out a gnat but swallow a camel!" v. 24
"you are like whitewashed tombs," v. 27
"you snakes, you brood of vipers," v. 33
"how can you escape being sentenced to hell?" v. 33

Jude's response is along very similar lines, making use of invective, analogy, sarcasm, and condemnation to demonstrate the unworthiness of his opponents and to predict their eventual, inevitable, and much-deserved punishment. Was it successful? As Neyrey notes, "The fact that we still have this document and revere it as the work of Jude suggests that the public verdict in this contest between rival authorities went in favor of Jude."[233]

Defending the Purity of the Community

Prominent in the various accusations leveled at his opponent are those having to do with purity and pollution. The opponents "pervert the grace of our God into licentiousness" (*aselgeian*), are "blemishes [*spilades*] on your love-feasts," who indulge "their own ungodly lusts" (*epithumias*). Referred to as "dreamers," they are said to "defile the flesh" (*sarka miainousin*). The community is called to have mercy but must hate "even the tunic defiled [*spiloō*] by their bodies." Even in the closing doxology the concern is manifest, as praise is offered to one able "to make you stand without blemish" (*amōmous*) in God's presence.

Jude's choice of analogies is also telling, in fact, particularly so. The angels "did not keep their own position, but left their proper [*idion*] dwelling." Sodom and Gomorrah, "in the same manner as they, indulged in sexual immorality and pursued unnatural lust" (literally "went after other flesh"; *apelthousai opisō sarkos heteras*). Korah sought to usurp the place of Moses, and in the tradition Balaam's name became attached to an attempt to entice and destroy the Israelite men (Num 31).

Why this great focus on sexual and general impurity? Because of the ongoing importance of codes, standards, and expectations of purity manifest in ancient Mediterranean cultures generally and most likely in Jude's community in particular. This is neither exceptional nor noteworthy; evidence of it is available

---

[233] J. Neyrey, *2 Peter and Jude* (1993), p. 52.

in most any book in the NT and as we saw is prominent in James. Two points are important here. First, purity and pollution are as much about place – "a place for everything and everything in its place" – as they are about stain or uncleanness or sexual transgression. Second, purity counts, for as Paul wrote to the Thessalonians, "God did not call us to impurity but in holiness" (1 Th 4:7). The opposite of impurity/uncleanness (*akatharia* in the passage just cited) is holiness, so that purity is part and parcel of holiness.

In Jude this is manifest as a concern to be spotless (v. 24) and to condemn sexual and other immorality (vv. 4, 7, 8, 14–15, 18). Nothing unusual here – it is common to the NT and to the morality of the age. What is unique, or at least noteworthy, in Jude is the emphasis on the purity/pollution of place, in particular the usurpation of place. This is clearly the basis for the condemnation of the angels/watchers (*1 Enoch* 6–18) in v. 6, at least in part for the condemnation of Sodom and Gomorrah in v. 7,[234] and certainly for the charge against Korah. Why does this matter so much to Jude? It doesn't, except as useful examples of his primary charge against his opponents. It is not immorality or sexual license that is the crux of the matter, but the usurpation of place, in particular, the attempt by the opponents to usurp Jude's place. The rhetoric of impurity serves to support the rhetoric of claiming and taking something other than one's rightful place, which is itself a form of pollution.

Jude's Eschatological Ideology

Jude's ideological orientation is not simply concerned with keeping his community free from sin and keeping usurpers in their place. He is concerned with these and other things for an overriding reason: his belief in the coming, imminently coming, judgment of the Lord. The letter is imbued throughout with an unmistakable eschatological spirit. For Jude and for his readers, these are the last days; the great day, the day of judgment, is near.

The first hint is in the first verse, when the beloved are referred to among those being "kept safe for Jesus Christ," a difficult phrase in Greek that makes more sense when the verb, *tēreō*, occurs again in vv. 6 and 21, where its eschatological sense is unambiguous. In v. 6 the angels did not keep (*tērēsantas*) to their proper place; now they are being kept (*tetērēken*) "in eternal chains in deepest darkness." If the imagery is not clear enough, Jude makes it explicit: they are being kept "for the judgment of the great Day" (*eis krisin megalēs hēmeras*). Reaching back into the tradition, Jude affirms the accepted understanding of the fate of Sodom and Gomorrah and the surrounding cities (an important awareness of the way the urban and rural economies were interdependent) – they "serve as an example

---

[234] See Weston W. Fields, *Sodom and Gomorrah: History and Motif in Biblical Narrative* (Sheffield, England: Sheffield Academic Press, 1997).

[*deigma*] by undergoing a punishment of eternal fire [*puros aiōniou*], itself an apocalyptic image.

Jude's eschatological perspective is perhaps best evidenced by the three "texts" he chooses to quote in the letter, the *Testament of Moses, 1 Enoch*, and an otherwise unknown saying of the "apostles of our Lord Jesus Christ" about the "last times" (*eschatou chronou*). Both the *Testament of Moses* and especially *1 Enoch* are important apocalyptic works dated at most a century or two before Jude, and they are well known, popular, and in the case of *1 Enoch*, well attested. That Jude claims their worldview and outlook for himself is significant indeed.

As we saw with James, whose eschatological perspective is similar to Jude's, the most distinctive element of Jude's outlook is not especially apocalyptic, but juridical. More in the manner of the classical prophets than the Apocalypse of John, the "great Day" is described in terms not of falling stars, wars, famine, plague, and peril, but of judgment. Assuming, as we must, that Jude was familiar with *1 Enoch* in its entirety, that he chooses to cite a passage specifically about judgment on ungodliness is important. The same is true of the reference to the Lord's rebuke in the *Testament of Moses* and the last time "prediction" of the "apostles." When given a choice, Jude chooses to talk about judgment and to do so in expectation of its imminence. This is also true of the penultimate saying about "snatching" from the fire (again note the parallel with James 5:19–20) and the concluding doxology, for to "stand without blemish in the presence of his glory" is truly to be ready for judgment.

Jude's eschatological emphasis is unmistakable and part of the reason for its likely early dating (see Introduction). There is no hint of delay in Jude's expectation.

SACRED AND HOMILETICAL TEXTURES

In the lectionary of the Episcopal Church's *Book of Common Prayer* Jude is not to be found – not even for the feast of Saint Simon and Saint Jude! Philemon, Titus, and even 2 Peter have their day. Only Jude and 2 and 3 John are slighted (and almost all of 1 John *is* read). Jude is so neglected that when preachers who do not use the lectionary offer a series on "forgotten books of the Bible" they rarely include Jude. The late Raymond Brown, SS, wrote a brief reflection on the meaning and message of each book except one – Jude – in his *Introduction to the New Testament*.[235]

Lewis Donelson has pointed out that alone among biblical material, we have a reading of Jude, and so Jude is both a reading of the tradition and a reading

---

[235] Raymond Brown, *An Introduction to the New Testament*, Anchor Bible (New York: Doubleday, 1997).

within the tradition: the interpreter is interpreted for later interpreters.[236] In this sense Jude is like our sermons, and the letter has no doubt suffered from this accessibility and vulnerability. Certainly the tendency of NT scholars to limit their interest in Jude to its relationship to 2 Peter has done little to help our appreciation of Jude on its own terms.

It is difficult to discern what we as preachers should take from our reading of Jude. Certainly his level of invective is not something to be imitated in our parishes. His ease with his tradition, however, is another matter, as is his skill to move between biblical, apocryphal, and contemporary material. His interpretation of his own situation in light of his inherited tradition evidences an appreciation for the tradition and an application of it, from which we may learn.

The simple truth is that we do not know the tradition, biblical and historical, as our predecessors in the pulpit once did. Surveys of Bible knowledge administered to entering seminary students show the lowest scores since the tests have been given. But the knowledge of Scripture in the pew is even worse. And this does not even speak of our awareness of the history of interpretation of the texts we preach on, or church history, theology, and the other divine arts and sciences.

Two approaches to this are possible. One, well evidenced in churches around the world, is to concede to the prevailing biblical and theological illiteracy and offer "messages" based on a mix of current events, popular psychology (self-help, self-improvement), movie reviews, and song lyrics. With a good Power Point presentation no one may ever know the difference.

The other approach is probably harder, requiring more work for preacher and listener: teach Scripture and tradition, then preach it. Assume that your audience does not know what you are talking about but also assume that they want to. So teach them Scripture and tradition, and then tell them why they are important. Renowned, and now retired, professor of homiletics Fred Craddock leads a Bible study on the lectionary texts before worship. Others incorporate the Bible study into worship itself, never "talking down" but always assuming most people in the audience have not spent the week thinking about the passages chosen or assigned for that day's worship, and would not mind a little "refresher course" from someone who has.

The first thing we learn from Jude, then, is a renewed commitment to the tradition, biblical and otherwise. The second thing we learn, or at least should learn to appreciate, is Jude's incredible passion. Jude cares deeply about the Gospel and about the community to which he is writing, deeply enough about both to intervene when it might have been easier to look the other way or to move on. Instead Jude moves in, challenging the integrity of his opponents and challenging his readers to a renewal of their faith in Jesus Christ.

Knowledge and passion. That is the legacy of the letter of Jude.

---

[236] L. Donelson, *From Hebrews to Revelation: A Theological Introduction* (Louisville, KY: Westminster/John Knox Press, 2001), pp. 87–105.

BRIDGING THE HORIZONS – PREACHING JUDE

Barbara Brown Taylor writes about preaching as well as anyone and better than most. As we consider preaching about and from the letter of Jude, consider these words:

> By calling someone to preach to them and by listening to that person week after week, a congregation gives their minister both the authority to speak and a relationship from which to speak, so that every sermon begins and ends with them.
>
> If that sounds too narrow, let me say that I also believe every sermon begins and ends with God. Because the word of God is what a preacher wrestles with in the pulpit, and because it is a living word, every sermon is God's creation as well as a creation of the preacher and the congregation. All three participate in the making of it, with the preacher as their designated voice. It is a delicate job for the one in the pulpit, a balancing act between the text, the congregation, and the self. If the preacher leans too far one way, he will side with the text against the congregation and deliver a finger-pointing sermon from on high. If the preacher leans too far the other way, she will side with the congregation against the text and deliver a sermon that stops short of encountering God.[237]

While Rev. Taylor was not writing with the letter of Jude particularly in mind, her comments are telling for anyone who chooses to "preach Jude." Lean one way, and Jude becomes a "pre"-text for announcing and denouncing one's opponents from the pulpit. Lean the other way, and Jude is a jumbled juxtaposition of eschatological expectations from a time long, long ago and an empire far, far away. Efforts to preserve the integrity and importance of the letter are further compromised by the likely ignorance of most hearers. The only "Judas" they are familiar with was the Iscariot, the betrayer. The only "Jude" they know was in an old Beatles song, and perhaps among Roman Catholics, the patron saint of hopeless causes, Saint Jude.[238] From this one might develop a sermon's opening gambit, but it is slight foundation for solid preaching.

So the interpreter and preacher may as well begin by assuming that her audience knows nothing about the contents, background, and occasion of the letter of Jude. As is so often the case, in whatever the form, we live in a time when *teaching* must precede *preaching*. The only way to balance the ignorance of the audience is a preaching style that is initially didactic. It falls to the preacher to provide the audience with the tools and information needed to join in the task of interpretation and appropriation.

This task need not be burdensome nor lengthy. The congregation does not need to know everything the preacher has learned, only enough to begin to share in the work of interpretation. In line with the reading of Jude found here, the letter needs to be placed in its first-century context. The turbulence of an

---

[237] Barbara Brown Taylor, *The Preaching Life* (Cambridge, MA: Cowley Publications, 1993), pp. 77–8.
[238] The name "Judas Thaddeus" is based on a patristic linking of one of the Twelve with one of the brothers of the Lord. For a remarkable study on those devoted to "St. Jude," see

emergent Christianity, the tensions with and within Judaism, and the role of the family of Jesus in the Jerusalem church should be highlighted but not belabored. Jude's rhetorical strategy – the emphasis on biblical and historical example, the use of invective, the closing turn to mercy, the glorious doxology – also should be noted and should inform the rhetorical strategy of the sermon itself. How so? The most obvious way would be to follow Jude's practice of using multiple examples from Scripture and tradition to make one's case.

Of course that assumes one has determined what case is to be made. Here the larger question of the purpose of the letter of Jude returns to the fore, and one's answer to that question by necessity guides the treatment of any particular section or verse. Influenced by Neyrey and Bauckham, we have read Jude as a response to an implicit or explicit challenge to the author's standing and authority within the community to and for whom he wrote. By calling on biblical and traditional examples to testify on his behalf, Jude bolsters his case against the "intruders" and rhetorically heightens his response through invective, sarcasm, and denunciation. But how does Jude's "case" speak to and for our communities today? Outside the closing call to mercy and doxology, where is the good news in the letter of Jude? And where, in a short writing filled with some of the strongest language found in the canon, should the preacher look for the rhetorical and homiletical clues to guide her or his own preaching?[239] Building on what has already been considered in these pages, it seems clear that the good news found in Jude is largely twofold and resides in its ethic and its eschatology.[240] From this emerges its homiletical strategy, a strategy that may be likened to the memorable description by Phillips Brooks of all preaching as "the bringing of truth through personality."[241]

There are many churches in which sermons focusing on either ethics or eschatology are rare, a homily dealing with both never heard. More the pity. Our discomfort with the end time expectations upon which Christian faith was founded and grounded and the ethical implications of that faith does not diminish the truth of those claims. Jude, like his brothers James and Jesus, was undeniably conscious of living in the last days and fully anticipated that the Lord's rebuke (v. 9) would be pronounced on his opponents sooner rather than later. Jude was also aware that such expectation of the close of the age could

---

R. Orsi, *Thank You, St. Jude: Women's Devotion to the Patron Saint of Hopeless Causes* (New Haven, CT: Yale University Press, 1996).

[239] On the relation between the structure of biblical texts and the structure of sermons, see Thomas G. Long, *Preaching and the Literary Forms of the Bible* (Philadelphia: Fortress Press, 1989).

[240] On Jude's ethic, see K. Lyle, Jr., *Ethical Admonition in the Epistle of Jude* (New York: Peter Lang, 1998). On Jude's eschatology, see R. Webb, "The Eschatology of the Epistle of Jude and Its Rhetorical and Social Functions" *Bulletin for Biblical Research* 6 (1996): 139–51.

[241] Phillips Brooks, *Eight Lectures on Preaching* [1879] (London: SPCK, 1959), p. 5.

have one of two ethical impacts – a loosing of all restraint or a heightened sense of moral requirement – and he accused his opponents of succumbing to the former while calling his readers to follow the latter. Both accusation and call were offered through the full force of his personality, characterized in the first verse as that of "a servant of Jesus Christ and brother of James."

To faithfully preach Jude the interpreter must be clear, then, on her or his own eschatology, ethic, and personality. For what does one wait, and how does such expectation inform how one lives? In a world as redolent of evil and good as the world of Jude, how does one understand the demands of the call of Jesus Christ? What friends and followers does one embrace, and for what enemies is one called to "have mercy" (v. 22)? The caution should be noted once more: Jude is not to be used as a cudgel in a church fight over, say, a new hymnal, or whether to have hymnals at all. Those who disagree with the preacher about a church project or program are not to be likened to Korah, Balaam, and the citizens of Sodom and Gomorrah. That is an abuse of Scripture and pulpit, and unless our "personality" is that of "a servant of Jesus Christ and brother of James" it is to claim an authority we do not have. The truth of our personalities are likely less grand. The truth of the Gospel is not. And it is the Gospel truth, as reflected in the letter of Jude, we are called to proclaim.

20 But you, beloved, build yourselves up on your most holy faith; pray in the Holy Spirit; 21 keep yourselves in the love of God; look forward to the mercy of our Lord Jesus Christ that leads to eternal life. 22 And have mercy on some who are wavering. . . .

24 Now to him who is able to keep you from falling, and to make you stand without blemish in the presence of his glory with rejoicing, 25 to the only God our Savior, through Jesus Christ our Lord, be glory, majesty, power, and authority, before all time and now and forever. (Jude 20–2, 24–5).

Amen.

Author Index

ANCIENT

Aristotle, 89

Eusebius, 12

Josephus, 3, 4, 30

Philo, 89, 90

Sophocles, 89

MODERN

Adamson, 5, 6, 99, 105

Bass, Dorothy, 83
Bauckham, Richard, 1, 2, 5, 6, 7, 10, 12, 51, 105, 151, 171, 173, 175, 182, 192
Baur, F. C., 2
Blomberg, Craig, 140
Borg, Marcus, 36
Brooks, Phillips, 192
Brown, Raymond, 14, 189
Buechner, Frederick, 55

Charles, J. D., 171
Craddock, Fred B., 104, 128, 190

Davids, 86
Deppe, Dean, 11
Dibelius, Martin, 5, 15, 34, 44, 56, 64, 72, 78, 84, 86, 89, 90, 91, 99, 101, 105, 124, 145, 147, 148, 151, 159

Dodd, C. H., 61
Donelson, Lewis, 189
Dowd, Sharon, 78
Dykstra, Craig, 83

Francis, Fred O., 141, 156
Frankenmölle, Hubert, 5

González, Catherine, and Justo A., 165

Hanson and Oakman, 184
Hartin, Patrick, 5, 6

Johnson, Luke Timothy, 1, 5, 6, 10, 12, 13, 15, 34, 41, 46–8, 51, 56, 60, 74–6, 78, 86, 88, 99, 100, 101, 106, 110, 111, 113, 115, 117, 120, 130, 132, 135, 141, 142, 143, 145, 146, 148, 151, 152, 155
Jülicher, Adolf, 15

Kern, F. H., 14

Laws, Sophie, 5, 34, 44, 46–8, 50, 56, 57, 60, 86, 99, 106, 110, 117, 125, 130, 135, 142, 143, 159
Lischer, Richard, 119
Lundbald, Barbara, 128

Malina, Bruce, 184
Martin, Ralph, 5, 73, 86–113, 143, 150
Massibeau, L., 15
Metzger, Bruce, 46, 88, 135, 182

195

Minear, Paul, 157, 162
Moo, Douglas, 5, 44, 86, 99, 125, 126, 142, 143, 146, 158

Neyrey, Jerome, 1, 2, 7, 182, 183, 184, 185, 192
Nouwen, Henri, 97

Perkins, Pheme, 5, 82
Pilch, John, 160, 184

Reicke, Bo, 5, 96
Robbins, Vernon, 2, 15, 151
Ropes, James Hardy, 56, 86, 99

Segovia, Fernando, 115
Sevenster, J. N., 4
Spitta, F., 15

Tamez, Elsa, 69, 136
Taylor, Barbara Brown, 191
Thich Nhat Hanh, 83

Wall, Robert, 5, 34, 49, 56, 68, 74–6, 86, 99, 105, 127, 142, 143, 148
Watson, Duane, 7, 80, 84, 166, 182, 183
Wheeler, Sondra, 140
Witherington, Ben, 36, 161
Wolthius, T., 171

Scripture and Extra-Biblical Texts Index

HEBREW BIBLE

Genesis
- 1:26–8   92
- 1:28   91
- 3:11–13   47
- 4:4–5   176
- 4:10   134
- 6:1–4   173
- 14:20   92
- 15:6   76
- 15:15   77
- 19:1   174
- 22:1–18   76
- 22:16   157

Exodus
- 4:18   77, 121
- 22:22   52
- 32   173
- 32:13   168

Leviticus
- 19   120
- 19:12   17, 150, 162
- 19:13   135
- 19:15   57
- 19:18   53, 59, 68, 118, 120, 121, 151

Numbers
- 14   173
- 16:1–40   177
- 22:21–9   177
- 31   187
- 31:16   177

Deuteronomy
- 6:4   75
- 6:4–5   75
- 26:12   52
- 29:5   133
- 34:5   168
- 34:6   175

Joshua
- 2   76, 171
- 6   171
- 6:17–25   76

Judges
- 16:6   77

1 Samuel
- 3:9   168
- 20:42   77

2 Samuel
- 7:52ff.   168

1 Kings
- 17:1   155
- 18:1   155–6
- 19:12   55

2 Chronicles

6:26	156
20:12	76

Job

1	145
2:1–10	145
2:3	118
2:10	47
42:10–16	145

Psalms

7:12 (LXX)	118
24:3–4	112
24:8	118
26:11	118
30:3 (LXX)	118
37:2	40, 136
41:13	92
46:10	55
49:6 (LXX)	118
49:20 (LXX)	117
69:2 (LXX)	118
78:12	173
86:1f.	64
90:5–6	40
100:5 (LXX)	117
102:4–11	40
103:15–16	40
105:23	173
105:38	173
109:31	64
121	112
129:6	40
132:15f.	64
136	173

Proverbs

3:34	111
10:12	157
12:13	88
13:3	88
16:27	89
21:23	88
25:14	178
27:1	124
29:11	49

Isaiah

1:9	135
1:9–10	174
1:17	52
1:18	131
3:16–24	112
5:8	136
9:14	90
10:10	132
13:6	132
14:25	118
14:31	132
15:2–3	132
15:6	40
16:7	132
23:1	132
23:6	132
23:14	132
24:11	132
34:2	118
40:6–7	42
40:6–8	41
43:6	123
51:12	40
52:5	132
57:20	179
59:1	118
65:14	132

Jeremiah

2:23	132
12:4	40
22:3	52
23:14	174
29:4	118
31:20	132
31:31	132
44:22	157

Lamentations

1:8	144
1:21	144
4:13	136

Ezekiel

16:1–17	109
16:46–56	174

21:17	132		Judith	
26:15	144		9:35	77
34:2–4	178			
			Sirach	
Daniel			2:5	133
6:28	118		5:11	49
			14:1	88
Hosea			15:11–12	47
2	109		19:16	88
2:5	173		20:18	88
5:1	131		22:27	88
7:14	132		29:10–12	133
			35:16	52
Joel				
2:12–13	112		Baruch	
			1:18	173
Amos				
2:6	136			
2:10	173		**PSEUDEPIGRAPHA**	
4:1	131		*1 Enoch*	
4:11	174		6–19	173
5:1	131			
8:3	132		*Testament of Moses* 10, 12, 13	
Nahum			4 Esdras	
3:7	144		2:19	52
Habbakuk				
2:11	134		**NEW TESTAMENT**	
Haggai			Matthew	
2:5	173		5:3	59
			5:9	101
Zechariah			5:17–48	68
3:1	175		5:21ff.	60
3:2	175		5:23–4	92
7:10	52		5:33–7	17, 150–1
11:2	132		6:11	66–9, 73
			6:19–20	133, 134
			6:30	41
APOCRYPHA			7:1	144
1 Enoch	10, 12, 13		7:7	34, 36, 39
			7:17–19	92
Tobit			7:24–7	115
1:8	52		10:28	118
10:12	77		11:21	176

Matthew (cont.)

11:29	42
11:28–30	50
12:33	92
13:55	3, 167
18:15ff.	161
20:1ff.	143
22:11–13	60
22:34–40	68
23	94, 187
23:8	94
23:10	94
24:37	143
24:39	143
25:34–5	59, 73
26:52	107

Mark

1:15	111, 143
1:19	29
1:22	184
1:27	184
1:28	184
1:39	75
2:1–10	185
2:9	161
2:16–28	185
3:1–8	185
3:19	167
3:22	75, 184
4:26–9	143
4:27	154
4:38	93
5:1–20	100
5:34	77, 154
5:38	132
6:3	3, 167
6:14	155
6:56	154
7:7	52
10:19ff.	60
11:12–25	122, 178
12:28	75
12:28ff.	118
12:31	59
12:38	93
13	107
13:4	148
13:21–3	181
13:29	144
13:37	175

Luke

1:51–3	43
4:25–6	156
6:16	3, 167
6:20	59
6:25	112
6:43–4	92
7:50	77
8:2–3	126
8:14	107
8:15	38
10:12	174
10:27	59
10:30	170
11:3	73
11:19	36
12:15	139
12:16–20	42
12:17–19	123
12:18	126
12:20	123, 127
12:28	41
13:34	145
14:1	61
14:7–14	61
14:11	40, 112
15:6	163
15:9	163
15:14	108
15:22–4	163
15:25	158
16:19–31	60
17:4–5	154
17:29	174
18:14	40
18:18	93
19	138
19:40	134
22:11	93
23:11	58

Scripture and Extra-Biblical Texts Index

24:12	52
24:41	133

John, Gospel of

1:1	97
1:9	154
1:39	184
1:46	5, 184
3:17	154
5:8	154
6:39–40	134
6:60	164
12:48	134
13:13	93
13:15	144
14:22	3, 167
14:26	172
20:5	52
21:16	168

Acts of the Apostles

1:1	169
1:13	3
2:17	134
2:38	154
2:46	178
3:6	154
3:16	154
5:37	3, 167
6:104	83
7:39ff.	173
8:28–9	89
9:11	3, 29
10:30	58
10:34	57
12:2	4–5
14:15	155
15	3, 5, 102, 158
15:22	167
15:22–9	69
15:29	5
16:14	126
16:18	154
19:13ff.	154
19:15	75
20:7	178
20:11	178
20:17	158
20:28	158
21	5
21:24	108
21:25	5
27	153
27:20	154

Romans

1:1	168
1:7	30, 168
1:9	30
1:30	117
2:11	57
2:17	125
3:28	81
4	78
4:19	153
5:3–4	142
5:3–5	35
5:5	
8:22	144
8:23	46, 144
9:29	135, 174
11:11	88
11:16	46
12–15	81
12:7	93
13:1	111
13:9	59, 60
13:14	50
16	130
16:5	46
16:25–27	182–3

1 Corinthians

1:2	168
1:3	30
1:26	126
8:7	153
11:20–3	178
11:20–34	178
11:23	6
12	96
12:28	87, 94

1 Corinthians (*cont.*)
- 12:28–9   93
- 12:29   181
- 13:1   125
- 13:4   142
- 14   96
- 15:1   6
- 15:15   154
- 15:20   46
- 15:23   46
- 15:27–8   111
- 15:33   45
- 15:44   100
- 15:46   100
- 16:6   52
- 16:15   46
- 16:17   143

2 Corinthians
- 1:2   30, 168
- 1:6   38
- 1:16–19   152
- 1:17   17
- 5:2   144
- 5:4   144
- 6:4   38
- 7:6–7   143
- 9:7   169
- 10:1   42
- 12:11   181
- 12:12   38
- 12:15   108
- 12:20   99, 117

Galatians
- 1–2   5
- 1:3   30, 92, 168
- 1:8   103
- 1:9   6
- 1:19   4
- 1:23   169
- 2   32, 102
- 2:4   169
- 2:9   69
- 2:10   69
- 2:12   79
- 2:13   66–9
- 2:16   81
- 5–6   81
- 5:3   60
- 5:6   81
- 5:14   59
- 5:20   99
- 5:22–3   50, 101
- 6:7   45

Ephesians
- 1:2   30, 168
- 3:20   155
- 3:20–1   182
- 4:11   93
- 4:24   50
- 5:27   178
- 6:9   57

Philippians
- 1:2   30, 168
- 1:25   81
- 1:27   81
- 2:6–7   168
- 4   130
- 4:2   169

Colossians
- 1:2   168
- 1:11   142
- 1:29   155
- 2:4   51
- 3:25   57
- 4:12   168

1 Thessalonians
- 1:1   168
- 2:19   143
- 3:13   143
- 4:1–2   6
- 4:7   188
- 4:15   143
- 5:1–4   142
- 5:6   175
- 5:23   143

2 Thessalonians
1:2	30, 168
1:11	81
2:1	143
2:8	143
3:17	4

Philemon
2	168
3	30
6	81

1 Timothy
1:2	168
2:7	93
3:14	111
5:1	158
5:2	158

2 Timothy
1:2	168
1:11	93
3:1	134
3:10	38
4:19ff.	130

Titus
3	130

Hebrews
3:13	52
5:12	93
7:9	112
11:23–9	173
11:31	76
12:1	50
12:23	118
13:17	144

James, Letter of (references are from Introduction and Chapter 6 of the commentary only)
1:1	168
1:2–5	16
1:2–8	20
1:6	179
1:9–11	18
2:1ff.	179
2:13	19
3:1	172
3:6	178
3:17	5–6
4:2	176
4:8	6
5:12	16
5:19–20	182
5:20	19

1 Peter
1:2	168–9
1:6	37
1:6–7	35
1:7	133
1:12	52
1:15	99
1:18	99
1:24	41
2:1	50, 117
2:12	99, 117
3:1	99
3:2	99
3:16	99, 117
3:21	50
4:8	157
5:1	158
5:6	112
5:12ff.	130

2 Peter
1:1	168
1:2	168
1:10	88
1:16	143
2:1	171
2:7	99
3	130
3:4	143
3:11	99

1 John
2:22–3	171
2:28	143

1 John (cont.)
- 3:12 — 176
- 4:20–1 — 92
- 5 — 130

2 John
- 1:3 — 168

Jude, Letter of (references are from Introduction and Chapters 1–5 of the commentary only)
- 3 — 7
- 4 — 17, 104
- 6 — 18
- 7 — 133
- 17 — 6
- 18 — 6
- 19 — 100
- 21 — 6
- 22–3 — 19
- 23 — 133
- 24–5 — 130

Revelation
- 1:9 — 38
- 2:2–3 — 135
- 2:9–10 — 45
- 2:16 — 107
- 3:20 — 144
- 9:7 — 107
- 9:9 — 89, 107
- 11:17 — 107
- 12:7 — 107
- 12:17 — 107
- 13:7 — 107
- 13:10 — 38
- 14:12 — 38
- 14:14 — 46
- 15:16 — 58
- 16:14 — 107
- 17:14 — 107
- 18:13 — 89
- 18:14 — 58
- 19:8 — 58
- 19:11 — 107
- 19:19 — 107
- 20:1–3 — 173
- 20:8 — 107
- 22:11 — 58
- 22:16 — 58

EXTRA-BIBLICAL TEXTS

Didache
- 11–12 — 103
- 11–13 — 94
- 11:1–2 — 94
- 13:2 — 94

Shepherd of Hermas
- 9.22.2 — 95

Stromateis (Clement of Alexandria)
- 6.8.65 — 182

Subject Index

Abraham, 75–6, 144
Akedah, 75–6
'am ha'aretz, 64
anawim, 64
angels/watchers, 170, 172, 188
Apocalyptic, 170

Balaam, 170, 177, 187
Bodmer Papyrus, 182
Book of Common Prayer, 189

Cain, 170, 176–7
church, 159
class, social, 64–5, 66, 113–14

desire, 107–8
Devil, 170, 173
Didache, 103, 115

Egypt, 172
Elders, 158–9
Elijah, 155–6
Enoch, 170, 172, 179
  1 Enoch, 171, 175, 189
eschatology, 72, 145, 146–7, 148, 188–9

faith, 56, 72, 80–1, 82, 140
forgiveness, 160–1
friendship, 115–16

healing, 153–5, 159–60
Hebrew Bible, 9

honor/shame, 70, 75–7, 137–9, 183–7

intruders, 170, 171

James
  in the New Testament, 4
  ossuary, 1
  as teacher, 95–6
James, Letter of
  genre, 7–8
  Jesus Christ in, 57
  Paul and, 12
  preaching and, 164–6
Jesus, sayings of, 10–11, 79–80, 153
Job, Testament of, 145
Jude
  Letter of: genre, 7; Preaching and,
    191–3; Second Peter and, 5, 190
  New Testament, in the, 3–4, 167

Kierkegaard, Sören, 104, 129
Korah, 170, 172, 177, 187, 188

law, 66–9, 118

Michael (archangel), 170
Moses, 170, 172, 187
  Testament of, 171, 175, 189

Nicaragua, 164

oaths, 150–2, 164

205

parables, 61
Paul, 78–82, 152, 169
poverty, 59, 66, 136–7, 138
practices, 56, 82–3
prayer, 116, 155
ptōchos, 65
purity, 187–8

Rahab, 75–6, 77, 144, 171
righteousness, 80

Scripture, 114
Second Peter, 190
Shema, 73, 75
slave, 167
socio-rhetorical interpretation, 2, 12, 15–20

Sodom and Gomorrah, 170, 172, 174, 187, 188
soteriology, 72
synagogue, 58, 62, 63

teachers, 93–5
tongue, 96

virtue, 101

wages, 134
wealth(y), 59, 114, 131, 133, 134, 135, 138, 139
wisdom, 10, 88, 100, 101, 119
works, 72

zero sum, 65–6, 138